Studies in Childhood and Youth

Series Editors: **Allison James**, University of Sheffield, UK, and **Adrian James**, University of Sheffield, UK.

Titles include:

Kate Bacon
TWINS IN SOCIETY
Parents, Bodies, Space and Talk

David Buckingham and Vebjørg Tingstad (*editors*)
CHILDHOOD AND CONSUMER CULTURE

Allison James, Anne Trine Kjørholt and Vebjørg Tingstad (*editors*)
CHILDREN, FOOD AND IDENTITY IN EVERYDAY LIFE

Manfred Liebel, Karl Hanson, Iven Saadi and Wouter Vandenhole
CHILDREN'S RIGHTS FROM BELOW
Cross-Cultural Perspectives

Helen Stapleton
SURVIVING TEENAGE MOTHERHOOD
Myths and Realities

Studies in Childhood and Youth
Series Standing Order ISBN 978–0–230–21686–0 hardback
(*outside North America only*)

You can receive future titles in this series as they are published by placing a standing order. Please contact your bookseller or, in case of difficulty, write to us at the address below with your name and address, the title of the series and the ISBN quoted above.

Customer Services Department, Macmillan Distribution Ltd, Houndmills, Basingstoke, Hampshire RG21 6XS, England

Also by Manfred Liebel

A WILL OF THEIR OWN: Cross-Cultural Perspectives on Working Children

WORKING CHILDREN'S PROTAGONISM (*co-edited with Bernd Overwien and Albert Recknagel*)

WORKING TO BE SOMEONE: Child Focused Research and Practice with Working Children (*co-edited with Beatrice Hungerland, Brian Milne and Anne Wihstutz*)

Children's Rights from Below

Cross-Cultural Perspectives

Manfred Liebel
International Academy at the Free University Berlin, Germany

with

Karl Hanson
University Institute Kurt Bösch, Sion, Switzerland

Iven Saadi
International Academy at the Free University Berlin, Germany

and

Wouter Vandenhole
University of Antwerp, Belgium

First published 2012 by
PALGRAVE MACMILLAN

Palgrave Macmillan in the UK is an imprint of Macmillan Publishers Limited, registered in England, company number 785998, of Houndmills, Basingstoke, Hampshire RG21 6XS.

Palgrave Macmillan in the US is a division of St Martin's Press LLC, 175 Fifth Avenue, New York, NY 10010.

Palgrave Macmillan is the global academic imprint of the above companies and has companies and representatives throughout the world.

Palgrave® and Macmillan® are registered trademarks in the United States, the United Kingdom, Europe and other countries.

ISBN: 978–0–230–30251–8

This book is printed on paper suitable for recycling and made from fully managed and sustained forest sources. Logging, pulping and manufacturing processes are expected to conform to the environmental regulations of the country of origin.

A catalogue record for this book is available from the British Library.

A catalog record for this book is available from the Library of Congress.

10 9 8 7 6 5 4 3 2 1
21 20 19 18 17 16 15 14 13 12

Printed and bound in Great Britain by
CPI Antony Rowe, Chippenham and Eastbourne

Contents

**Part IV   New Frameworks for Children's
Rights from Below**

Acknowledgements

The basic ideas expressed in this book were developed within the framework of the European Network of Masters in Children's Rights (ENMCR). In particular, they draw on my experience of working with the Movements of Working Children and Adolescents in Latin America, for whom I have been an advisor since the early 1990s.

The guest chapters were written by my colleagues Karl Hanson, Wouter Vandenhole and Iven Saadi, who have worked with me in the ENMCR and have been excellent collaborators for many years. I thank them for enriching this book with their contributions.

I have had extensive discussions with Iven Saadi, in particular, over the past months. He commented on most of the chapters I wrote and made suggestions about literature I should consult. He has improved the chapters in various places with his suggestions for honing my argument, and his contributions have enhanced the book considerably. Chapters 7 and 10 were amended to such an extent that we decided we should be listed as co-authors.

I am equally grateful to Rebecca Budde, who, with me and others, established the European Master's in Childhood Studies and Children's Rights (EMCR) at the Freie Universität Berlin and who still coordinates the programme. She has encouraged me again and again to continue work on this book and was, like Iven Saadi, invaluable in helping me overcome the language barrier of English.

My chapters for this book were written mostly in German, with some portions being written in Spanish. Rebecca Budde, Iven Saadi and Jessica Walsh did the majority of the translation into English and linguistic editing. Shorter passages were translated by Philip Angermeyer and Malina Wieland. Without their diligent work it would not have been possible to publish this book. In addition, Malina Wieland helped me in creating the index.

My thanks also go to graduates and students of the EMCR at the Freie Universität Berlin, whether they contributed actively to discussions during my seminars, or made me the supervisor and reader of their often excellent Master's theses, or supported me in finding literature and other technical works. I would like specifically to mention Noëmi Fivat and Johanna Richter, who were among the first group of graduates in 2008 and are now working in the EMCR team.

Last, but not least, I am grateful to the reviewers of the proposal for this book and the sample chapters. I would also particularly like to thank Barry Percy-Smith, who made essential recommendations for revising the first draft of the book. And I thank the staff at Palgrave Macmillan for their cooperation in the smooth publication of this book.

Abbreviations

ACRWC	African Charter on the Rights and Welfare of the Child
AMWCY	African Movement of Working Children and Youth
ASBO	Antisocial Behaviour Order
CEDAW	UN Convention on the Elimination of All Forms of Discrimination Against Women
CHH	child-headed household
CLM	Children's Liberation Movement
CRC	UN Convention on the Rights of the Child
CRC Committee	UN Committee on the Rights of the Child
CRIN	Child Rights Information Network
CRP	child rights programming
CWC	Concerned for Working Children (India)
ENMCR	European Network of Masters in Children's Rights
FGC	female genital cutting
FGM	female genital mutilation
HIPC	highly indebted poor country
IGA	income-generating activity
ILO	International Labour Organisation
LHR	localising human rights
MANTHOC	Movimiento de Adolescentes y Niñas Trabajadores Hijos de Obreros Cristianos (Movement of Working Children and Sons and Daughters of Christian Workers (Peru))
MOLACNATs	Movimiento Latinoamericano y del Caribe de NATs (Movement of Working Children and Adolescents from Latin America and the Caribbean)
MYWO	Maendeleo ya Wanawake Organization
NATRAS	Niños, Niñas y Adolescentes Trabajadores (Movement of Working Children and Adolescents of Nicaragua)
NATs	niños, niñas y adolescentes trabajadores (working children and adolescents)

NGO	non-governmental organization
PATH	Programme for Appropriate Technology in Health
TRIPS	Trade Related Aspects of Intellectual Property Rights
UNATsBO	Union de Niños, Niñas y Adolecentes Trabajadores de Bolivia) Bolivian Union of Working Children and Adolescents
UNICEF	United Nations Children's Fund
WHO	World Health Organization
WTO	World Trade Organization

Contributors

Karl Hanson is a socio-legal scholar and an associate professor at the Children's Rights Unit, University Institute Kurt Bösch, Sion, Switzerland.

Iven Saadi is a political scientist and lecturer on the European Master's in Childhood Studies and Children's Rights programme at the Free University Berlin, Germany.

Wouter Vandenhole is a legal scholar and UNICEF Chair in Children's Rights, Faculty of Law, University of Antwerp, Belgium.

Introduction

Manfred Liebel

With this book, we want to reconsider children's rights in the sense of how children themselves can exercise and enjoy these rights, in what ways they need the support of adults to do so and how they can make a claim to such support. We are not interested in revisiting the controversial philosophical and legal debates about whether children can or should actually have rights or whether it makes sense to grant them specific rights.[1] Our intention is more practical. The starting point of this book is the premise that children nowadays have rights and might need more of them, and that their rights must be understood as human rights, to which children are entitled in the same way as adults. Following the assumption that 'there is a distinction between "having" rights and being allowed to exercise them' (Freeman, 2009: 387), we want to investigate what must happen so that children's rights become relevant for children, and children themselves recognize them as relevant and use them for their current and future lives.

We will address what we consider a problematic trend in large parts of the debate on children's rights, namely, a focus on the responsibilities of states (and derivatively of adults) and legal procedures. The framework and starting point for many authors are the rights enshrined in the UN Convention on the Rights of the Child (hereafter CRC), and much of the analytic interest lies in the ways of implementation and exercise of the rights codified therein (see the critical remarks by Alanen, 2010). We certainly agree that these are necessary ingredients to an analysis of children's rights. But for several reasons we also consider that this focus severely hinders an adequate re-conceptualization of children's rights, since little attention is given to their broader meaning and implications, the social and political contexts and conditions of their creation and exercise, and their significance for children and their relationships with a right-bearing status.

One especially important critique is that this approach to children's rights does not address the meaning and impact that these rights might have for children living in different social and cultural contexts. 'Children's rights are presented as the new norm in policy and practice without questioning

1

or making a problem of this new norm. ... The debate on children's rights has become a technical debate on the most effective and efficient way to implement children's rights, how best to monitor this implementation and how this can be organized' (Reynaert et al., 2009: 528). Closely linked with this 'technicalization' of children's rights is, still according to Reynaert et al., its 'de-contextualization'. 'A de-contextualized discourse does not take into account the living conditions, the social, economical and historical contexts in which children grow up, which can be very diverse, and which are the environments in which children's rights are to be realized' (Ibid.). According to other authors (Veerman & Levine, 2000), it is time to shift the discussion from the 'Geneva scene' to the grassroots level where children's rights must be realized in their actual context.

The main analytic prism for a sociological understanding of children's rights applied in this book consists of framing children's rights as rights held and necessarily exercised by children, particularly rights that open up an ensemble of concepts, practices and methods that can be and are used by children themselves in ways contributing to their own welfare. This specific approach answers a shift in human rights scholarship giving more importance to the ways in which rights-holders themselves relate to and use their rights, and what constraints limit the modes and the extent to which they do so. While the specific social statuses of children can certainly be identified as an important factor in why children have difficulties making use of their rights, we will try to show that there are other reasons why children's rights are still an alien concept for many children. Among these reasons is that not only the content and significance of the CRC were not adequately conveyed to children from the beginning of the drafting process, but also the fact that children can only appreciate their rights as meaningful if these are interlinked with their lives and if children themselves can put them to an empowering use. One key question we want to discuss in this book, therefore, is in which ways children's rights can be understood as subjective or agency rights of children and whether they can be enforced by children themselves.

In order to ensure that children embrace rights and make use of them for themselves, they must be conceptualized in a context specific way and give answers to the children's life experiences. The task cannot be only to 'implement' formally existing children's rights, but they must rather be reflected according to their cultural, political and structural coherence and weighed against the possible consequences for the children's lives. In doing so, the large differences amongst living situations of children across the globe, between girls and boys, between privileged and marginalized, must be considered and can lead to different meanings of the same rights. If need be, the rights must be specified and extended with children significantly participating. In emphasizing the necessity to contextualize and localize children's rights, we do not only aim to conceptualize and present children's rights in a child-friendly way and by this to make them also more attractive for children, but rather to understand children's rights also as expression and part of children's agency. Our basic thought on children's rights from below is that children themselves can influence the contexts in which their rights come to life and have practical implications for themselves as well as for the society or the community they live in.

Generally, the necessity for special children's rights is argued with children being more vulnerable as adults and therefore requires special provision and special protection by adults or state institutions. We do not want to question this argument. However, we want to emphasize beyond this aspect that children can exercise their rights and that possibly conditions must be created to enable this. If the principle established with the CRC that children are understood as subjects of rights is to reach practical meaning, children also must be understood as social subjects who can do something with their rights and achieve and implement changes in their 'best interest'.

The underlying assumption of children's rights that children are different from adults cannot be reduced to the biological aspect that children are yet 'incomplete' human beings, who must first develop and are therefore dependent on, and possibly inferior to, adults. The difference is also socially 'constructed' in the sense that the life world of children is separated from the adult world and that children are made dependent on adults. Understood paternalistically, even children's rights can bring about and intensify this dependence. We, however, understand children's rights as a possible way to reduce socially constructed children's dependence, to strengthen their autonomy and make their agency a reality.

Before giving an overview of the structure of this book, some considerations should be expressed about the cross-cultural intentions of the book and the main terms used in this context. We do not intend to suggest that there is an exact overlap between culture and society, but instead we assume the existence of a multiplicity of different cultures also within a society, with which any individual is associated in different ways, including cultures that reach beyond the boundaries of a single society (see Benhabib, 1999). Still, we argue that in relation to cultural representations of childhood and the involvement or 'agency' of children, one can, in most societies, identify dominant norms or conceptions of what is adequate or not, and that these norms do not always correspond to the dominant idea of childhood in the minority world.

The differentiations of 'Western' and 'non-Western' cultures, or minority and majority world societies, used in this book, are certainly not without problems. They suggest the existence of two distinct and internally relatively homogenous social or cultural 'worlds' that furthermore exist in total separation from each other. Actually, they are neither homogenous nor uninfluenced by each other. The self-image, idea and materiality of the minority or 'Western' world are inconceivable without its 'other', the non-Western world (see Hall, 1992). In this book, the distinction is used in a *heuristic* sense, pointing to the fact that certain characteristics relevant for an understanding of children's participation and rights are more likely to be articulated either in or outside Europe and North America. In this regard, we also take into account that a claim to universal validity of certain ideas is closely related to relations of dominance and their constant reproduction. When looking at the relevant ideas, we must be aware of the fact that when gazing on the 'other', thus 'strange' societies, one always tends to implicitly stylize these after one's own standards and thereby to falsify them.

This book is structured in four main parts. In the first part, we explain the perspective on children's rights taken in this book. In the first chapter, we give an overview on our main arguments for a sociologically inspired cross-cultural rethinking of the children's rights discourse. In the second chapter, we look at aspects of the history of children's rights that have, until now, remained largely hidden or have been given only little attention. Then we go on to discuss some pitfalls in reference to children's rights, as well as to analyse what the prerequisites are for making rights accessible and valuable to children, from their own perspective as rights-holders. We will show that one essential prerequisite is an understanding of children's rights that reflects social, cultural and political contexts.

The second part includes four chapters and is dedicated to theoretical perspectives that may contribute to further conceptualizations of children's rights. First, guest author Karl Hanson discusses different approaches to children's rights, here understood as schools of thought, namely paternalism, liberalism, welfare and emancipation. Second, guest author Wouter Vandenhole proposes the framework for an approach to localize children's rights and explore how it may help to bring in a bottom-up perspective in the understanding and implementation of these rights. Third, we discuss age-based forms of discrimination so far mostly neglected in debates and research on children's rights as well as literature on discrimination, and propose theoretical paths to better understand and, if needed, overcome them. Fourth, with a view to children's rights, we identify some shortcomings of the present state-focused human rights system and conceive of possible 'immanent' and 'transformative' innovations. One key question is how rights could be understood as subjective rights, and how they could possibly be enforced by children themselves, particularly those in experiencing specifically severe situations of social disadvantage and exclusion.

The third part centres on more practical questions. First, we look at what drives children to frame demands in a language of rights and how doing so they can also go beyond existing codified rights, and why it could be important to recognize and to enforce them. First, we present various examples of self-formulated children's rights, differentiating between individual and collective expressions, and referring to different continents. Second, taking as an example the working children's movements and organizations in different continents, guest author Iven Saadi considers whether these movements and their activities constitute an argument for also understanding children's rights as a 'work in progress', possibly leading to a modified corpus of nationally and internationally acknowledged children's rights. Third, we discuss concepts and practices of participation in different cultural, economic and political contexts and ask, on the one hand, whether the 'participatory rights' codified in the CRC can be understood and implemented in an intercultural sense, and, on the other hand, if children's agency in 'non-Western' cultures can be understood as a manifestation of potentially transformative rights exercised by children. Fourth, understanding children's citizenship as a specific aspect of children's participation, we discuss what it would require to become a reality and explain why any meaningful concept of citizenship must take into account power structures in society and must show how it can contribute to more social equality and social justice.

In the final part of the book, we try to conceptualize new frameworks for children's rights from below. First, referring to children's initiatives and social movements, we explain what might be the role of children in shaping new contexts of children's rights, including some considerations on 'alternative' economic and research activities by children themselves as a way of improving children's agency and own voice in representations of social reality. Second, we investigate what role adults could play in supporting children's rights from below and discuss circumstances under which 'advocacy' by adults might be useful or risky for the children. We argue that advocacy only makes sense where it is aimed at counteracting the subordination of children and, wherever possible, at strengthening their social position. Our assumption is that adults who want to act as advocates for children in this way will not only have to insist on their independence, but also understand themselves as 'co-protagonists' of children.

Note

1. On this, see the debate about whether rights are to be understood as 'legal' or 'positive rights' or as 'moral' or 'natural rights', and, with a view to its motivation, the debate between 'will theory' and 'interest theory' (see, e.g., van Bueren, 1998; Archard, 2004).

Part I

Contexts of Children's Rights Discourses

1
Framing the Issue: Rethinking Children's Rights

Manfred Liebel

Scene 1: Sarah is the 12-year-old daughter of the author of this book. Because she sometimes shares her father's home workspace, she is not unacquainted with the topic of children's rights. When one day her father tries to motivate her to use the Internet-portal on children's rights newly established by a youth association, she answers: 'Why should I? I am not a child anymore.' Should her father remind her that, according to Article 1 of the UN Convention on the Rights of the Child (hereafter CRC), she can remain a child for six more years und claim specific rights? Or would she interpret this advice as presumptuousness of an uncomprehending adult?

Scene 2: Two years earlier, a fellow pupil at Sarah's school met a stranger to the school in the girls' bathroom and felt threatened by him. 'Nothing' happened, and the man's motivation remained unclear, but the class got very excited. During a parents' meeting convened shortly thereafter, demand was voiced to lock down the school building after the beginning of the classes. When a teacher spoke about this request with the children, they disapproved of it and instead proposed to pay attention themselves to persons unknown to the school and to accompany each other to the bathroom from then on. Children's rights were not mentioned during these discussions. But did the children implicitly act in terms of children's rights?

Scene 3: A large road junction with traffic lights in a Latin American city, on which children sell sweets and newspapers. After signing an agreement with the International Labour Organization on eradicating the 'worst forms of child labour', the government decided to demonstrate its determination to combat poverty by not tolerating these types of children's economic activities anymore. In response, the children feel prevented from continuing to assist their families and insist on being able to work. Instead of being chased away from their working places by the police, they demand to be protected from aggressive drivers. Additionally, they make specific propositions about ways to improve their working situations at the traffic junctions: the lines between traffic lanes should be broadened in order to diminish the risk of accidents, and shelters should be built on the roadsides as resting places and to protect the children from the sun. How do these claims match the children's right to be protected from economic exploitation established with the CRC? Or do they constitute an example of how children call upon this right as well as upon their rights to participation and apply them to their specific circumstances?

Scene 4: A children's meeting in Western Africa. Convened by a non-governmental organization, it was supposed to acquaint children with the CRC and the African Charter on the Rights and Welfare of the Child. The children present in the meeting quickly tired of this agenda and instead started to come up with their own ideas of rights. Some of these rights differed significantly from those granted to children in international and regional treaties. For instance, the children claimed the right to stay in, and return to, their villages of origin and the right to 'light and limited work'. Have they disregarded existing children's rights? Is there any basis for the claims raised by them to be called 'rights'? Do they infringe on the idea of human rights as elaborated in international law, and eventually harm themselves by developing competing ideas about the content of children's rights? Or does their invention of new rights claims give reason to examine the existing children's rights system in terms of its weaknesses and limits?

Scene 5: In Calcutta, India, as in most markets in countries of the majority world, many children are busy collecting or stealing leftover vegetables and fruit from market stands. One morning, some children brought a small boy to the meeting point of an aid organization and reported that he had been caught by a vendor and then severely beaten by the policeman arriving on the scene. The boy was bleeding profusely and seemed to be in very serious condition. When the boy was somewhat restored, he was told that the policeman had violated his rights and should be punished for his actions. After listening carefully, the boy said, 'Aunty, it would have been much worse if he had arrested me. They would have put me in the lock-up until I got bail, and in the lock-up worse things would have happened. He was doing his job and helping me by beating me at the market itself. I know him because during the times that I have fought with someone at the shelter and decided to sleep on the station platform, he often asked me to run small errands for him and gave me a blanket to cover myself at night.' Would it have helped the boy if he had insisted on being protected from the violence and maltreatment at the hands of the policeman, and to be presumed innocent until proven guilty according to the law in accordance with Article 40 of the CRC? Or in this case do existing rights and laws reach limits that make farther-reaching interventions and changes necessary, without which a children's rights-based claim could turn the situation from bad to worse?

The right of children to have rights

Following the rationale of human rights, granting and exercising rights cannot be made conditional on verifiable cognitive competences or on rationality and reason. With some caveats to which we will turn later, we are convinced that the CRC as well as other internationally codified human rights 'decouples rights entirely from the concepts of rationality and responsibility [and instead] establishes children as rights-bearing subjects enjoying full humanity from birth' (Grugel & Piper, 2007: 112). Neither do we think that the relatively more limited autonomy of very young children can constitute a legitimization for temporarily withholding or entirely denying them certain rights, as they are not less human than older children.

> Although the implication of exercising particular rights, particularly participation rights, may shift as children become older and perhaps better able to deal with longer term perspectives and abstract concepts, this is not an argument for denying children the exercise of the right. (Van Bueren, 1998: 3)

Arguments against the appropriateness of making what are considered individual qualities and competences the measure of eligibility for children's rights are manifold and can be found beyond normative-philosophical debates on the link between humanity and human rights. As evidenced in the rich literature on disability (for instance, Jenkins, 1998), classifications and measurements forming the basis to judge individual (in)competence, (dis)ability, autonomy/dependency and similar concepts are socially constructed and subject to sizeable variations *amongst* different historical and socio-cultural contexts, as well as significant incoherence and inconsistencies *within* societies. To base the eligibility of individuals to hold and exercise human and children's rights on such classifications seems, the very least, problematic.

In a related, but more child-specific, argument, Michael Freeman reminds us, with reference to Alderson, Hawthorne and Killen (2005a; 2005b), that evidence from newer empirical social research on children strongly refutes dominant assumptions about young children's incompetence and incapability to exercise agency:

> Rights are important because those who have them can exercise agency. Agents are decision-makers. They are persons who can negotiate with others, who can alter relationships and decisions, who can shift social assumptions and constraints. And there is now clear evidence that even the youngest amongst us can do this. (Freeman, 2011: 22)

On the same note, Tom Campbell (1992: 19) states that 'lack of physical independence at these early stages is erroneously confused with lack of the capacity for choice autonomy which is an everyday feature of a child's life even in conditions of extreme dependency'. Nonetheless, the question remains how to deal with the rights of children who are incapable of, or hindered from, defending their own rights, be it because of individual attributes or because of the specific social relations and living conditions they experience.

We are aware of the impossibility of applying every human right to children in exactly the same manner as it is applied to adults. This impossibility is linked both to the fact that children are regarded as embodying a specific life stage regardless of how exactly childhood is socio-culturally conceived of in the society they are part of, and to the specific social positions children occupy in societies in which they grow up. In order to enable children to make use of their rights, they must be treated with a minimum of respect,[1] and they must dispose of institutionalized avenues for making rights-based claims. But in most societies, children experience such institutionalized legal, political and social exclusion that it is hardly conceivable how they could overcome the 'immense difficulties in winning, for themselves, a discursive recognition of their rights or policies that aim to challenge their ... social marginalization' (Grugel & Piper, 2007: 153).

Related to their marginalization, thinking in legal terms and in the language of rights itself is unusual to children. With regard to codified law, children are largely excluded both from 'legislating' and 'administering' law. When they come into contact with the legal world, they mostly experience it in a negative way because it tends to be constraining and disciplining. From the perspective taken in this book, it is therefore not sufficient to 'give' rights to children. Children must also perceive these rights as their own, i.e. they must be able to establish a relationship between their rights and their lives. In addition, children must have the opportunity to have their rights realized; that is, they must also be able to claim their rights and have them recognized. This can only happen if children find recognition as competent subjects and trustworthy counterparts, as actors who, on the one hand, are capable of taking their rights seriously and, on the other hand, can play an essential role in contributing to their realization, including children who are particularly socially disadvantaged and who find them-selves extremely marginalized.

Approaches narrowing the field of vision down to rights 'existing on paper' and to the best legal means to implement and enforce these, while excluding interrogations on their wider contexts, are not exclusive to the field of children's rights but reflect a general tendency within human rights scholarship and practice.

According to Makau Mutua (2002: 4), the 'major authors of human rights discourse seem to believe that all the most important human rights standards and norms have been set and that what remains of the [human rights] project is elaboration and implementation'. Similarly, Tony Evans (2007: 109) describes the human rights discourse as characterized by an 'overwhelming focus ... on legal instruments, practices and institutions', and notes that critiques of human rights regimes 'are commonly concerned with refining, polishing, and elaborating accepted norms, standards, and practices in an attempt to make the regime more elegant, sophisticated, imposing and magisterial' (ibid.: 110), leading to what Upendra Baxi (2006: 184) terms a 'violent epistemic exclusion'.

In contrast, an increasing number of authors from different disciplines and with a variety of theoretical backgrounds have come to question the adequacy of such top-down approaches to human rights. First, they under-line the highly politicized history and continuous development of human rights and remind us that before they became codified into international conventions or declarations and entered the mainstream discourse, the principles and demands forming their basis were 'part of struggles for self-definition and for social justice ... , seen as something that needed to be fought for' (Cornwall & Nyambu-Molyneux, 2004: 1420). Turning towards the social foundations and prerequisites for the realization of rights, Woodiwiss (2006: 37) rightly points out that 'for rights to work far more than law itself is required', as most importantly, 'to be effective the legal enforcement of human rights ... *must mobilize the supportive elements and/or processes present within the social routines of everyday life*' (ibid.: 34; emphasis added). To paraphrase Woodiwiss's remarks on the 'disproportion between human rights related legal events and social events with a potential human rights content' (ibid.), we can assume that on any day in a country like the United Kingdom, there are hundreds of thousands of potentially children's rights-related legal events, but millions of other social events with a poten-tial children's rights content also take place on the same day. While a legal-ist and/or statist perspective might be adequate for analysing the former, we need different conceptual and analytical instruments for understanding the latter.

Therefore, what we are arguing for in this book is an approach to chil-dren's rights aware of the limitations of the statics and legalism pervading large parts of child rights-oriented literature and practice and which reflects children's rights as field of academic inquiry requiring more encompassing analytical instruments than those prone to the 'technicalization' and 'contextualization' mentioned in the introduction.

Although the CRC was the result of a normative struggle that expanded over many decades, involving conflicting conceptions of childhood and children, their needs, their appropriate place in family and society and, accordingly, competing conceptions of the rights they should obtain, the eventual document came into being without the active involvement of children. Seen from the perspective of children, the rights enshrined in the CRC constitute granted rights, in whose elaboration children had no role. For children to become rights-holders in the sense of the use of rights, we believe it is necessary that they gain influence as to the way in which these are understood and put into practice. However, attention to children as active rights-holders should not be limited to their involvement in the interpretation and application of existing, already codified rights (see VeneKlasen et al., 2005: 7). If we take the aforementioned conceptualizations of human rights as the products of struggle seriously and apply it to children's rights, we must also consider the possibility that children could demand and contribute to modifications or expansions to the rights available to them, and where necessary, replace them with better and more appropriate rights. They must also be permitted to formulate rights themselves and to insist upon their recognition and implementation. As we will try to show later in this book, contrary to a widespread assumption, children are actively involved in the interpretation, realization and reworking of children's rights.

We can assume that rights thought up and formulated by children themselves would have a more direct and concrete connection to their lives and their ideas of a just and equitable existence. Such rights would certainly not be equally important to all children. But, arguably, measured against an important insight of newer social childhood studies we will turn to later, namely, the inadequacy of speaking of one childhood in the face of the large variety and diversity of lives lived by children, the expectation that rights can be formulated and codified with a claim to universality, and be of equal interest to all children, can only be mistaken. From a perspective which takes into account the large variety of childhoods, any generally formulated rights would therefore have to be combined and completed with more specific rights.

Even if claims by children for not-yet-existing rights were eventually translated into codified rights, they would remain largely inconsequential without general recognition by society. They might give children the satisfaction of having become active and having created something of their own. But since any practical effectiveness of rights depends on the nature of wider sets of social relations and transformations within them (see Woodiwiss, 2006: 37), both in the case of rights that have their origin in children's rights claims and rights that adults granted to children, the task does not stop at their legal codification. Furthermore, if we assume that the social conditions and relations that make children's rights in general, and specific rights in particular, necessary are constantly being transformed, the adequacy of rights must be constantly questioned and, where necessary, existing rights must be modified and developed further.

Relevance and limitations of the CRC

We appreciate the CRC as a 'convenient benchmark' (Freeman, 2009: 388) which contributes to fundamental improvements in the life of children all over the world. But considering that the convention is 'a beginning rather than the final word on children's rights' (ibid.), it seems also important to us to reflect on its limitations. It is essential to bear in mind that the CRC does not, first and foremost, aim at providing rights being used by children. As with all international human rights law, the CRC primarily addresses the state as guarantor of children's rights. In parts, the CRC devolves obligations and responsibilities to the family, parents, private social welfare institutions and other adult individuals or institutions. Critically, even children's rights to participation which are established for the first time in an international human rights treaty do not guarantee any weight in decision-making but are limited to the right to be consulted. While the participatory rights established with the CRC doubtlessly indicate a very important shift in terms of conceptualizing children as actors and not only as passive objects of adults' agency, it is still far from providing a basis for equal respect between adults and children.

Similarly, there is little guidance on how exactly the core principle of the 'best interests of the child' should be interpreted and implemented. In practice, it probably most often depends on who exactly has the authority to interpret this principle and how this authority is put into practice. However, a fundamental question lies in 'whether the best interest of the child is served by focusing exclusively on the child's welfare or whether children are entitled to participate in decisions affecting their own destinies' (van Bueren, 1998: 16). If the latter is taken seriously, ways must be found for children to play a substantial role in the interpretation and invocation of their rights. Accordingly, it would not be sufficient to conceptualize children as abstract legal subjects, but they would have to be understood as social subjects, for whom rights have a meaning and a practical value.

According to Campbell (1992), the best interests of the child can be understood at least in three different ways: a) as interests held by children as persons regardless of their age; b) as interests held by children in relation to their present life; and c) as future-oriented interests children have as 'future adults'. Newer social approaches to childhood research have raised attention to the fact that 'children often suffer discrimination through an overemphasis on their position as future adults and an underemphasis on their status both as persons and as children' (ibid.: 4). In the meantime, we know that it comes to an underestimation and devaluation of children's 'agency' and to a 'downgrading' of their status in society, when children are only seen in their role as 'becomings' instead of being recognized and treated in their role as 'beings' as well.

In this regard, the CRC allows for ample interpretations. Art. 12, for instance, says that the exercise of rights and consideration of the children's views and opinions must be 'in accordance with the age and maturity of the child' and it is made dependent on the fact whether a child 'is capable of forming his or her own views'. These restrictions give way to random interpretation of whether or not or to what extent children's views ought to be considered or even asked for by those with decision-making power.

In this sense, it is important to think of Gerison Lansdown's (2005) reflections on the 'evolving capacities of the child' (gathered in Art. 5 of the CRC). Following her argumentation, in accordance with the evolution of the above-mentioned capacities, an appropriate direction and orientation is needed so that the child can exercise his or her rights; a direction and orientation that does not require certain competencies for assuming responsibility and taking decisions on their own life, but rather implies that the children develop them also through the assumption of responsibility and by making own decisions. For Lansdown (2005: 15), the 'evolution of the capacities' is based in three conceptual frames that have a complex relationship with each other:

1. As a *developmental* concept, recognizing the extent to which children's development, competence and emerging personal autonomy are promoted through the realization of the CRC rights.
2. As a *participatory* or *emancipatory* concept, denoting children's right to respect for their capacities and for shifting the responsibility for exercising rights from adults to children in accordance with their levels of competence.
3. As a *protective* concept, which acknowledges that because children's capacities are still evolving throughout childhood, they have rights to protection from exposure to activities likely to cause them harm both by parents and the state.

It is also necessary to mention that the limitations are, in fact, generally not caused by a lack of good will but rather are dependent on the given external structures which hinder children from interpreting and exercising their rights themselves.

Furthermore, it is important to ask why in particular in relation to children such emphasis is placed on the issue of them having to formulate their own points of view (and on which basis can be judged whether this is their 'own') and why there are restrictions especially to children's freedom of expression as they should limit their statements to matters affecting them.

(Hasn't the child already been affected when it wants to express herself, and how do those matters which affect children differ from those which do not?) Additionally, one must ask critically, why it is especially important with respect to a child, that she expresses her 'own' views (who can measure the 'individuality' of her perspective against what kind of criterion?), and why must children limit the expression of their opinions to matters that affect them. (Isn't the child 'affected' when she wants to express herself, and how do the 'affecting' matters differ from those who do not affect a child?)

Apparently, the half-heartedness and ambiguities of the CRC's definitions of participation express the great reservations that many official state representatives who participated in the final drafting of the CRC had towards strengthening the children's social status and reveal that compromises were needed. The understanding of a child who effectively has become accepted assumes that he or she is per se inferior to an adult and lagging behind in her capacities. In juridical interpretations, this is revealed in chronological age determinations. The fact that the participation of children is tied to such conditions questions the understanding of children's rights as inalienable, i.e. unconditionally effective human rights. The underlying risk is to discriminate against children because they have not yet reached a certain age. (On the advantages and disadvantages of fixing the limits of age or their elimination, see Lansdown, 2004).

The question of how to interpret and identify the 'best interests of the child' is to be posed not only in life-course or generational perspectives but also with respect to differences among children. The 'child', as defined in terms of the CRC, as a member of the age group younger than 18, only exists as an abstraction. In social reality, there are major differences between younger and older children, as well as between children of different life situations and social or ethnic background. These can play even greater roles than those between children and adults. Such differences exist not only in regard to the 'agency' which is certified and granted to children, but also in regard to their own location in the respective society or community. To detect and understand the particular interests of children, their situation and self-perception must also be considered.

Contribution by the new social childhood studies

As we have already pointed out, reflections on the social preconditions and contexts of rights are largely missing in the children's rights debate and practice. To address this gap, it could be helpful to take account of the development of new sociological approaches that seem adequate to theoretically back a less paternalistic and more participatory understanding of children's rights.[2] These approaches all conceptualize childhood less as a biological fact than as a social-historical category, and they all consider children as social agents. In sociology, social psychology, anthropological, historical, cultural, media and literary studies as well as in history, philosophy, economic science, geography or social policy (just to point out the most important disciplines) the concrete conditions for children's organization of their daily life have increasingly become the focus of concern. The primary interest hereby is not, as it has been until now, the mutuality of children growing up, but the historical, cultural and economic differences. The goal is to find out how the empirically detectable diversity of living environments influences behaviour, emotions and attitudes of children (see Alderson, 2005: 128).

Instead of concentrating on the biological incompleteness of children, these new approaches concentrate on aspects of performance of 'childhood'. Thus, childhood is no longer understood as a naturally given span of time of maturing and development, but as a social category or construction which in principle can be carried out differently. Closely tied to this assumption is the idea that children are seen not only as recipients of adults' services and, as such, as objects or products of their efforts of socialization, but also as independent social subjects and active stakeholders.

The acceptance of childhood(s) being strongly influenced by the times and spaces in which they take place, characterizes the tenor and mainspring of new childhood studies. They began to question components of a 'correct' childhood which had been taken for granted, such as being raised in the family of origin, school attendance, pedagogical attendance, desexualization, disentanglement from economic relationships or their sentimentalization (Zelizer, 1985; 2005; 2011). Historical as well as ethnological studies account for the cultural diversity of childhoods. From a perspective that understands childhood in its particular social construction, facts that had been perceived as general truths can be identified as characteristics of certain dominant cultures or social groups. The model of a 'correct' childhood predominantly found in Europe can thus be proved to be further developments of an idealized middle-class concept of protected childhood in family, whose worldwide implementation is a goal.

The insight into cultural heterogeneity and (co-)existence of different childhoods had the consequence that children who did not fit in the existing model of childhood were generally not dismissed as deficient anymore. Consequently, the differences within the childhood(s) of the same society also became a matter of interest. Here, different environmental influences such as social status, sex/gender and ethnic affiliation, shape different cultures inside a single society and thus lead to diverse and varying experiences of childhoods. The empirically detectable models of childhood challenge the implicitness with which conditions of growing up have been judged either as child-friendly and positive, and thus as good and right, or as dangerous for the development of the child, and thus as wrong. The many presuppositions of what belonged to a 'correct' childhood and therefore was indispensable for growing up well and prosperously (for instance, that children ought to grow up with their father and mother, children ought to go to school, children should not earn their own livelihood and children ought to play) thus become inconsistent.

However, the new childhood studies do not adopt an arbitrary relativism that brings no practical benefit for children aside from the quest for truth. To the contrary, precisely by unfolding the social standardization of childhood, the opportunity has arisen to recognize more clearly the potentially underlying hegemonic interests. Only if children in socio-scientific childhood research are understood as a social group that lives under specific conditions in a surrounding society, structural social disparities can be recognized and questioned. As we will show, this is of great importance for understanding the subjective relevance of children's rights according to different living conditions, and for recognizing the necessity of their contextualization.

Opposing the conception of children as 'developing' or 'unfinished' persons, recent childhood studies have perceived and valued children as 'beings' and as active social stakeholders. Instead of understanding children merely as future members of society who will start playing a decisive role when they come of age, they are considered self-determined members of society who readily act in their own interest. Thus, far more than only the long-standing debates of pedagogues about a new 'image of children' to which education is oriented will be discussed. In fact, it means to take a radically different attitude towards children: They are seen as subjects who have a right to be taken seriously, not only in the future but also in their present. It is surely recognized that children's acting is restricted by defined social demands, specific norms and conceptions as well as legal regulations; nonetheless, they can not only be considered as objects to, or victims of, these structural conditions. Rather, it is accepted that they play an active role in the organization of their environment.

In this context, it seems important to revisit not only the notion of 'childhood' but also the use of the related concepts of 'child' and 'children', especially as both the habitual language use and sciences mostly do not differentiate them well. As each of the concepts refers to another aspect, and thus to another set of problems, conceptual specification is necessary. The currently widely accepted basic principle of new social childhood studies has adopted an understanding of the term 'childhood' as a description of a structural pattern which includes 'children' collectively. There is a tendency to 'clump children together as members of a category' without considering the diversity of childhoods (James, 2007: 262). But inside of this collective and institutionalized (living) space of 'childhood' and the associated group called 'children', each single 'child' acts individually and as an independent stakeholder (James & James, 2004: 14; James, 2009). The use of the generalizing expression 'child', when reference shall be made to 'children' as group or category, expresses a lack of sensitivity towards children as serious individuals. Such generalizations are usually only used for groups that are denied or not granted individuality. An 'adult' would justly refuse such generalization for himself or herself.

New childhood studies assume that children are subjects who make experiences, who reflect these experiences, and who are able to communicate them. Thus, children are seen as social stakeholders who organize their environment actively on the basis of their knowledge, by means of their possibilities and according to their interests. It is presumed that they interact with people, institutions and their different purposes and positions in their daily routine and that by doing so they assert their respective position in social space in their own manner (Prout, 2000: 7). Accordingly, children do not only have their own will, own wishes and needs and do not only stand in a reciprocal exchange with their environment, as it has long been accepted in pedagogy and cognitive developmental psychology. (See Woodhead, 2009). Moreover, new childhood studies explore how children, through their individual and collective actions, can make a difference 'to a relationship, a decision, to the workings of a set of social assumptions or constraints' (Mayall, 2002: 21). What this focus on children's agency has achieved, therefore, 'is a re-conceptualization not only of what "childhood" is, but also of the ways in which children themselves can be understood as active participants in society' (James, 2009: 34).

As the influence of children is certainly strongly restricted due to their marginalized and relatively powerless social status, new childhood studies see their challenge in making the children's voices heard. Unlike other socially 'minorized' groups (for instance, women or ethnic minorities), children have no collectively adoptable means to 'assert their claims concerning specific inventories of knowledge with respect to themselves' (Alanen, 1994: 97). This is not, as could be argued from a developmental point of view, a question of lacking competence or maturity, but a question of disparate relations of power and acceptance. With regard to proper concepts of reality, there is no reason to assume a quasi-'natural' difference between children and adults (ibid.).

By conceiving childhood as social category, and by recognizing children as social subjects, new childhood studies have opened a new view on children and childhood(s). They represent a paradigm shift that could advance the equality of children and adults on the level of social co-determination without negating the particular situation and special needs of children. However, in some areas of childhood studies, the idea that the form of 'modern childhood' generated in Europe is more developed than other cultural manifestations of childhood has remained, and there is a lack of unbiased empirical studies concerned with childhoods outside the western cultural area. (Exceptions include Penn, 2005, and Montgomery, 2008)[3] Furthermore, it must be considered that up to now, 'the new sociology of childhood has not enabled significant progress either in research techniques or in adding to data related to children's rights. ... The picture gained from the available literature is of scattered, poorly-documented and non-comparable studies, which seldom involve children in systematic data collection, much less in planning research and designing research tools' (Ennew, 2011: 135, 137).

Cross-cultural perspectives on children's rights

Like all human rights codified in UN conventions, the children's rights formulated in the CRC claim universal validity. Nevertheless they are criticized especially by people from the majority world who consider them a manifestation of western hegemony and partly incompatible with certain other cultural traditions. It is necessary to question whether, and the extent to which, this criticism is a qualified one, and how the claim for universality of children's rights can involve cultural diversity. We are especially interested in finding out in which way further developments of children's rights can promote culturally specific ways of living and the equality and acceptance of children as subjects with their own positions and interests.

In relevant literature, the views and answers to this question vary. Some authors, and especially the UN Committee on the Rights of the Child, emphasize the openness of the CRC to different cultures and point out that cultures are not stable, self-contained entities but 'adaptive systems' (see, e.g., Alston, 1994; Brems, 2007). In this sense, the CRC and the UN Human Rights systems, too, are understood as an adaptive system in a permanent process of change. However, it is often expected from 'cultures' to 'open up' to the idea of human and children's rights, i.e. to align by further development, and by what we might call 'becoming human rights-oriented'. This perspective has been formulated particularly explicitly by agents of development work focussing on sensitization and 'capacity building' towards human rights.

Other authors equally assume that the CRC and the concept of human rights are open to different cultures, but they consider the specific interpretations and attempts at implementation of human and children's rights more critically. Among other issues, their criticism refers to the fact that the discourse on human and children's rights is exploited by certain power groups, who act as 'moral watchdogs' with the aim of 'modernizing' and 'civilizing' allegedly backward cultures and ways of living (e.g. Pupavac, 1998; Bentley, 2005; Valentin & Meinert, 2009). In their objections to this way of handling human and children's rights, the authors are not necessarily led by considerations of cultural relativism; rather, they believe it to be crucial to distinguish 'real culture' as interpreted by the people living the culture themselves and 'the culture presented to outsiders by governments and intellectuals' (Freeman, 2002: 30; see also Harris-Short, 2003). Thus, the objections are directed against the quasi-exercise of human and children's rights from above by governmental actors and power elites; a 'localized' notion of rights and 'dialectic' approaches are set against this view. By doing so, the diversity and meanings of cultures and ways of living are acknowledged and promoted instead of denigrating them as fundamentally backwards. In this book, we take up the aforementioned thoughts and inquire about possible alternatives of a culturally differentiated and context specific dealing with children's rights.

With regard to children's rights, we want to ask whether the instrumentalization we tagged as problematic is intrinsic to the design of the CRC. It has been pointed out various times in literature that the CRC is based on a certain concept of childhood, whose founding principles have been developed in the European enlightenment and bourgeois society, and whose global normative validity is now claimed (see, e.g., Boyden, 1997; Pupavac, 1998; 2001; Harris-Short, 2001; Ennew, 2002; Cussiánovich, 2010b; Holzscheiter, 2010). Mostly, it is given the name 'modern childhood' and is conceptualized as a historically particularly sophisticated stage of childhood (for critical remarks on this, see Alanen, 1992). Childhood – in this case up to the age of 18 – is strictly separated from adulthood and is defined as a stage characterized by particular vulnerability and lack of maturity. In relation to the vulnerability, the implicit point of reference is a society that harms the child if he or she is not protected from it (i.e. the focus is on the child's protection, embodied in the so-called protection rights). This is completed by the idea that a child, first and foremost, must be attended to; i.e. the relationship between adult and child is conceived as one of one-way dependence rather than one based on interdependence (embodied in so-called empowerment rights).

The adult, who is presented as perfect, or at least as superior to the child, is the standard for measuring the lack of maturity. Thus, a system of power focussed on adults is confused with personal characteristics, a fact that finds expression even in the conception of the so-called participation rights. These merely concede a child the right to be heard but not the right to independent decision-making or self-determination. The right to be heard hereby only comprises the idea that opinions of the child (as far as he or she is considered capable of judging wisely) shall preferentially be taken into account by those governmental institutions and adults in power. According to this understanding, it must be said that, for the first time, the child as a legal subject is endowed with certain civil liberties, but he or she is still not provided with political power (for instance, voting rights).[4]

With this critical remark, we do not want to de-emphasize the fact that in the CRC, children are guaranteed the status of juridical person according to international law, for the first time ever. Still, we want to point out its constraints and conditionality (sometimes also opposed to the principles of human rights). We also do not want to deny that the CRC contains some phrases which imply recognition of other cultures and their ways of practising 'childhoods'. According to the preamble, the public agreements and all activities made in the CRC are to be understood with 'due account of the importance of the traditions and cultural values of each people for the protection and harmonious development of the child'. Yet, the CRC leaves little space to imagine other childhoods, that do not conform to the structural pattern of 'modern' childhood, and that indeed are practised in some cultures or do transcend the societies and cultures we usually have in mind and which children possibly create themselves.

Approaches and problems of participatory children's rights practice

The principles of the CRC – understanding the child as juridical person and the explicit establishment of participatory rights – have driven a considerable number of civil society organizations to reorientate their practices. Instead of supplying 'needy children' directly – and selectively – with commodities and services, they have come to favour advocacy and empowerment approaches, for instance public actions for children's rights and informing children about their rights to trigger more participation. Contrary to formerly dominant charitable approaches, the new approaches are propagated and discussed under the notions of 'Rights-based Approach' or 'Child Rights Programming' (see, e.g., Save the Children, 2002; Theis, 2004; Tobin, 2011).

   The charitable approach starts from the assumption of neediness and considers the assistance for disadvantaged and needy people as (voluntary) moral self-commitment of those who are 'better off' and who dispose of more resources. The rights-oriented approach, on the other hand, emphasizes the general right of all humans to claim certain services and benefits from the society they live in and the obligation of those persons and institutions in power to take (a share of) the responsibility for the powerless.

   The action approach of Child Rights Programming occurs in the basic principles of *responsibility, participation* and *equality* and implies different elements and areas of social and political reality that can be important to its successful implementation. On the one hand, the responsible authorities – above all, the state – shall be admonished to protect and respect children's rights (and human rights in general), and they shall be encouraged to improve their structural conditions and capacities to fulfil their obligations. On the other hand, children and their families and local groups of civil society, respectively, shall be supported in claiming children's rights against the state and other powerful authorities of society. It is important that the 'political space of action' grow and that all people of all ages, either gender and any social origin can participate and strengthen their potential for action equally and free of discrimination.

   With regard to the state, laws directed against any form of discrimination and promoting equality of opportunities and 'inclusion' are aspired.

Appropriate political agendas shall enhance cultural diversity, tolerance and options in daily life. Economic and social policy shall contribute to accomplishing human rights (for instance, by improving standards of labour law, by progressive taxation or by promoting fair trade) and guarantee equally distributed access to social services for everyone. On the other side, campaigns and educational work should increase the sensitivity and alertness towards violations of human rights in 'civil society' and awaken its interest to speak up for more participation in all social and political concerns.

These guiding principles are based on the assumption that the implementation of children's rights can only be achieved in a society that is characterized by, or at least strives for, democracy and social equity. On this basis, the power relations between adults and children also need to be changed, in the direction of increasing equality and reciprocal respect. On the one hand, adults (parents, teachers, educators and functionaries in governmental and non-governmental organizations) shall be sensitized to the rights and basic needs of children, and on the other hand children shall be encouraged and empowered to advocate for their rights. In particular, children coming from groups who are discriminated against or otherwise socially disadvantaged shall be encouraged to claim their rights and to participate fully in society.

By now, the approach of Child Rights Programming has been put into practice mainly in countries of the majority world. In several cases, this has produced new initiatives of child policy among governments and communal authorities, as well as among organizations of civil society that have been beneficial for children. However, some problems have become apparent during the implementation of this new approach. After all, it is an approach designed from the perspective of people and organizations who 'know how' and want to 'enlighten', and thus it contains the political message of a developmental backwardness in certain countries, cultures and population groups which ought to compensated. Therefore, according to John Tobin (2011: 67), we want to stress that 'there is no logical impediment to a rights-based approach embracing alternative sources of human rights standards which could be drawn from regional or domestic human rights instruments (or indeed a moral or political theory of rights that has not been transformed into law)'. Tobin makes this point 'because whenever the phrase "rights based approach" is invoked the question must be asked, which rights?' (ibid.).

Furthermore, there is no clear and generally accepted concept of what should be understood by *participation of children*, to which area it can extend and under which conditions children really can take an active role in the realization of their rights. It has become increasingly evident that objective and subjective conditions for effective participation differ to such an extent amongst different countries, cultures, living conditions, genders and ages of children that particular approaches and forms of implementation must be found in each case.

In many countries, participatory approaches of international organizations are dismissed with the argumentation that they are an expression of
western ideals and not compatible with local culture. (See, e.g., van Beers
et al., 2006: 13) One reason for this can be the wish to preserve paternalistic customs and structures, but it can also be a reaction to paternalistic
practices of organizations that are headquartered in the richer regions of
the world and that consider there to be no alternative to their own interpretation of children's rights. Indeed, these organizations often impose their
perceptions as a condition for further aid on those local groups that are
financially dependent on them (Valentin & Meinert, 2009). Therefore, it is
necessary to confront local cultures without the preconceived judgements
that they have anti-child and anti-participatory attitudes, and to observe
accurately the ways in which children are integrated into communal life.
Sometimes children already play a far more active and responsible role then
envisaged in many models of participation inspired by the 'West' (See, e.g.,
Burr, 2006; Smith, 2007).

While the clauses on children's participation contained in the CRC point
towards the obligation of such a participatory exercise of children's rights,
case studies from the majority world point towards the possibility that the
specific conception of participation underlying the CRC may constitute an
a priori limitation on the child-empowering range of these rights. If children's participation was understood as not only consisting of being heard
and having a voice, but also as taking part in vital economic and political
processes, new opportunities could arise for the positioning of children in
the community and society. Children's participation thus is not depicted as
a particular form of communication arranged selectively and with specific
aims in mind by adults for children, but as an element of the daily, meaningful and essential agency of children themselves. While this agency is
embedded in social relationships, it is essential to understand and respect
children not only as executing actors but also as independently-acting
subjects with their own rights.

Another problem results from the fact that the 'participation of children'
has become a fashionable trend from which children often benefit less than
a new class of NGO specialists. Instead of strengthening the position of children within their life contexts and enlarging their influence on living conditions, 'participation' is sometimes celebrated and exercised in convenient
places with small groups of precisely-selected children. In this way, some
local NGOs decorate themselves with their particular activities for children's participation. But where children and young people want to develop
their own approaches and become active on the spot, they are accused of
aimless activism, and help is denied. Moreover, the necessity of including
those children and young people in project activities who do not comply
with the norms of the project-leading organization immediately or without
questioning them or who find it difficult, at first, to play to the gallery

openly, is underestimated or denied. They are considered 'difficult cases' or even 'unable to participate' and are excluded or handed over to charitable organizations.

Such problems in handling the participatory rights of children are found predominantly in countries of the majority world, in which children, even more than in countries of the minority world, are confronted with difficulties and animosity in their everyday lives. However, these problems are by no means restricted to that region of the world.

Outlook on children's rights' future

The development of children's rights has come to a crossroads. While for the longest time the question of how adults and the institutions and organizations formed by them can be brought to recognize and implement children's rights has been dominant, now more interest is put on ways in which children themselves can make use of their rights and can possibly contribute to their modification. According to Geraldine van Bueren (1998: 1), there are three different stages in the development of children's rights then, which are even more distinguishable than those in the development of human rights in general.

The first stage has been the recognition by the international community that all individuals, including children, are subjects of international law requiring international legal protection. The second stage, which is still evolving, is the granting of specific substantive rights to individuals, including children. The third stage, which is also still developing, is the acknowledgement that in order to ensure that individuals are able to enjoy the exercise of their fundamental rights they must be acknowledged to possess the necessary procedural capacity to exercise and claim these rights and freedoms. Where the international law on the rights of the child differs from the general body of international human rights law is in the development of the second and third stages. Although recognizing in principal that children are entitled to enjoy the full range of civil rights, this has not always been acknowledged in practice by states or by human rights tribunals. ... A similar reluctance has marked the international community's recognition of the rights of the child to possess sufficient procedural capacity to act on his or her own behalf.

During the last decade, 'awareness has been growing that children can play a key role in the realization of their rights' (Vučković Šahović, 2010: 8). Efforts to include children in measures aimed at implementing their rights and to strengthen children's active contribution to child-rights practice have significantly increased. Numerous NGOs have designed concepts to that effect, and the UN Committee on the Rights of the Child has encouraged children and youth to claim their rights themselves and to participate in the activities of the Committee. Only recently, in its General Comment No 12 (2009) on 'The Right of the Child to be heard', the Committee has called on states parties to enable children to form groups and organizations so that they can express their views on matters affecting them. The Committee also asks states parties to listen to children, including their collective speech. States parties should enable continuous participation of children in decision-making processes through organizational structures, such as student councils and representation on school boards and committees. Further, the Committee underlined the important role of NGOs in developing practices to support children by safeguarding transparency of representation and countering the risk of manipulation or tokenism.

The Committee and NGOs have thereby responded to a number of initiatives that have come from children and youth themselves. 'The past decade has seen growth in children's organizations, some established and run by children and adolescents themselves' (Vučković Šahović, 2010: 8). A leading role in this has been played by children and young people from the majority world, especially working children and their self-organized movements and organizations (see Chapter 9). Since 1998, two working-children's organizations in India have turned to the Committee with their own reports, reflecting a trend in which increasingly children's groups prepare and submit alternative reports. In only two years (between 2007 and 2009), the Committee received reports from children from more than 20 countries, including Australia, Austria, China, Denmark, India, Ireland, Japan, Kenya, Latvia, Lesotho, Mali, Moldova, Netherlands, Norway, Peru, Senegal, Serbia, Sierra Leone, Sweden, Thailand, Uganda, the United Kingdom and Uzbekistan (Vučković Šahović, 2010; Simeunovič Frick, 2011; for recent examples, see AGJ, 2010; Funky Dragon, 2011). In these reports, children sometimes raise issues or provide evidence on subjects not raised in official states' or alternative reports submitted by NGOs.

These and other interventions by children and youth in different parts of the world are important indications that young people increasingly claim and want to use their rights. But they should not be understood in the sense that the influence of children on the interpretation and implementation of their rights has already substantially been strengthened. The obstacles hindering children from appreciating children's rights as a viable and relevant way to improve their lives still exist. 'A review of state party reports and concluding observations indicates that implementation of legal standards remains the weakest area among the general measures of CRC implementation. For instance, the right to be protected from violence or exploitation cannot be enjoyed in the absence of an independent, professional and child-sensitized judiciary, which few countries have' (Vučković Šahović, 2010: 9). For some rights, among them the core participatory rights, the perspective for a timely and meaningful implementation could, arguably, even have diminished in the face of wider societal changes in which decision-making centres importantly affecting lives of children are increasingly remote and out of the reach of local or national democratic processes.

It is not only the lack of institutions to which children can turn with a reasonable expectation to be listened to and taken seriously that constitutes a barrier for them to take up children's rights as their own cause, but also a lack of contextualization and localization of children's rights themselves. In many cases, it is relevant to consult with children about whether they believe their rights are being fully recognized and realized. Interviewing children and promoting them as researchers (with appropriate ethical considerations and safeguards) can be important ways to learn about key aspects of their lives, such as the extent to which they enjoy respect for their civil rights, including the right to have their views heard and given due consideration, in the family, schools and the community (see, e.g., Knowing Children, 2009).

Notes

1. In the sense of taking what they have to say seriously.
2. The following considerations refer in parts to Hungerland, 2010.
3. This is clearly stated in relevant anthologies (Qvortrup, 2005; Qvortrup, 2009) and in *The Palgrave Handbook of Childhood Studies* (Qvortrup, Corsaro & Honig, 2009).
4. The UN Committee on the Rights of the Child has recently begun attempts to recognize the right to be heard as a collective right of children (by way of the General Comment No. 12, 2009), something that definitely strengthens the position of children as social group and disrupts the adultist power relations.

2
Hidden Aspects of Children's Rights History

Manfred Liebel

> We respect our masters and are willing to work for our living and that of our parents, but we want more time to rest, to play a little, and to learn reading and writing. We do not think it right that we have to work and suffer from Monday early to Saturday night to make others rich. Honourable Gentlemen, enquire carefully into our situation!
>
> (Children's petition to the House of Commons, England, 1836)[1]

The discourse on children's rights has many facets and meanings. They can be understood as a special form of human rights or as guidelines that separate childhood as a phase in life and as a status from adulthood. Under the United Nations Convention on the Rights of the Child (CRC), a differentiation is often made among protection, provision and participation rights or rights to freedom. Besides rights to secure the basic needs of children, rights that serve to ensure the development of children are emphasized. Therefore children's rights can be understood as 'welfare rights' which are enforced by adults on behalf of, and in the interest of, children or as 'agency rights' which are used and enforced by children themselves. Analogous to general human rights, children's rights can be distinguished as civil, political, economic, social and cultural rights. Finally, it is possible to speak of 'unwritten rights' (Ennew, 2002) of children besides the codified rights that are based in international treaties or national legislation. They are thought of or invented and demanded by children or other people.

In discussions on children's rights, these different meanings are often not distinguished enough. In practice, however, they can also overlap, depending on the intentions with which they are handled; for instance, when weighing state duty against children's claims to autonomy. Here, the emphasis should be put on a concept of children's rights that, first and foremost, sees children' rights as *human rights in the hands of children* and as a means to *strengthen their social position* and to *extend their scope of activity*.

The development of children's rights

If we understand children's rights as a specific set of human rights, their beginning is to be found in the European Enlightenment, i.e. in the 18th century. However, when we take a closer look at the different aspects of children's rights, we can neither view them purely as a European achievement nor limit their beginnings to the last 250 years.

Rights to *protect* children probably have the longest and most widespread history. They emerged from the conviction that the life of a newborn deserves protection; that children are not equal to a thing that can be handled discretionally. This can be seen particularly well in regulations prohibiting the killing of children. The reasoning behind this attitude towards children can be found in the common belief held by all of the world's major religions that children do not belong to individual persons who have power over them but that they are God's creations. In Europe in 1530, Martin Luther (1483–1546) was probably the first person to voice that children do not belong to their parents but to God and to the community (see Alaimo, 2002: 6). About 150 years later, at the end of the 17th century, the British liberal philosopher John Locke (1632–1704) also questioned the parents' right of disposition over their children (see Archard, 2004). However, even into the 19th century, this applied only to male descendants. In those days, farmers in France, for instance, would say, 'I don't have any children, only girls.' In Naples, it was very common to hiss a black flag when a girl was born, as a signal to everyone that congratulations were not appropriate (see Verhellen, 2000: 12). In some parts of the world, for instance, in China or India, similar customs are still in place and sometimes lead to avoidance of female births, using modern reproductive medicine.

Provision and *participation* rights or *freedoms* seem to be of a younger age, with one remarkable exception: The English radical and advocate of the common ownership of land Thomas Spence (1750–1814) was the first who, in his pamphlet 'The Rights of Infants' (1796), explicitly ascribed to children natural rights on 'full participation of the fruits of the earth'. Yet it also would be limiting to view them as an achievement of the European Enlightenment or even the modern welfare state. In many non-Western cultures, it has been a custom for centuries to assign capacities to children and to assign certain tasks to them which, according to Western understanding, are reserved for adults who have reached 'legal age'. In some African and South American regions, children were assigned a piece of land or cattle at a very young age, which they were to handle and take the responsibility to care for. To some extent, these practices served to learn necessary life skills at an early age, yet they also express the belief that children have their own qualities which are to be respected and promoted. In the highlands of Bolivia and Peru, a tradition is still upheld by which children at the age of 10 or 12 are elected to be mayors, as the belief is that children can give specific impulses for community life (For an overview see Liebel, 2004: 83–99). No one in these villages would think that the children lack the necessary competences for this task, let alone the legally set rights to vote and to be elected. Children in the same villages tend to work in the fields as well. And no one would think that they have to go to school first to do so or to have reached a certain minimum age for working.

In the indigenous cultures of South and Meso-America, as in other old cultures on other continents, it is not common to separate children and adults strictly by age; both are seen as an integral part of the community, each with their specific characteristics. Children are seen as 'small persons', who are to be taken seriously just like 'adults'. They are ascribed different capacities that are important for communal life and which 'adults' might not have (anymore) to the same extent. Since they are 'small', they are also looked after, and normally no tasks are assigned to them that would overwhelm or harm them (see PRATEC, 2005). Nonetheless, these customs are not seen as 'individual rights' of children which they can refer to in case of conflict. They are also not codified in legal texts that are renewed by formalized legislative procedures but are, rather, embedded informally in centuries-old traditions which are kept alive in a ritualized way. (Legally formalized procedures can certainly take on the character of rituals as well.)

In Europe, the idea of provision rights was based on the common belief from the enlightenment days in the 18th century (similar to the idea of child protection) that children are different to adults in basic needs and that these needs are to be taken into special consideration. Another idea that fuelled this was that the child must first 'develop' to become a full-fledged adult and that he or she had to be prepared for this in special institutions. Generally at this stage, there was (and still is today) an 'investment motive' behind the thinking on children's rights: 'society's concern for the child is seen very much in terms of the child's usefulness to society. Children are objects of invention rather than legal subjects' (Freeman, 1992: 30). Understood as such, the child's right to education was, for example, not formulated as the right of the child to choose an education but as a responsibility of the parents to send their children to school, which the state had established for their (obedient) education.[2]

The belief that the child should have more independence is intertwined with the idea that the community – represented by the state – ought to care for the well-being and the development of the child to become an adult who is capable of working. Whereas the history of general human rights – at least in Europe and North America – started with freedom rights, the beginnings of children's rights were marked by *protection* of children, not by their freedom. This can be seen most clearly in the history of the legislation on child labour, which has been focused on the prohibition of children working for money. It did not bring the children rights that they could claim or use as they wished, but rather put the duty on factory owners and parents to safeguard children from situations and actions that could harm their health or development.

If, by contrast, we understand the quintessence of children's rights to be that they are rights of *children*, i.e. rights that children can enforce and claim themselves (or guaranteeing that nothing may happen against the will of children), then their history is still at its beginning. Although there have been several initiatives since World War I to provide children these rights, under state law they did not surpass declarative intentions or only had validity intermittently in limited ways. Only in 1989, with the CRC, were children granted such rights in a binding way under international law. Yet even here, we should keep in mind that the rights were not formulated by children but by adults *for* children and that they are specked with reservations. 'There is no evidence that children, or children's groups as such, participated in drafting or had any real influence in preliminary discussions' (Freeman, 2009: 383).

In the history of children's rights, two main strands can be distinguished: on one hand, those who emphasize the protection of children and later the guaranty of their dignified living conditions, and on the other hand, those who strive for the equality and active participation of children in society (see Renaut, 2002).[3] The two strands do not oppose each other absolutely, yet they have each developed separately until very recently. Internationally, the first strand found its first marked expression in the Geneva Declaration on the Rights of the Child, which was signed by the League of Nations in 1924. This tendency was continued in many international agreements and led to the CRC. As this strand of children's rights history has already been described many times before,[4] we will not elaborate on it any further here. Rather, we would like to refer to the other, less-known development, in which children's rights are foremost seen as an expression and means of the emancipation and equality of children. As they generally go hand in hand with social movements, which aim at changing social and political conditions, we will name them 'children's rights movements'.[5]

Children's rights movements since the beginning of the 20th century

Parallel to the efforts to establish international treaties for the protection of children, in some countries, movements emerged at the beginning of the 20th century that expressly promoted the self-determination rights of children. They became the basis of endeavours to achieve more (political) participation of children and to recognize them as equal citizens in society. These endeavours were not limited to so-called freedom rights; rather, they were at times also extended to the social and political rights of children. They emerged either in the context of political revolutions and reformist attempts or had social movements of disadvantaged population groups as role models.

The organization 'Free Education of Children' can be seen as the pioneer of children's rights movements. Founded during the Russian revolution of 1917–1918, it had introduced a 'Declaration of Children's Rights' at the first national conference of the 'Organizations for cultural enlightenment (*Prolet'cult*)', which took place in Moscow from 23 to 28 February 1918.[6] This declaration went much further than anything understood as children's rights in Europe at the time.

Moscow Declaration of Children's Rights (1918)

1. Every child that is born, regardless of his parents' social situation, has the right to existence, that is to say he has to be guaranteed a certain set of living conditions, including child health care and those which are necessary for the preservation and development of his organism and for the successful fight of the latter with life threatening factors.
2. Guaranteeing the provision of the living conditions required to secure child health care is the responsibility of parents, society as a whole, and the state. The role of each of these factors and their relation to each other in granting the child these conditions is regulated by corresponding legal ordinances.
3. Each child, regardless of his age has a separate personality and is not to be treated or seen under any circumstance as the property of his parents nor as property of the society or state.
4. Every child has the right to choose his closest educators and to secede from his parents and leave them if they reveal themselves as bad educators. The child has this right to leave his parents at any age whereupon the state and society have to ensure that no change in this aspect has the effect of a worsening of the child's material situation.
5. Every child has the right to education and upbringing according to his individuality. The realization of this right has to be guaranteed by allocation of the according institutions for education and upbringing for him at all ages, where all sides of his nature and his character can find the most appropriate conditions for his harmonious development.
6. No child can be violently forced to attend an educational institution. All stages of upbringing and education is a matter which the child can decide upon freely. Every child has the right to reject an upbringing or education that is contrary to his individuality.
7. Each child participates in the necessary public work from the earliest possible age, in the way his strengths and skills allow him to do so. This work may however not harm the children's mental health or be a hindrance to his mental development but must rather be united with the whole system of upbringing and education. The participation in the necessary public productive work opens up the possibility of realizing one of the most important rights of the child- not to feel like a parasite but to be a stakeholder and builder of life and to realize that his life does not only have a social value in future but also already in the present.

8. The child is equal to the adult of-age persons in freedoms and rights at all ages. If these or those rights are not realized by the child, this must be solely due to the lack of the necessary physical and mental abilities. If these are not lacking, age may not be an obstacle to the use of these rights.

9. Freedom is being able to do anything which does not inhibit or harm physical and mental development and does not harm people. By this, each child can enjoy his natural rights, them being only limited by the self-dictated laws of his normal physical and mental development and anything that endangers the guarantee of these rights to the other members of society.

10. This or that group of children can be given rules for their interaction with each other or with the surrounding adults that prohibit actions harming the society as a whole. Anything not prohibited in these rules may not find any obstacle in its fulfilment. None of the children may be forced to do anything which is not prescribed by these rules.

11. All children must be granted the right to participate in the compilation of rules by which their life and capacities are regulated.

12. Nobody – neither the parents nor the society or the state – can force the child to be taught a particular religion or to be forced to conduct its rituals: religious education ought to be completely free.

13. No child may be limited due to his beliefs, only the expression thereof may not harm the same rights of the other members of society- adults and children alike.

14. Each child can express freely his opinion in writing or orally, to the same extent as the adults also have this right, that is to say, solely limited by what is dictated by the well-being of society and the personalities that is it made up of, and which must be according to the child's mental abilities and must be precisely regulated in the law.

15. Every child enjoys the right to establish organizations, associations or similar social connections with other children or adults and have this right to the same extent as adults. The possibilities for limitation, which are dictated by the best interest of the child and his normal physical and mental development, must be strictly regulated by law.

16. No child may be imprisoned or punished. The transgressions and blemishes of the child must be fought with appropriate education institutions by means of clearance and cure, but not through punishment or other measures of repressive character.

17. The state and the society must see to it, using all means, that all of the rights of the child written in the above paragraphs do not suffer limitation in any way; they must safeguard these rights from any attempts of an attack on them and must force everyone who does not fulfil their duty to the young generation to do so.

Source: Pridik, 1921: 40–2; translation from German.

In contrast to the then-dominant idea (which is still prominent) that children are to be *protected* first and foremost from the dangers of urban life and industrial work, the Moscow Declaration is guided by the basic idea of *strengthening* the position of children in society as well as attaining their equality with adults, regardless of the children's age (one reason, perhaps, why there is no hint given in the declaration as to the age through which a young person is to be considered a 'child'). The responsibility of parents, society and the state towards the children is not understood as care and provision. Rather, conditions for living and acting should be created for the children, which allow for a life of dignity and the free fulfilment of their needs, strengths and capacities. For the first time, children were not only seen as 'becomings', who count only in the future (i.e. as adults), but as 'beings' who, already now, in the present (i.e. as children) deserve social recognition. The children's rights are expressly understood as rights that cannot be claimed by anyone, but rather by the children themselves, a truly revolutionary thought for that time (yet also nowadays).

These basic thoughts are expressed by the rationale that no child may be forced against his will to undergo a specific education or religious ritual, that he may chose his educators and may even separate from his parents, that he may freely express his opinion, may organize himself with other children or adults and may participate in all (political) decisions which, in his view, concern him. A right of children to participate in socially necessary work in dignified, i.e. in non-exploitative conditions, is advocated with the remarkable argument that children could thus understand themselves as active subjects of life and recognize that their own life is meaningful already.

The declaration had a short life and very quickly disappeared in the cellars of history. The 'Committee for Education of Children, Youth and Young People', which was founded during the *Prolet'cult* conference, rejected the declaration as 'unacceptable, as it speaks with the voice of natural law, which is not accepted by Marxism and which shows signs of anticollectivism'. The conference pursued the committee's advice, but as they felt the declaration on the rights of the child was an issue which could not be delayed, they contracted the Prolet'cult organization 'to immediately start elaborating a declaration which reflects both the proletarian view, Marxism, but which also meets the interests of the child' (cited acc. Pridnik, 1921: 42–3). We were unable to determine whether such a declaration was actually elaborated, and therefore we also do not know how this masterpiece would have been managed to unite the conference's idea of a 'proletarian world view' and 'Marxism' with the 'interests of the child' that were apparently seen as conflicting. Further along in the development of the Soviet Union, a children's policy and education was enacted, which was definitely repressive in character and left no room for children's own rights.

With its proposal for a Declaration of Children's Rights, the Russian association 'Free Education of Children' had taken up thoughts which circled among European countries and North America at the turn of the twentieth century. They had developed mainly from the critique of authoritarian repressive schools, which was partly driven by pupils themselves and which manifested itself in various alternative school foundations as well as socialist and anarchist education concepts. Generally, the book

Century of Childhood is seen as the first manifestation of this new thinking, which set a focus on children's needs and aimed at a 'pedagogy from
the child'. It was written by the Swedish pedagogue and feminist Ellen Key
(1849–1926), published first in 1900 and translated into many languages (in
English first in 1909), attracting a lot of attention.[7]
Although Ellen Key held to the romantic childhood myth for the most
part, by which children are idealized as innocent, 'good' creatures by nature
and in which childhood is viewed as an ideal world (see Dekker, 2000), in
her 1911 volume of essays (in English) *Love and Marriage*, she also started
to demand rights for children which result from their living situation. She
demanded equal rights for children born out of wedlock and the right of
children to physical integrity and respectful treatment. Children also had
the right to be 'bad' (or rather did not have to be only 'good' all of the time),
and they had the right to think for themselves and to have their own will,
opinion and feelings.

Whereas the aims of Ellen Key and most other reformist pedagogues
revolved around the thoughts on how the behaviour of educators may be
influenced, how the pedagogical institutions could be reformed in view of
the children and how better development and learning conditions could
be achieved for them, the Polish pediatrician, writer and pedagogue Janusz
Korczak (1878–1942)[8] went a step further. As director of the Jewish orphanage in Warsaw, he actively promoted the independent and active role of the
children he cared for, but he also explicitly fought for more individual rights
and a stronger position of children in social life. As early as 1919, in his first
major pedagogical work, *Jak kochak dziecko* (How to love a child), he pro-
claimed in a 'Magna Charta Libertatis' for the child three elementary rights:
the 'child's right to his death', the 'child's right to the present day' and the
'the child's right to be itself'. The right to death sounds strange at first glance,
but from the remarks and explanations, it becomes very clear what Korczak
meant: it is the demand for self-determination and self-experience which is
often cut short by the excessive care of many parents. With the other two
rights, Korczak underlines his belief that children do not become persons
but already are persons and have the right to their *own* lives.[9]

Based on this belief, Korczak criticized the 'Geneva law makers'[10] a few
years later in his essay *The child's right to respect* (Polish original, 1928; recent
English edition, 2009), arguing they had 'confused duties with rights; the
tone of the declaration is one of persuasion not insistence: an appeal to goodwill, a plea for kindness' (Korczak, 2009: 34). The child is neither given nor
trusted to be able to act on its own: 'The child – nothing. We – everything'
(ibid.: 25). The relationship between adults and children is 'demoralised
by the child's poverty and material dependency' (ibid.).

A beggar can dispose of his alms at will. The child has nothing of his own
and must account for every object freely received for his own use. He is

forbidden to tear, break, or soil; he is forbidden to give anything away as a present; nor is he allowed to refuse anything with a sign of displeasure. The child has to accept things and be satisfied. Everything must be in the right place at the right time according to his regimen. ... Since he has no vote, why go to the trouble to gain his good opinion of you? He doesn't threaten, demand, say anything. Weak, little, poor, dependent – a citizen-to-be only. ... The brat. Only a child, a future person, but not yet, not today. He's just going to be. (Ibid.: 25–7)

Instead, Korczak rigidly demanded a comprehensive participation of children whose 'democratism' obviously does not know any hierarchy (ibid.: 26). They ought to be trusted and allowed to 'organise' as 'the expert is the child' (ibid.: 33).

Children's liberation movements of the 1970s and 1980s

The thoughts and demands of Janusz Korczak or the Russian organization 'Free Education of Children' were not considered or taken into account in children's rights debates of the following decades (see Kerber-Ganse, 2009). They were, with the early exception by Alexander Sutherlnd Neill (1953) in Britain, only taken up again in the 1970s, initially in the United States with the developing *Children's Liberation Movement* (CLM).[11]

Richard Farson, one of its public mentors who in 1974 published the polemic book *Birthrights*, was inspired by the civil rights movement, which 'alerted us to the many forms oppression takes in our society', beyond the oppression of blacks (Farson, 1974: 2). After various ethnic minorities (and, not last, women) claimed their equal rights in US society, children are understood as the 'last minority', whose emancipation is still due. The rights demanded for the children are to guarantee that children are no longer treated as a special group but can become an accepted and integrated part of a democratically constituted society. 'In a free and democratic society, there is no valid basis to exclude children from the decision-making process' (ibid.: 178). They should have the same rights to freedom and democracy as adults.

The CLM in the United States judged that the traditional practice of child protection reinforces a 'paternalistic view' (Farson) and harms the children more than being useful to them. It would be a better support to the children if their full civil rights were guaranteed by persistent and insistent work instead of always interfering for their protection. Instead of always looking at what the children are not (yet) able to do, one should look for the 'children's potential' with intuition and empathy. In addition, conditions are to be established that allow children to identify and to express themselves. Adults can only get to know children comprehensively if they 'develop a new appreciation for their rights and a new respect for their potential' (ibid: 13).

Thus, the CLM also opposes any form of 'infantilization' of children, i.e. any attempt to make them 'smaller' than they are, and to measure them only by criteria fixed by high-handed adults. According to such criteria, the 'ideal child is cute (entertaining to adults), well-behaved (doesn't bother adults), and bright (capable of early admission to her parents' favourite college)' (ibid.: 2). That also requires a new evaluation of children's behaviour which, until now, has been regarded as problematic. For example, 'we may view differently the incorrigible child, the stubborn child, the runaway child' (ibid.: 194). Instead of only regarding such a child as 'troubled', one must ask whether it is not 'the good, well-adjusted child [who] may be less far along in his own consciousness-raising, in his own development towards maturity' (ibid.).

The CLM in the 1970s was not satisfied with regarding the child in a new light and with proclaiming children's rights. It also asked what had to be done so that children could really claim their rights. First, it was assumed that children's rights only have a chance to be finally put into effect if the children themselves fight for them in an organized way. In a society in which children are at the disposition of adults, it cannot be expected that adults have a special interest in the realization of the children's rights, because that would limit their own right of disposal. Therefore, children are dependent on developing 'greater strength and vision as a group' in order to 'act on their own behalf' (ibid.: 8). Like the members of other powerless social groups, children cannot emancipate themselves individually, but only 'as a class' (ibid.: 16).

Secondly, a 'right to economic power' is claimed together with the other rights. Only this right gives the children the necessary power to enforce the other rights as well. In present society, children are so weak and dependent, above all because they are kept 'unproductive and out of the economic mainstream of society' (ibid.: 155). By the income resulting from their work, children 'stand to gain not only financial rewards, but the dignity which derives from work and achievement. With it will come a new measure of respect from adults and, more importantly, a new measure of respect for themselves' (ibid.). The child would have better chances 'to make constructive changes in his environment and to pursue self-determined life goals' (ibid.: 109).

With John Holt (1974), another public representative of the US Children's Liberation Movement who had worked as a teacher for a long time, the argumentation for children's rights got a stronger (anti)pedagogical accent. The target of his critique is the 'institution of childhood' which came into being with bourgeois society. It has 'infantilized' children and locked them into a privatized area where – for the better or the worse – they became dependent on the goodwill of adults. By separating children from the adult world, it is made 'difficult or impossible for young people to make contact with the larger society around them, and, even more, to play any kind of active, responsible, useful part in it' (Holt, 1974: 26). This is especially clear and vehement in the modern school. The children's abilities would also be reduced and underestimated. By observation from everyday life, Holt demonstrates that a child clearly can 'be able to do what we think of children as being wholly unable to do until they are much older' (ibid.: 100). If one would regularly give three- or four-year-old children the opportunity to explore their surroundings on their own, they would be able to draw a mental map and would be able to find their way around independently.

In view of the Children's Rights Movement of the 1970s and 1980s, some criticize that the differences between children and adults are not taken into consideration and that children are treated like adults (see Moosa-Mitha, 2005). This critique does not take into account that the children's rights movement sees childhood not as a natural category but – like today's subject-oriented childhood sociology – as specific and historically created and therefore as a changeable social construction. The aim of the movement was not to demolish differences between adults and children but rather to question the power difference and privileges of adults deriving from this concept of childhood and to insist, despite existing differences, on the equality and equivalence of children (see Rose & de Bie, 2007: 432–3).

In Europe, the demands of the US American Children's Rights Movement were taken up in the 1970s. The protagonists were people who were critical towards traditional child protection and who rejected any form of education as an 'attack on the growing generation's freedom' (Kupffer, 1974: 25). Most of them were active in alternative and anti-pedagogic initiatives. Their goal was to reform 'all objectively child-phobic laws' so that 'children and young people have the unlimited and direct enjoyment of agreed basic- and human rights' (Stern, 1995: 16).[12]

In contrast to the US American Children's Rights Movement, the European initiatives neither gave much thought to the preconditions necessary to reach equality for children, nor was it asked how children themselves could contribute to this endeavour. Instead of asking – as in the US American debate and as Janusz Korczak had also already done – under which 'economic' preconditions the children could (re-)acquire autonomy and play an active, participatory role in society, they limited themselves to appeal to the child-friendliness of adults and to demand a 'rethinking' in relation to children.

Outlook on today's children's rights movements

Today, children's rights movements exist almost everywhere around the globe. Even though earlier children's rights movements played only a marginal role in the development of the CRC,[13] today's children's rights movements would not exist without it. Most of them explicitly refer to the CRC yet do not see their task being its mere 'implementation' but rather to develop their own ideas on children's rights and the role of children in society, which sometimes go beyond the Convention or contrast to it. They emphasize, as did earlier children's rights movements, the necessity for children's equality and oppose any form of discrimination due to an unreached legal age. They particularly insist on creating conditions which allow children themselves to effectively make use of their existing rights and, if need be, create new rights which seem important to them and to receive social and legal recognition for them. However, the emphasis is not put on lobbying work – as, for instance, the many so-called *National Coalitions* that exist in many countries do, or as national networks for the implementation of the CRC do – but they rather attempt to acquire validity for their rights and interests, mainly by self-organization. Therefore, they can not be compared to NGOs, as they play a major role in children's rights debates today, but are rather a form of social movements or organizations in which children themselves are active or which they even direct.

Some examples are the working children's movements which arose in the 1970s in Latin America, and since the 1990s, also in Africa and Asia (see Chapter 9). Their self-conception is crystallized in the term *protagonismo infantil* (children's protagonism) and influences the children's rights discussion and practice in particular in the majority world (see Liebel, Overwien & Recknagel, 2001). Whereas the children's rights movement in Latin America was directed against the persecution and oppression of the so-called street children, today's movements are directed mostly towards the social role of working children and demand to connect criticism on economic exploitation with the recognition and respect for their productive contribution to their families and societies. They promote dignified working conditions and social relations that are not based on the exploitation of mankind.

In Latin America, the children's rights movement has also found an amazing echo in the legal debate. The Colombian law professor Ligia Galvis Ortiz (2006: 12) remarks:

> The consideration that children are to be understood as active rights holders deserves a profound and radical reflection. Because of this the necessity could arise to reform the classical institutions of law and to create new approaches, in which cultural pluralism spreads on the recognition of the children's world as a universe with its own characteristics. In this world we find elements, languages and symbols with which the children express and exercise their rights.

Galvis Ortiz sees the biggest barrier for the recognition of children being active rights holders in the rights discourse 'being limited to the verbal language(s) mastered by adults and the distinct articulations of children are not seen as sensible and meaningful forms of language' (ibid.: 33–4). The intelligent lifestyle of children is expressed in the speech that matches their life cycle. The problem is not the expression of children but rather the incapacity of the adults to understand the messages which can be read in the looks, the gestures, the movements and the sounds they make.[14] Galvis Ortiz (2007: 61) requests to overcome the established hegemony of a mindset that judges the world and lifestyle of children solely by the views and in the language of adults:

> Once we have finally freed ourselves from the adult centrism, we enter a colourful world of languages a world of diverse actors and mediators. This leads us to break with the doctrine and the entire philosophical, psychological and legal literature, which turn children into objects and we get to a place where we allow children a psychosocial status as active persons. Only in this way can we recognize their capacities and messages, by which they reconstruct the world, create, change or resist it.

In the meantime, the thought and the expectation that children (can) play a major role in the creation, formulation and implementation of their rights has gained influence in other parts of the world. The following chapters give an idea of the aims, the self-image and the growing importance of this new children's rights movement.

Notes

1. Submission from Manchester's Factory Children Committee, sent to the House of Commons in 1836, http://www.spartacus.schoolnet.co.uk/IRmanchester.child. htm, date accessed 5 May 2011.
2. Unfortunately, it is not possible to give a deeper insight into the obviously very different motives and reasons in the history of compulsory school and class attendance in different countries here.
3. Today, this idea is mainly connected to the idea of children's 'citizenship' (see Chapter 11).
4. Relevant descriptions are (amongst others): Veerman, 1992; Detrick, 1992; Verhellen, 1994/2000; van Bueren; 1995; Freeman & Veerman, 1997; Alston & Tobin, 2005; Dillon, 2010; Invernizzi & Williams, 2011.
5. In more recent years, children's rights movements, which we refer to here, are sometimes distinguished as 'radical' children's rights movements compared to 'reformist' and 'pragmatic' movements (Verhellen, 1994: 59–60). In this sense, here we mostly refer to the 'radical' ones. The distinction between 'children's rights movements' and 'children liberation movements' made by Veerman (1992) seems problematic to us, because in both movements there is a particular understanding of children's rights. According to Reynaert et al. (2009: 521), we understand children's rights movements as 'counter-movements' against movements mainly centred in paternalistic notions of child saving and child protection.
6. On the history of the *Proletkult* movement see Mally, 1990. The author refers to the Declaration of Children's Rights in only a few words but, based on original sources, she reports of the formation of 'Children's Proletkults' (*Detskie Proletkul'ty*)

as a kind of autonomous movements or clubs of children ages eight to 16. One of these clubs (in the city of Tula) published its own newspaper, staffed and edited by the young participants themselves. The articles reveal children's hostility to the confines of conventional family life. Enthusiastic children 'expressed their hopes for a special proletarian culture for children that would be based on a highly developed sense of children's self-worth and autonomy. In these articles, children and youth appeared as the real revolutionaries who needed to inspire recalcitrant, backward adults to revolutionary acts. "We have to do more than awaken and organize other children", wrote one fourteen-year-old girl. "We have to awaken and organize our fathers, mothers, older brothers, and sisters to come to the defense of the revolution." According to the organization's young leader, Dmitrii Pozhidaev, the Children's Proletkult would liberate young people from the despotism of the petty-bourgeois family and give them useful social tasks' (ibid.: 181).

7. Already in 1892, the American feminist Kate Douglas Wiggin (1971) had fought for respect for the child as an autonomous individual.

8. Korczak was murdered in the extermination camp Treblinka by the Nazis, together with the children of the orphanage he directed.

9. In the biography on Korczak *The King of Children*, Betty Jean Lifton (1989) depicts all the rights that Korczak had formulated in his works.

10. Korczak refers to the 'Declaration on the Rights of the Child' initiated by Eglantyne Jebb, president of the British Save the Children Fund and adopted 1924 by the League of Nations in Geneva.

11. See Adams, 1971; Gottlieb, 1973; Gross & Gross, 1977; Cohen, 1980; Hawes, 1991; Veerman, 1992.

12. Referring to the 1980s, Campbell (2011) also mentions the creation of Working Groups for Children within Amnesty International national sections.

13. This was manifested mainly in activities of so called Non-Governmental Organizations (NGOs), which had come together internationally in the 1980s specifically to influence the elaboration of the CRC.

14. In this respect, Galvis Ortiz looks to the meaningfulness of toddlers' body language and reminds of the French philosopher Jean-Jacques Rousseau, who had declared the latter to be the 'universal language' in his main work *Emile, or On Education* (1762/1979).

3
Children's Rights Contextualized
Manfred Liebel

> Just because I have holes in my trousers and worn-out shoes they
> think they can do anything they want with me.
>
> (Estéban, 12 years, Nicaragua)

Today, children are understood as 'subjects of rights' or 'rights holders'.
Accordingly, they have their own rights and are not simply reliant on the
benevolence of those on whose support they depend. Insofar as children
continue to be dependant, this dependence is cushioned by their own rights
which aim at controlling any arbitrary behaviour towards them and strive
to gradually secure autonomy for their actions. According to this concept,
children are no longer only 'minors' who possess very few or no rights, but
persons who partly share equal rights and partly other or additional rights
they can exercise. The question is, *what determines whether these rights can
actually be exercised?* In this chapter, different aspects of pitfalls in reference
to children's rights are discussed, as well as what can or ought to be done in
order to make rights accessible to children and to turn them into something
that is, in their view, valuable for them. To achieve this, an understanding
of children's rights that reflects politics and context is needed.

Understanding children's rights as agency rights

At first, the rights system resulting from liberalism and bourgeois societies
only recognized children as 'minors', and because they 'by definition lack
the capacity to act, it made it impossible for them to engage in any kind of
economic trade relations' (Barranco Avilés, 2007: 16). With the liberalist idea
that all men are equal (before the law), no distinctions were made between
differing circumstances and needs, with the exception of the one, stating
that one is still not 'legally mature' at a certain age. 'Under the same liberal
framework, neither the existence of different people with different needs
is taken into account nor are any temporary situations between full capacity and total dependence foreseen. Until the moment in which majority

is acquired, the child is seen as unable to enforce his rights' (ibid.: 16–17). This framework was revised only with the UN Convention on the Rights of the Child (CRC), which recognizes children in an internationally binding legal way as subjects of own rights. The prerequisite was that two changes be made in the European history of law, which María del Carmen Barranco Avilés (2007: 17) describes as 'generalisation' and 'specification':

> The process of generalisation was based on the extension of dignity with the consequence that now there were subjects who were rights holders, whom one would not have thought of before as such. This process lead to the dissolution of the concept of an 'abstract human being' which was connected to the first declarations on human rights and which resulted in not matching any human being. But it also became clear that dangers exist that threaten human dignity, and that can not be scared away by establishing formal rights on equality and freedom. ... The process of specification starts with the thought that some needs are not shared by all persons. The dignity of some human beings requires satisfying needs which others do not have. The process of specification opened the discourse on vulnerable groups and established instruments by which one could give some – yet not all – human beings specific rights.

The distinction in the CRC is based on the assumption that children have different *needs* than adults. These should be satisfied by rights to special protection and provision, or rather developmental rights. In legal theory, rights that are deduced from needs (for instance, special vulnerability) are generally called *moral* rights (Archard & Macleod, 2002). Regardless of their codification in formal rights systems, the historically developed 'moral' (self-) commitment of society to care for the especially 'needy' or 'weak' or is manifested. These legal concepts do not foresee that children (or other 'weak' persons) can claim these rights themselves or ensure their implementation. In the CRC, they are voiced as children's rights, but as the CRC is an international rights treaty (in whose process of establishment children did not participate), they are, in fact, treated as *state obligations*.[1] Therefore, in academic legal debates, somecontest that these rights are actually children's rights (Griffin, 2002), or they are called *welfare rights* and are distinguished from *agency rights* (Brighouse, 2002).

By also envisaging participation rights for children for the first time, the CRC breaks clear of this logic. Participation rights cannot be justified by *needs* but are based on the assumption that children have special *interests*, which they can recognize and represent themselves. From a theoretical legal perspective, this discrepancy raises questions. Does it mean that participation rights stand alone, or are they effective in dealing with the other rights groups? Stated differently, do the participation rights ultimately imply that children have a special sphere in life in which they act as subjects and can manage their affairs, or do they suggest that (also) agency rights have to emerge from the welfare rights? The CRC does not provide clear answers to these questions. In the usual interpretations and in dealing with the CRC in practice, both rights groups are treated separately. They do not have anything (or, at the most, little), to do with each other. This is expressed by the fact that the participation of children, where it is thought of at all, is limited to 'children's affairs' and is seen as a sort of playground to practise and prepare for adulthood. In the following, however, we intend to demonstrate, why all rights groups are also to be understood and treated as *agency* rights of children.

If the so-called welfare rights are only understood as state obligations, they lose their meaning as special rights of children.[2] As rights, if they are to be used in practice, always require interpretation and concretion, their construction and the decision about their importance and implementation would be in the hands of adults only and would be subject to their good will to act according to these rights. The fact that they are justified by the needs of children does create the impression that this is an objective criterion, which can be determined without any doubts, yet needs are changeable and are not necessarily perceived or understood in the same way by adults and children. Therefore, over and above the needs, (differing) interests also must be taken into account. These, again, can only be expressed and realized if children can participate in a meaningful way in the interpretation, concretion and implementation of protection and provision rights. We shall elaborate, taking the example of protection rights.

Generally, it is assumed that protecting children is mainly an adult task, as adults are more farsighted and have more means, power and influence to protect children against dangers. However, the protection of children can lead to limiting their freedom and space for decision-making. This can go as far as increasing children's helplessness and need for protection despite all good intentions, as they are asked to settle into dependence and to rely on adults. Even if this limitation can be justified, it can be used by adults to implement their own interests and to make use of the power advantage or even to extend their scope of power.[3] This can be seen, for instance, in the efforts to observe children around the clock – even by using new surveillance technologies or by using special 'security services' – so that nothing happens to them or that they do not 'get out of hand'.

In order to prevent a one-sided instrumentalization of protection by adults, it is indispensable not only that children be objects of protective measures, but also that they be able to decide ways in which they ought to be protected or whether in certain situations they might not need protection at all. Such participation also ought to be practised because all protection becomes all the more effective the more it is accepted and supported by the children being protected. Children can contribute actively to their protection, by, for instance, informing themselves or letting themselves be sensitized, learning certain rules or techniques of prudence, getting together with other children, or defending themselves better. Apart from the question of efficiency, the specific interests of children would be taken into account.

In the CRC, it is clearly postulated that the premise when interpreting and implementing children's rights must be the 'best interests of the child'. Since the invention of this concept, there have been controversial debates about ways to identify it and who can do it appropriately (see, e.g., Zermatten, 2007). As needs or interests are not timeless and should not be defined without taking into consideration the circumstances under which they occur, also the points of view of the subjects. In this case, those of the children must be considered. In the CRC, this is expressed as the child's right to be heard in all decision-making concerning him/her. Such decisions are not limited to select ambits or rights but include all areas which affect the child's life now and in the future, and all rights which belong to children. Consequently, children must have the opportunity to represent all of their rights without exceptions; that is, at least to participate in a significant way in their construction, interpretation and implementation.

Arguing along this line, the separation of welfare rights from agency rights is meaningless in (legal) theory but not necessarily in (legal) practice. One reason is that the so-called protection and provision rights continue to be seen in a paternalistic and individualizing way, as if they were a selfless performance by (adult) society for the children, and as if they had equal value for everybody and would be good for all children equally. A second reason is that in the existing political systems, in which political decision-making is a privilege of adults, children are inhibited from participating in the conceptualizing and, if required, (re-)design of the protection and provision rights according to their interests and thereby from connecting them to their experiences and perspectives on life. In the following, both reasons are critically evaluated and discussed.

Connecting children's rights with political practice

The debate on children's rights is mainly limited to the question of how children can come by and enjoy *legal rights,* that is, how they can use them. The codification of rights in the CRC or in national law is regarded as the highest attainable 'endpoint of the dialog' (Rose & de Bie, 2007: 434). Seen as such, only one question remains to be discussed: how the codified rights can be 'implemented'. The way of solving specific problems seems to be based more on formal regulations than on the dialogue between involved persons. Yet if all focus is put on implementation, there is a tendency to ignore or even hide social contexts and inherent unequal power structures. There is a danger to lose sight of the possible and widespread instrumentalization of rights as well as their paradoxes. This can only be avoided if the debate on children's rights is contextualized and understood as part of political practice.

Traditional dealing with human rights in general, and children's rights in particular, is marked by two problems:

1. Basic structural problems are approached in an individualized way.
2. The supposed equality of rights ('all have equal rights') in reality *does not* mean that all can take equal advantage of these rights.

The assumption inherent to human rights and children's rights discourse, that rights can be individually claimed by autonomous persons and can be used in their own interest, can have paradoxical or rather undesired consequences and can aggravate marginalization for people who are already in a weak and socially marginalized position. The assumption that a person has rights and needs only to claim them, can lead to making this person responsible across the board for her situation. In the case of children, the assumption that they can participate significantly in decisions about their life through participation rights granted to them in the CRC, can lead to making them responsible for actions beyond their reach. Further actual existing dependencies, as well as structural reasons for their marginalized status or their social or rather generational disadvantage, are thus easily negated or underestimated.

In particular, connecting participation rights with provision and, specifically, developmental rights can have a depoliticizing effect. This is the case where the impression is created that social problems can be avoided or even globally eradicated merely by claiming individual rights. Thus, the right to participation is in fact separated from its political roots and conventionalized to a seemingly arbitrary personal issue. Therefore, every so often, there are pleas for a 'differentiated' and 'relational' understanding of participation. According to this, participation is seen not as a societal norm that must be fulfilled but rather as a possible precondition in order to come closer to achieving goals yet to be clearly determined. Although all people participate in social life, the questions are the extent to which and the reasons why this happens. This includes the thought that participation can also have negative or marginalizing effects.

> Participation does not automatically lead to emancipation, but emancipation is defined as the antidote of marginalization. The mission of participatory work is then to breach marginalization. Participation remains a key concept in this approach, but not as a goal or method. Participation, in this view, is defined as an essential condition in the definition of social problems. (Vandenhole et al., 2008: 13)

In this sense, the participation approach serves to turn the dominant politics into the subject of analysis and to push for changes if need be. In doing so, the main aim is to secure human dignity. In this way, different approaches and forms of participation are to be questioned as to whether and the extent to which they contribute to securing or achieving human dignity.

Like citizenship, participation is to be seen neither as a status which needs to be attained nor as a goal to be reached, but rather as a continuous learning process. This process always takes place in a certain context and is therefore to be understood as *contextual practice*. This does not imply that participation and citizenship are only learning processes in an educational sense, but it should be emphasized that in both cases the process is never ending. Their meaning is to be measured by the practical goals achieved by their means and by how they are reached. In the case of participation and citizenship of children, the issue at stake is whether they actually contribute to granting social recognition and human dignity to children. Therefore, it is most important that children be accepted as equal co-actors in the dialogue about their 'best interests' (see Rose & de Bie, 2007; Liebel, 2008).

Frequently, children whose human rights are violated in the most aggressive ways are seemingly indifferent to them and seldom claim them. This raises the question of whether the legal debate and the practice of children's rights bypass the actual life experiences of these children, and how they can be procured to them. We elaborate on this question by looking at four examples of marginalized groups of children: Dealing with human rights violations towards children living on the street in Guatemala and India, child refugees in Europe as well as AIDS orphans in Africa who live in so-called child-headed households.

Guatemala: persecution and oppression of children living on the street

Children who live on the streets are often subjected to repressive and arbitrary actions of police bodies or paramilitary groups. In Guatemala, a country in which human rights violations towards these children have shown particularly brutal forms,[4] Angelina Snodgrass Godoy (1999) researched the question why the human rights work of a very engaged children's welfare organization found such little resonance with children. For her research, she drew on a model that needs further discussion and understands the conscious and goal-directed perception of one's own rights as the result of a step-by-step process, which goes from *naming* to *blaming* to *claiming* of rights (Felstiner et al., 1980/81).

It is usually assumed that rights violations are so seldom *named* by the victims because they do not know their rights. In her research, Snodgrass Godoy actually found that, generally speaking, this does not hold true. Much more important seems to be that the children experience violence as so common and so frequent that it seems normal to them. Consequently, they no longer see the violence as a problem which is worth paying attention to and therefore do not talk about it either.

Mostly, criticism of the rights violation (blaming) does not occur because the children feel guilty and accuse themselves, instead of making others responsible for the violation. Most of the interviewed children had internalized the existing moral norms to such an extent that life on the streets seemed an aberration of 'normal life' or a 'correct childhood' to them. A girl, for instance, emphasized that she wanted to leave the streets 'because the street doesn't bring us anything good, and now I want to be a normal person'. Another girl answered the question of whether her boyfriend also lived on the street: 'No, he's honourable'. A boy expressed the internalization of existing norms clearly when he said, 'We are, as people say, the garbage of society' (all citations: Snodgrass Godoy, 1999: 431).

Other interviewed children distinguished themselves from 'the other street children' by which they wanted to emphasize that the 'real' street children are the others. As an answer to the question, 'What best could be done to protect these other street children from police attacks?' some children answered that it would be best for them to leave the streets, 'because then they wouldn't be a problem' (ibid.). They accept that they themselves or the 'other street children' are responsible for their situation, not only as individuals but also as a group. Snodgrass Godoy sees not only a self-accusation in this, but also an attempt to escape the stigma of victimhood. By calling themselves 'responsible', they define themselves as acting persons, who themselves hold the reigns. However, this can lead to ignoring the attacks as well as the violation of their rights.

Based on our own research and that of others, it can be seen that even children who permanently live on the streets hardly ever call themselves 'street children' and often fight against this labelling. They feel that this is a word construction imposed on them to separate them as group from other children and to turn them into a subsumable object of 'helping' interventions or to even defame them as 'deviant' group and scandalize their way of living. The explicit non-regarding of oneself as a street child can therefore be an expression of self-esteem as well as a documentation of the claim to be able to determine one's own way of life.

The violations of rights and human dignity that children living on the streets are exposed to are intertwined so closely with their daily life that 'one's entire existence [is seen] as a never-ending series of violations' (ibid.: 432) and that they would have to continuously define themselves as victims if they were to see all the actions directed towards them as human rights violations. 'As outsiders, it may be easy for us to consider these youths eternally vulnerable; but for individuals whose daily lives are a struggle to survive, it may be important to maintain at least the illusion that one is in control' (ibid.).

Upon talking to these children, Snodgrass Godoy sensed that they avoided complaining about their situation and the experienced abuses in order to maintain a positive self-image. In particular, boys believe complaining about their situation to be a weakness. One boy, for instance, rejected the offer of legal aid from a child-help organization, saying, 'I handle my problems by myself. To each his own.' Another boy disclaimed assistance because 'we don't like to be complaining, like women' (ibid.). To this boy, filing a claim means asking those who have the power in society for help and thus admitting to vulnerability and weakness. Some who renounce seeking support have, in fact, offered support to others. This again shows that they actually are willing to reconcile if they do not automatically land in the role of the victims in the process.

To claim one's rights means to address a public office in the hopes that it can end the experienced abuse or injustice suffered. The children Snodgrass Godoy interviewed mostly named two reasons why they do not choose to do so: fear of repression and a feeling of futility. The fear of repression (e.g. by the police) is not to be underestimated; it has been proven by many diverse experiences. In order to file a claim, a child must go to the police, whose members the children experience first and foremost as their perpetrators. The feeling of vanity is not in the least an expression of lacking confidence in one's own capabilities to achieve change, but rather reflects the loss of confidence in the legitimacy of the entire (legal) system and is also often based on habitual experiences. The boys and girls living on the streets are conscious of living in a society and of being confronted with institutions that are not there for them and of which they have nothing positive to expect because of their marginalized and stigmatized social position.

It is enlightening to look at the few cases in which the children living on the streets did actually accept the legal aid offered by child help organizations and did claim their rights. These children did not have fewer reasons than their peers to fear consequential repressions or to doubt the effect of their claim. They also were not better educated or better informed on their rights. The main difference must be seen in whether they kept up contact with institutions of the existing society, be they family, school, a legal labour market or (most frequently) the church. The less they felt that they were part of society, the less prone they were to claim existing rights or to file a claim.

Some of the most marginalized children did fight against the violation of their rights but did so without claiming existing, formal rights. Instead, they took the law into their own hands, so to speak. A 16-year-old boy, who had given up all contact with his family years ago, explicitly referred to his 'own law'. It is based on the loyalty to the 'street gang', where 'we are all united. We all take care of each other, and any problems, we all join together for one (of us)' (ibid.: 434).[5]

Snodgrass Godoy concludes that: 'unfortunately, this means that human rights principles and mechanisms tend to serve only those who are well off enough to see them as relevant to begin with – a whole segment of the population essentially leaves itself out of the human rights paradigm' (ibid.: 436). In order to transform legal principles into rights practice, she therefore demands to translate 'the international human rights discourse into everyday lived experience' and 'to take into account a more contextualized, "bottom-up" understanding of rights, privileging the perspectives of those whose rights are in question over the abstract premises of political philosophy' (ibid.: 437).

India: children living and working on the streets

As in all countries of the South, in the 1990s aid organizations in India also discovered children's rights and included them on their agendas. They were explicitly asked to do so by international NGOs or by UNICEF, who finance the local children's projects. Based on the CRC, programmes and action forms were developed that branded the difficult situation of the children as a violation of their rights and that often were to animate the children to fight for their own rights. In three examples of street children projects in Calcutta, the Indian social researcher Sarada Balagopalan (2012) shows unexpected and headstrong ways in which the children understood their rights and how they dealt with them.

Example 1: A local NGO that worked with street children had invited children to demonstrate that they have rights in a public sketch. An educator suggested to a group of 20 street children: 'This sketch should show the audience that all children have rights, you too. You have a right to food, education, to sleep beneath a mosquito net.' Shankar, one of the older boys who liked to perform as an actor, said: *'We are doing this skit so people really understand the way we live, the way we stay.'* Liton, a smaller boy who seldom said a word, interfered with the question: *'Will they give us money when we tell them that we have rights?'* Immediately the other boys took this up and argued loudly how this could be done. The educator answered loudly, 'NO all we want is their understanding.' Liton, keen not to lose out on the role, added: *'I know the perfect first line for the play. I can open the dialogue saying to the rest of the boys as if my character is not one of them, "Why should the babus (middle-class) listen to you? After all they make money from people like you"'* (ibid.: 13).

Example 2: Some NGOs wanted to organize a demonstration for children's rights together with children. All children who attended had, as far as they could, dressed up. Whereas normally they would have walked in simple sandals, some of the children had somehow obtained shoes this time. Or they wore pretty shirts that never been seen before. At the demonstration, which went through the business district of the city and through a wealthy residential area, the children held up banners and shouted slogans which the educators had given and taught them. After 15 minutes, the interest of the children had ceased, and the older boys handed the banners to the younger ones and complained that there was nothing to drink. Observed by the disapproving views of the educators, some began to collect pieces of metal they had found on the street, which they obviously thought they could use. The demonstration ended in a high school which none of the participating children had ever attended. There, a stage was set up, from which NGO officials held speeches against child labour. Some children started collecting plastic cups and empty Coke bottles that were lying around while the speeches were being made, so that they could watch a movie at night with the money they earned by selling them. When asked, some older children who only observed the activities said that they would rather not dirty their nice clothes as they were not meant for working.

Example 3: As in all markets in countries of the South, in Calcutta many children are busy collecting leftover vegetables and fruit. Sometimes, they also nip things from stands. Mostly they appear in groups and split the work amongst each other. Whereas some collect or steal, others carry away the loot in small sacks in order to distribute it amongst each other later or to resell the goods in other corners of the market. One morning, some children brought a small boy to the meeting point of an aid organization and said that he had been caught by a tradesman and had been beaten up by the police right then and there. The boy was bleeding in many places and looked very bad. When the boy was somewhat fixed up, he was told that the policeman had acted in an unjust way and must be sanctioned for his behaviour. Having listened carefully, the boy said, *'Aunty, it would have been much worse if he had arrested me. They would have put me in the lock-up until I got bail, and in the lock-up worse things would have happened. He was doing his job and helping me by beating me at the market itself. I know him because during the times that I have fought with someone at the shelter and decide to sleep on the station platform he often asks me to run small errands for him and gives me a blanket to cover myself at night'* (ibid.: 17).

Obviously the children thought it to be of little use to be made aware of their rights. They could not imagine how reference to these rights could help improve their situation. However, it would be short-sighted to see a lack of understanding of children's rights in this. The problem is, on the one hand, the manner in which children were imparted their rights and how they were introduced to them, and on the other, the children's marginalized status which makes it nearly impossible for them to understand themselves as subjects of rights.

In the case of the sketch and the demonstration (Examples 1 and 2), children were to show their rights to more fortunate people in order to demonstrate clearly that their situation is unjust and to reach understanding. This approach contradicted their whole life experience. The 'wealthy' people, whom they were to address, are mainly experienced as ruthless and even as the origin of their problems. How were they to expect from these people, who exploit and abuse them, that they *do* anything *for* them? In addition, the children probably felt hurt in their pride and dignity by this approach, as they must have felt like some sort of beggar asking for pity from the better off. It is not a coincidence that most children hate begging and that they would rather steal or be active in some other way to deal with their misery.

In the case of the sketch, the children interestingly did not reject the idea of having their own rights but rather gave this idea an unexpected interpretation of their own. They took them up, not to promote understanding for them but to point out those responsible for their situation and, ironically, to make fun of them. The children did not trust that the rights speak for them or have any effect but wanted to show that the law is often used by the powerful to their advantage at the expense of the children. What seems like a violation of rights in our eyes is, for the children, the normality of the social and rights systems in which they live.

The children obviously participated in the demonstration not because they were convinced of its sense, but rather in order not to disappoint the educators. That they dressed up (and likely stole again to be able to do so) shows that they interpreted their role differently from the organizers of the demonstration. Whereas the NGOs wanted to achieve authenticity in recognizing children's rights by showing the visible misery of ragged children, the children made sure to be seen in their best light and to avoid the impression of being dependent on other people's pity. Instead of trusting in verbal appeals to businessmen and well-to-do pedestrians, some children seemed to find it more effective to use the anonymity of the demonstration to do something for their living and enjoyment.

The small boy's refusal to insist on his rights towards the police who had abused him (Example 3) shows that generally formulated rights can have very different meanings according to situation and experience. The boy had not only had more complex experiences with the police than his caregiver could have, but he also had more in mind than only the recently experienced abuse. As he had to fear further encounters with the policeman in his daily (and nightly) life, it was very obvious for him to weigh the advantages and disadvantages of a legal claim. Far from an attitude of submissiveness, he proved to have an extraordinary sense of the actual existing dependencies and power hierarchies and knew how to use them to his own advantage.

The behaviour of the children shown in the three examples may be disappointing for some children's rights advocates, yet it demonstrates even more clearly the necessity of not propagating rights without taking into account the actual life context of the children and to be sure of the experiences and views of the local children. Sarada Balagopalan, whom we thank for these examples, clearly states that she does not intend to regard children's rights principally as useless and senseless for children living on the street in India because of their liberal 'Western' origin. She also does not want to give way to impunity and rights violations and accept the existing power hierarchies and injustices or trust in survival tricks of the less powerful. However, she does insist on addressing children's rights (and human rights in general) in a contextual and situational way.

Our conclusion is: children's rights cannot be only 'implemented' but must be culturally 'translated' and imparted with local ways of reasoning and according to local customs as well as legal views and practices. This includes understanding children's rights not only in the sense of individual claims, but also as mutual connections and obligations between members of different generations. This further includes, notwithstanding the cultural and regional specifities, taking care that rights do not come into force merely by being 'naturally' ascribed to persons or being written in laws and regulations. To refer to them is useful only if they are not undermined by factual power and ownership differences. In view of their often marginalized status, this holds particularly true for children who live in extreme poverty and oppression.

Like the children in Guatemala and India, whom we discussed in the previous sections, there are many children around the world whose rights are massively violated and who have little reason to believe in the 'power of rights'. Many of these children are not willing to give in to being seen and treated as victims of adverse circumstances but rather, lacking other possibilities, try to find solutions for their problems themselves. Taking the example of child refugees, who came to Europe 'alone' and the example of AIDS orphans, who mainly live in Africa in child-headed households, the following two sections aim to show why only a context-specific understanding of children's rights and an according practice can do justice to the children and be helpful to them.

Europe: separated child refugees

For children who fled from their home country without any relatives, the terms 'unaccompanied' or 'separated minor refugees' have become commonplace. These terms should express that the children are in an extraordinary situation and that they require special protection and care. The program *Separated Children in Europe* (Save the Children, 2004b) talks of *separated* children because this term reflects more adequately the true situation of many children. Their basic problem is that they are separated from their parents or their legal guardians and that they suffer from this separation, socially as well as psychologically. The term 'separated child' recognizes that some children may appear 'accompanied' when they arrive in Europe, but in practice the accompanying adult may be either unable or unsuitable to assume responsibility for their care. The authorities in the country they arrive in, however, regard both terms in a way that does not treat the situation of child refugees justly and does not solve their problems but rather magnifies them.

In order to reach legalization of their status in the new country, children must prove that they are unaccompanied or separated. Children are considered 'alone' or 'unaccompanied' by the authorities only if there are no relatives with them or if their residence is unknown. For the children, this often means that they must deny their family or pretend that they do not know of any relatives who could care for them. This can lead to the children feeling even more left alone and to their doubting their own moral integrity, often with traumatic consequences. However, the frequent 'silence' of the children, which can be seen as an attempt to make themselves invisible, need not be interpreted in a psychopathological way but also can have a protecting function. 'It allows them a psychological space to reflect on their experiences, and make some sense of them, before using their emotional energy to move on in their new worlds' (Kohli, 2006: 710).

In addition, the children see themselves as confronted with the suspicion that they function as a kind of bridge or anchor for relatives ('anchor children'), who are only waiting for legalization of the children in order to follow them soon by way of family reunification, or to take material advantage of the children's stay in the new country (see Engebrigtsen, 2003: 194). This suspicion is never expressed clearly in official speeches or documents but is always present when addressing issues of child refugees.[6]

Equal to the construction of being alone or unaccompanied, that of 'anchor children' is based on a certain cultural model of childhood, parenthood and family care which has its place in European bourgeois thinking and forms the basis for the welfare systems here (see Panther-Brick & Smith, 2000). According to this, the lone or unaccompanied child appears as a threat to the ideal of security and control. The 'correct' childhood is seen as being connected to living in a home, has its place in the family and is marked by children being dependent on adults who care for them. This ideal inhibits the perception and recognition of other childhoods that are located at the margins of society and outside of families and where children possibly act on their own authority and care for themselves. Measured by the European ideal of a family childhood, refugee children are abnormal beings who are to be mistrusted and 'domesticated' or discarded (see Bhabha, 2007: 209).

At the same time, this ideal of childhood has controversial consequences for the perception of families the children supposedly come from. By assuming that they have left their children or have sent them on an uncertain journey, they are seen as irresponsible. 'Although children should, according to the ideal model, be emotionally tied to and live with their parents, once separated, the quality of the parent is questioned rather than the precarious situation that makes such separations necessary' (Engebrigtsen, 2003: 195). The parents are seen as unqualified to follow their children to the new country and care for them, yet good enough to send the children back to them (if they can be found at all). The result is that refugee children often become a playing field for official decisions. It is claimed – not seldom by making explicit reference to the CRC – that the child's well-being or the best interest of the child is the premise, yet in the end, the state's interests in having an uncomplicated, smooth official procedure or in the 'securing of the well-being' of the native population is the actual premise on which decisions are made. For the affected children, reference to the right, or even their alleged own, interest becomes mockery.

Africa: child-headed households

Taking the example of children who take on the full responsibility for leading households ('child-headed households'), we want to depict the extent to which, also here, only a contextualized understanding of children's rights can do the children justice and can be seen by them as support. Similar to the separated child refugees, child-headed households create an unease, as children are actually not supposed to take on parental responsibility (as one of the most recent examples, see UNICEF, 2007: 62). Parenthood is seen as an adult task. Any living arrangement which deviates from the norm has the tendency to be seen as a source of maldevelopment. Instead of recognizing a justified interest and innovative survival strategy of children, officials and NGOs who dedicate themselves to orphans tend to discriminate against and marginalize these children further (see Ennew, 2005; Cheney, 2012).

Hereby, no consideration is made of the fact that, in many countries, children are involved in taking care of younger siblings, many of whom are still very small. They learn this alongside their parents and relieve them by caring for the physical and psychological needs of their younger brothers and sisters and taking on household chores. Many families see looking after siblings as part of a normal development and as essential preparation for adult life. In some societies, the raising of children without adult participation is quite widespread. For instance, Judith Ennew (1985) found that sibling groups in the slums of Lima, Peru, were at least as common as two-parent families. Luis Aptekar (1991) concluded (in a study done on 'street children' in Colombia) that the strong supporting relations between children originated in the care of younger siblings, which they knew from their families.

The gathering of children on their own authority has a long tradition in many non-western cultures. Sometimes it is part of some sort of initiation rite under which children are left to themselves for a period of time, in order to prove themselves in 'autonomous' child groups and to make themselves fit for life together (see Liebel, 2004: 93–6). In many parts of Africa, groups of children take on very clearly defined social functions, for instance, maintenance of wells or mosques (in Muslim communities), keeping villages clean, assisting the sick and handicapped or the support of victims of hard rainfalls or fires (see Sall, 2002: 89). The widespread phenomenon of child-headed households nowadays is, however, due to emergency situations. A particularly high number of such households can be found in countries that are strongly affected by the HIV/AIDS pandemic (van Breda, 2010). Also, as a result of the genocide, there are an estimated 60,000 child-headed households in Rwanda (Tolfree, 2004: 163). South Africa is the first country where a special legislation on child-headed households is to be established (Couzens & Zaal, 2009).

The following statements of children from Rwanda and Tanzania who lived in such households illustrate well what affects these children (quoted by Tolfree, 2004: 162):

> *I am fourteen years old, and I am a child. But if I ever get married, I know I will always continue to take care of my children. How could a family abandon its children? To me, a family is a group of people who care for each other when they are hungry or sick. I have a family, I just need a home.*

> *I am too young to be a mother, but I am a mother, and I would never leave my brother and sister alone.*

> *I am twelve years old and came here with my parents, who all passed away one year ago, and I don't like to be separated from my young sisters and brothers, we stay together, I take care for them, especially the young one who is one year old ... In order to care for him, I have been compelled to drop from school ... But we enjoy when we are together without being interfered by anybody outside our family.*

Such preferences are usually not respected by organizations that, in the name of children's rights, promote the protection of, and provision for, abandoned children and children living apart from adults. David Tolfree (2004: 161) reports that, for instance, children living in such households in Tanzania were hard to convince to confide in a foster family despite enormous difficulties encountered in the own house. In Malawi, other members of the communities principally view child-headed households as inappropriate, even if the oldest 'child' is already 18 or older.

Children who live in child-headed households must cope with many difficulties. As they experience little recognition for their way of living and are hardly supported, they often have difficulty earning their living. Sometimes they lack needed experience to direct their day-to-day lives and to solve problems that arise. A 15-year-old boy uses these words (quoted by Tolfree, 2004: 165):

> *What choice do I have? I am 15 years old. I do not know how to raise these girls. I do not know how to look after them. I can take care of myself, but I*

cannot take care of them. Sometimes I do not know what to do. Without me,
they would have no food to eat, no place to sleep. But what can I do?

When these children find neither protection nor support, they are in particular danger of being abused and exploited. The children themselves very
often complain that they have no one who speaks for them and defends
them against accusations. They feel left alone frequently and say, for example: *'If you are alone, you are discouraged'* (ibid.: 166). The children who care
for their survival and that of their siblings find very little time and few
opportunities to be with other children and, when they grow older, to find
a possible partner for life.

Nonetheless, child-headed households can be more than an emergency
solution and can bring some advantages for the children. They enable siblings to stay together and strengthen mutual relations that are also important later in life. David Tolfree (2004: 163–4) reports that some children
particularly mention the fear of being separated from their siblings and
of being maltreated when living in foster families or homes. This is partly
based on their own experiences. Sometimes, living together can also be a
way of not losing the house or of continuing work and practices established
there, which are indispensable for survival. Older children emphasize that it
is especially important to them not to lose economic independence in order
to have a more advantageous starting point for adult life.

When children are reliant on helping themselves, as in the cases of the
'unaccompanied' refugees or the AIDS orphans, their interests are best met
if they find recognition and support for the form of living they feel appropriate. Only then will they see any sense in children's rights and possibly
use them to their advantage.

Conclusion

In order to ensure that children embrace rights and make use of them for
themselves, they must be conceptualized in a context-specific way and in
accordance with the children's life experiences. The task cannot be to 'implement' formally existing children's rights; they must, rather, be reflected
according to their cultural, political and structural coherence and weighed
against the possible consequences for the children's lives. In doing this,
the large differences between living situations of children across the globe
must be considered and can lead to different meanings of the same rights.
If need be, the rights must be specified and extended with children participating in a significant way. The children are to be respected as persons who
(co-)construct their rights and participate and design the handling of their
rights.

If rights are not understood as a weapon of the powerful, but as 'power
held by the powerless' (Federle, 1994: 345), then the child rights discourse

held until now is in serious need of revision. Rights are important because they signal to those who hold them that they need not see themselves as beggars or objects of good deeds granted to them. But 'rights without remedies are of symbolic importance, no more' (Freeman, 2007: 8). As Katherine Hunt Federle (1994: 343–4) stated years ago, based on her experiences in the US, it holds equally true that:

> Having the right means having the power to command respect, to make claims and to have them heard. But if having a right is contingent upon some characteristic, like capacity, then holding the rights becomes exclusive and exclusionary; thus, only claims made by a particular group of (competent) being will be recognized. ... Children, however, have been unable to redefine themselves as competent beings; thus, powerful elites decide which, if any, of the claims made by children they will recognize.

Children's rights become rights of the children and can be understood and practised as such only when children themselves reach the necessary power and means to set their own priorities and to use the rights according to their own discretion. In the following chapters, we will discuss how this can be achieved, from different perspectives.

Notes

1. In the concept of democratic states, the idea is that 'civil society' (generally limited to adults with voting rights) also participates in state decisions.
2. If 'welfare rights' were understood as children's rights, it would be more suitable to speak of *responsibility rights* or *recognition rights*.
3. Therefore, the North American children's rights activist Richard Farson (1974) demanded as early as the 1970s not to protect the children but their rights.
4. Other countries with similarly brutal human rights violations towards these children include Brazil and Colombia.
5. The interview is documented in detail in Snodgrass, 1999: 434, 438; see also Stephenson, 2001; McAdam-Crisp et al., 2005.
6. The author refers to experiences in Norway, where reference to children's rights has an especially long tradition, and official decisions are generally legitimized with the remark that they served the 'best interests' of the child.

Part II
Theoretical Perspectives

4
Schools of Thought in Children's Rights

Karl Hanson

A consensus on the extent, priorities or even precise content of children's rights is not readily available: children's rights are a morally sensitive domain having to deal with strong, and often competing, normative and ideological perspectives. Working in such a context is particularly challenging, not only for policy makers and activists but also for researchers (Reynolds et al., 2006). This chapter aims to reflect on the differences amongst conceptions of children's rights by proposing a heuristic structure which presents the various approaches as 'schools of thought' in children's rights. After we question the supposed generalized consensus on children's rights, we will discuss four dimensions or key issues on which opinions diverge and that are pivotal for understanding variations in approaches to children's rights. These dimensions are the childhood image, the debate on competence, the rights of children and the difference dilemma. As a next step, and according to positions taken on the key issues, we suggest differentiating approaches to children's rights in the form of four schools of thought: Paternalism, Liberalism, Welfare and Emancipation. In conclusion, we will point to some possible implications of this proposed framework for child research.

A false consensus

In the 1970s and early 1980s, the notion of 'children's rights' was a much more homogeneous concept than it is today. Persons who then labelled themselves as children's rights advocates adopted a consistent ideological position in their actions against discrimination and unfair treatment of children and young people. In step with contemporaneous emancipation movements such as the women's movement or the civil rights movement, children's rights advocates wanted to liberate children and argued in favour of children's equal rights. Their claims were directed against both family and state, whose paternalistic approaches to children were considered an impediment to young people's pursuit of autonomy and full participation in society. Illustrative for the unison and the prevailing aim of the children's rights movement to free children from adult's oppression of that time is the subtitle of one of the emblematic books of the children's rights movement, edited in 1977 by Beatrice and Ronald Gross, *Overcoming the Oppression of Young People*.

The positions and actions of the children's rights movement of that period, also labelled the *children's liberation movement* or *kiddie libbers*, were until then directed against dominant protectionist and welfare approaches towards children. The child protectionist or 'child-saving movements' (Platt, 1969) had come into being at the end of the 19 century in the context of uncontrolled industrialization and its dire consequences for the living conditions of poor working-class children. The child savers saw it as their moral duty to alleviate the plight of vulnerable children whom they considered passive victims and mere objects of intervention, emphasizing the need to offer children protection against all sorts of dangers as well as to offer them welfare provisions arranged for by well-intentioned adults. These social groups have been instrumental for the creation of child-protection laws and institutions, leading to the establishment of professional practices and academic interests in child protection. However, their concepts did not as much speak of *rights* of children but referred to the need to protect children's health, welfare or decent upbringing – even if the 1959 UN Declaration on the Rights of the Child did refer to the rights of the child terminology to focus on social welfare rights. It was only since the advent of the 1989 UN Convention on the Rights of the Child (CRC) that persons and organizations traditionally associated with a welfare approach to children started to begin making use of children's rights as an overall concept to frame their actions. Illustrative of this shift is the initial reluctance of both UNICEF and the International Union of Child Welfare, which was the major federation of child-focused NGOs at the time, to participate in the drafting of the CRC (Cantwell, 2007). It was only during the last stage of the drafting process that UNICEF enhanced its involvement and took up a crucial role in facilitating the acceptance of the new international children's rights document.

Since 1989, 'children's rights' have received considerable and widespread attention by international organizations, governments and civil society at large, not least as a consequence of the adoption and subsequent almost universal ratification of the CRC.[1] The concern for children's rights continued throughout the 1990s and persists today, where children's rights have gained an established place in society. Across all regions, and in a considerable number of ratifying states, the CRC has set in motion a process which promoted national legal and institutional reforms aiming to advance the cause of children's rights (UNICEF, 2004). With this, an increasing number of professionals must deal with this Convention as well as with other international legislative documents on children's rights. For example, to meet the needs for extensive knowledge, in part resulting from the wide-reaching impact of the CRC, an increasing number of universities and research institutes are offering academic children's rights programmes.[2]

The expansion of the children's rights field and of its number of supporters also gave rise to a proliferation of views on the meaning and content of children's rights. In academic children's rights literature, various subjects are being discussed not only from a wide range of disciplinary perspectives but also from diverse ideological positions. Thomas W. Simon (2000), for instance, substitutes the 'wrongs to the child' for the 'rights of the child' and places the primary focus on children's protection rights. For him, children's rights deal with a universal moral obligation for all individuals to avoid that the gravest harm is inflicted upon children, and hence limits children's rights to the right of children to be protected by well-intentioned adults. Katherine Hunt Federle (1994: 365) rejects such a view of children's rights which does not empower children through rights, but 'empower[s] ourselves to intervene in their lives'. According to her, the value of rights is that they enable children to rely on their rights to challenge existing hierarchies and can contribute to shifting power away from those who have it, to children, and thus can equalize relationships. The two authors, who have both published their views in one of the main academic journals on the subject, *The International Journal of Children's Rights*, refer to children's rights discourses for defending radically different views on the subject. Moreover, the contrasting views of both authors illustrate that although everyone seems to agree about the importance of children's rights, a true consensus on the meaning and content of the concept is often far away. The aphorism launched in 1973 by Hillary Rodham, 'The phrase "children's rights" is a slogan in search of definition', has lost none of its relevance.

Key issues under discussion

For analysing the conceptions of childhood among philosophers in the Western tradition, Turner and Matthews (1998) propose three headings 1) what children are, 2) what they know, and 3) what they deserve. A fourth issue, common to these headings, compares children to adults. Each gives rise to particular questions and tensions:

> Firstly, are children beings in themselves or merely potential beings? Are they animals of instinct or rationality? Secondly, are children capable of consequential reasoning or are they capable only of living for the moment?...Thirdly, do children merit any of the freedoms or protections adults enjoy, or should they content themselves with the obedience and servitude, as well as the vulnerability that belong to the lives of non-human animals? Should their freedoms be drastically limited to protect their vulnerabilities and foster their development? Or do strong protections stunt their development and assault their dignity? (Turner & Matthews, 1998: 3)

The questions in the debate amongst philosophers coincide with the key issues which are discussed in the children's rights field. For our analysis, we will have a look into each of the following key issues: childhood image (what children are), the debate on competence (what they know), rights of children (what they deserve) and the difference dilemma (comparing childhood with adulthood).

Childhood image

In his landmark study on the history of childhood, the French historian Philippe Ariès (1960) relativized what had been, until then, prevalent conceptions of childhood. Ariès defended the thesis that there is not one, 'natural' view of childhood, but that time and space offer many different ways of conceiving children and childhood (James et al., 1998; Archard, 2004). Over centuries, children had been considered, by and at large, not to be fully fledged citizens but 'unfinished human beings' or 'citizens in the making'. John Locke (1632–1704), for instance, illustrated a long Western philosophical tradition of understanding children as persons who lack that which defines adults, for instance, reason or physical independence; in general terms, he saw childhood as a preparatory stage on the way to a terminus called 'adulthood' (Archard, 2004). Verhellen (2000: 16) points out: 'In this way, children were gradually put in a *position of not yet being*; not yet knowing; not yet being able to; therefore not yet able to express themselves, not yet responsible. ... Their master status became one of *not-yet-being* ... .' These childhood images refer to a teleological perception of the world, which considers humans, animals and others as moving towards a final optimal state (Hart, 1998). According to such a teleological world view, evolutions or changes can be explained and are valued as events which 'ought to have happened', as steps in the direction of the appropriate and therefore desired end goal or *telos*. The image of the child as 'inevitably' developing and maturing towards an optimal end goal has received further emphasis via dominant discourses of traditional development psychology, which constructed the model of 'the naturally developing child' (James et al., 1998). Children are natural, rather than social, phenomena who develop through a series of hierarchically structured and defined development stages. The status of the child is reduced to 'an inadequate precursor to the real state of human being, namely being "grown up"' (ibid.: 18).

Such a teleological childhood image has been seriously questioned in a range of realms and in various academic disciplines, including sociology, socio-legal studies, psychology, history and anthropology. A representation of the world where beings develop in order to reach their optimal 'natural' state does not take into account the possibilities for human beings to intervene in their own lives as actors. Moving towards an optimal predefined end goal supposes a belief in an agenda of the optimal end state which has been set by nature or divinity, rather than a rational explanation for human developments and evolutions. Also, where development theories can give an explanation for 'normal' development of the 'normal' child, it offers only little help for those who do not follow the standard procedure of development, such as children with mental or physical disabilities (James et al., 1998). Childhood sociology contributed to the deconstruction of the 'natural developing child' and emphasizes that children are social actors, human 'beings' rather than human 'becomings'. In opposition to considering children as 'becoming', contemporary sociologies of childhood urge 'that children be treated equally, at least in terms of recognizing that children have views and perspectives of their own. On this view, all humans, regardless of chronological age, are and should be treated as "beings"' (Lee, 2001: 3).

The debate on competence

A second fundamental discussion deals with the question of the extent to which children are deemed capable of consequential reasoning or only capable of living for the moment. Are children physically, intellectually and emotionally sufficiently mature? Do they have sufficient experience to take well-founded decisions? Or are children insufficiently developed to make rational judgments on what is and is not in their interest (Verhellen, 2000)? To better understand the debate on children's competence, we suggest differentiating amongst at least three dimensions in the debate, each built upon a particular set of arguments.

A first dimension is a practical or empirical one and deals with how children's competence can be evaluated in particular settings on the basis of empirical findings and arguments. Instead of relying on common wisdom about children's competency, people argue about children's competence or incompetence based on scientific research. One influential person for the empirical verification of children's competence is Jean Piaget (1896–1980), who argued on the basis of his empirical findings that children gradually acquire intellectual skills which he subdivides in stages of intellectual development. These stages are ordered temporally and arranged hierarchically on a continuum from infantile figurative thought to adult operative intelligence (James et al., 1998). According to Piaget's findings, children would be capable only from around 12 years old as this is the age at which they attend the concrete operative stage where they have the cognitive competence to make their own rational and moral judgements. These findings are referred to as giving empirical evidence for the image of the 'naturally developing child' who is less competent compared to adults (who are at the end of the development stages) and therefore give weight to arguments calling for a neat distinction between children and adults based on competence.

However, not only authors who rely on children's incompetence, but also those who argue in favour of recognizing a greater competence for children refer to Piaget's findings. For Leo Apostel (1989), this is not a surprise, as Piaget's findings would encourage neither the first nor the second ones.

Piaget was mainly interested in studying the ordinary succession of the stages rather than in the precise ages at which each stage appears. There is also abundant evidence that development stages are context-dependent, whereby children may be far more advanced for certain decision-making tasks than for others (Apostel, 1989). Competency not only deals with a person's the cognitive abilities but is a function of contextual and interpersonal factors. Philip Jaffé and Hélène Rey Wicky (1996: 99) explain that 'competence is a notion that does not exist per se *in abstracto*, but is displayed *in concreto*, and takes on individual significance only when evaluated in context and analysed from an observer's perspective'. Empirical research on children's competence in practical decision-making generally concludes that children's competence depends on children's own measurable competence, but rather from the willingness, the training, the mandate and the talent of the adult who was assigned to help children demonstrate their competence (Jaffé & Rey Wicky, 1996). Other important contextual factors include children's degree of power and their emotional and economic dependency. Children, just like adults, might need support to exercise their intellectual and practical capabilities, depending on both their age and the situation in which a particular decision is to be exercised (Mortier, 1996).

A second dimension looks at the values and various interests at stake and addresses children's competence/incompetence from a particular ideological position. In this respect, many legal arrangements and individual decisions concerning children prescribe the use of age limitations and/or competence tests in order to allow or prohibit children from accessing certain goods or services, for instance, buying alcohol or cigarettes, the right to vote, obtaining a driver's license or being recognized as a reliable witness in court. Albeit referring to the competence debate, many of these age limitations are based not as much on empirical data concerning children's competence but rather on underlying social interests and ideological preferences. In this respect, Martha Minow (1986: 6) observed that:

> ... the inconsistent legal treatment of children stems in some measure from societal neglect of children. The needs and interests of children, difficult enough to address when highlighted, are too often submerged below other societal interests. The dominance of these other interests helps to explain the inconsistent treatment of children.

The children's rights movement has made every effort to counter the arguments supporting the theory of incompetence, by disputing their validity, relevance and soundness (Verhellen, 2000). For adults, being competent or not is not considered a valid argument to grant or deny certain rights. Moreover, according to the child liberationists, the incompetence of children is an ideological construction and a characteristic feature of the modern conception of childhood (Archard, 2004). Furthermore, the presumption of children's incompetence is self-confirming. 'Presumed unable to do something, children may simply not be allowed to show that in fact they can' (ibid.: 96). From a protectionist perspective, children 'deserve' to be protected, precisely because they have not yet developed the cognitive abilities to make rational decisions.

Reasons why children's incompetence is so often highlighted do not deal as much with facts or justice, but with ideology and power. For Katherine Hunt Federle (1994), the competence criterion plays to the advantage of the elites, of those who are actually in power. To ignore children's claims on the basis of their presumed incompetence, or if only some of their claims are recognized, also means that 'those deciding which claims are worthy of attention have tremendous power' (ibid.: 344). Literature on judicial practice across the globe highlights that arbitrary norms, non-objective ideas and prejudices are very often used to justify decisions (Jaffé & Rey Wicky, 1996).

Third, there is also a strategic dimension in the debate on competence, dealing with the question of where the burden of proof should lie, in particular with who has to give proof of children's competence or incompetence (Verhellen, 2000). In a particular setting, should children have to demonstrate their competency, or, conversely, must it be shown that they are insufficiently competent? Victor L. Worsfold (1974) elaborated a philosophical justification for children's right based on John Rawls' (1921–2002) theory of justice and thereby referred to the presumption of rationality as a principle of fairness.

> This point has major implications for children's rights, shifting the burden of proof to those who would deny children the exercise of their own rights. Although there are no doubt many areas where children are justifiably denied the exercise of freedoms, the correctness of his denial is no longer taken for granted. On the contrary, it must be shown to be just. (Worsfold, 1974: 156)

In the legal realm, it is argued that a presumption of children's incompetence must be replaced by a presumption of their competence, placing the burden of proof no longer on children and their allies but on the opponents of recognizing children as competent (Rodham, 1973).

In most discussions on competence, the empirical, ideological and strategic dimensions intersect, whereby it is not always possible to distinguish clearly between the kinds of arguments. Results from empirical findings are, for instance, used and even reinforce pre-established ideological positions. Conversely, the ideological position from where children's competence is studied influences the outcome of the findings. However, the separation of the arguments provides a useful analytical frame for improving an understanding of the debate on children's competence.

Rights of children

The next key issue considers the question of what children deserve – what rights they have and what kind of rights they should have. The Convention on the Rights of the Child recognizes both children's general human rights as well as a number of special rights of children. Its content can be summarized by the so-called three Ps, including protection rights (for instance, against violence or exploitation), provision rights (for instance, education or health care provisions) and participation rights (for instance, freedom of expression or right to information). The provisions of the CRC must be considered holistically, which means that the CRC gives equal importance to the different kind of rights of children and that there is no hierarchy amongst the provisions which all belong to one of the three Ps (Verhellen, 2000).

Several authors refer to the distinction between 'child liberation' and 'child welfare' to provide further insight into how protection, provision and participation rights might be combined (see, e.g., Archard, 2004; Franklin, 1986; Federle, 1994). *Child liberationists* take as a starting point the claims to autonomy of children and emphasize the importance of their rights to self-determination. From the point of view of the welfare of children, *child welfarists* point to the importance of taking care of children and predominantly emphasize the child's right to protection. However, this dichotomy often leads to an ideological debate of truths or develops into a war of position with two camps, the 'advocates' and the 'critics' of rights to self-determination and of rights to protection.

In order to transcend this diametrical opposition between defenders of the rights to freedom and of the rights to protection, different authors seek to find a balance between both approaches. They do not consider the protection of children as the antithesis of advocating their right to self-determination or vice versa. 'Protecting children and protecting their rights are therefore not necessarily oppositional but can be complementary objectives' (Franklin, 1986: 17). The right to freedom and self-determination as well as the right to protection and care should both therefore be recognized. With respect to young children, who first need protection and care, rights to protection should be emphasized. As children grow older, their rights to self-determination become more important, and their rights to protection may less immediately lead to a restriction of their rights to freedom. A gradual acquisition of rights is defended to give shape to the complementarity between freedom and protection.

The division of children's rights into two categories, i.e. rights to self-determination and rights to protection, can, *in abstracto*, generate an overview of children's rights. However, not all discussions on children's rights can be described by using the categories 'to protect children', 'to respect their autonomy' or 'to gradually find a balance between both'. Working children, for instance, claim the right to participate (self-determination rights) in the measures to be taken to enhance their working conditions (protection rights) and seem to be unconcerned about the dichotomy between autonomy and protection (Hanson & Vandaele, 2003; Hanson, 2012).

An alternative conceptualization of rights which leaves more space to cover the complexity of the discussion on children's rights can be found in the writings of Rodham (1973), who distinguished two general approaches of claims for children's rights: the extension of adult rights to children and the search for a legally enforceable recognition of children's special needs and interests. Rodham did not intent to simply equalize adults and children. In some cases, the rights of adults can be applied to children in the same way as for adults, whereas in other cases, they must be adjusted to the needs and situations of children. According to this conception, children's rights involve a double claim, including 'equal rights' and 'special rights'. First, children's rights reaffirm children as full members of the human family and assert that children have an equal right to the protection of their fundamental human rights without discrimination based on age. Second, they acknowledge children's developing capacity as well as their vulnerability, and encompass additional, special rights for children.

Difference dilemma

One final key issue which crosscuts the previous ones is the question on resemblances and differences between children and adults. Children are both different from adults and equal to adults. The question now is: what differences between adults and children are relevant in what cases? Martha Minow (1986: 14) saw a remarkable parallel with the debate about women's legal rights. She wrote:

> Rights' may be claimed to underscore children's similarity to adults – but rights may also be invoked to call attention to children's differences. The notion of 'Children's Rights' could – and has – been seized by advocates of both separate, protective treatment and identical, equal treatment for children and adults. This confusion bears a striking parallel to the special versus equal treatment debate about women's legal rights.

Within the women's rights movement, generally three strands can be discerned (Brems, 1997; Raes, 1992). Liberal feminists, whose major concern is the equal treatment of men and women, claim a consequent application of the non-discrimination principle contained in most human rights treaties. Cultural feminists (or 'different voice feminists') underline biological, psychological and social differences between men and women, rather than the equality of the sexes, and base women's values not on individualism or autonomy but on responsibility, care and connectivity. They claim the recognition of rights based on female values, such as the rights to food, shelter, education or to be protected against violence within family relations. Difference-feminists emphasize that relevant differences occur not only between men and women but also amongst women and amongst men. Questions on equality and difference must be contextualized, taking into account 'differences that make a difference'.

The dilemma of difference, as developed within feminist theory (Minow, 1986) can be easily translated to the children's rights context for coining debates on resemblances and differences concerning children. The *difference dilemma* in children's rights can be phrased as follows: Should children (or those who defend them) on the one hand, choose rights similar to the rights of adults (equal rights), with the risk that these equal rights are not adjusted to children, and risk insufficiently taking into account children's specificity? Or should they, on the other hand, defend special rights, on the basis of their particularity, while running the risk that these special (and different) rights may lead to new forms of discrimination?

As for all dilemmas, no definite solution exists. In one case, children should be granted special rights, whereas in another it may be important to defend children's equal rights. In other words, rather than making general abstractions to resolve the *difference dilemma,* an assessment of concrete contexts dealing with children's equal rights or special rights is always required. The discussion then no longer deals with the choice between some rights of children and others, but with the mutual contribution and the interrelation of children's general and special rights. When, and how far, should children's special, rather than general, rights be recognized? Which rights should be given priority, and to what extent, if there is a conflict between both? In what cases, to what extent and on the basis of which criteria can children's preferential rights extend, or otherwise restrict, their general human rights? Special rights should, in this respect, enable the recognition of the individuality of children and the defence of children's interests, whereas equal rights – to a greater or a lesser extent, adjusted to the situation of children – emphasize the equality of children and adults.

Approaches to children's rights

The childhood image, the debate on competence, the rights of children and the difference dilemma all leave room for a broad range of approaches to children and their rights.

> In between the view that children are what adults are, know what adults know, and deserve exactly what adults deserve and the view that children are the negation or the opposite of adults in being, knowledge and desert, is an as yet unfathomable range of possibilities that merits exploration and mapping. (Turner & Matthews, 1998: 6)

In our endeavour to explore and map the children's rights field, we suggest differentiating amongst four 'schools of thought' in children's rights, as shown in Table 4.1, according to a series of positions taken on each of these issues. Hereafter, we will briefly discuss the major points of each position with illustrations from practice and literature.

Paternalism

From a paternalist position, children are considered as dependent, future citizens (becoming) who are generally incompetent to make rational decisions. Their rights are limited to the right to be protected, be it by parents, the state, professional or voluntary benefactors, who can rely on legal arrangements, institutions and welfare organizations to treat children paternally. In the paternalist view, control over children has been justified by the need to protect children from themselves and others; children are considered lacking, by their very nature, an adequate conception of their own present and future interests (Worsfold, 1974). Because what children are, can be and deserve are considered essentially different from adults, paternalism does not have to deal with a dilemma. In the paternalist view, children only need special treatment and special, different rights which are intended to preserve their future well-being. What is in the best interests of children is completely decided by caring and loving adults who offer their help and exercise their authority over children.

Paternalism has long-standing historical roots, both in philosophy and in activism on behalf of children and youth. Illustrative for paternalist approaches towards children are many social and political reform movements in the late 19th century and in the first decades of the 20th century, such as the child-saving movement that helped to create special judicial and correctional institutions for the management of 'troublesome' youth (Platt, 1969) or the US National Child Labor Committee (NCLC), which conducted

Table 4.1 Schools of thought in children's rights

	Paternalism	Welfare	Emancipation	Liberation
Childhood image	Becoming	Becoming and being	Being and becoming	Being
Competence	Incompetent	Incompetent, unless	Competent, unless	Competent
Rights of children	Protection rights	Protection rights Provision rights Participation rights	Participation rights Provision rights Protection rights	Participation rights
Difference dilemma	Special rights	Special rights – equal rights	Equal rights – special rights	Equal rights

major campaigns to abolish child labour (Dimock, 1993). In his historical study of the US American child-saving movement, Anthony M. Platt (1969), for instance, described this movement not as an effort to dignify and liberate youth, but as a punitive, romantic and intrusive effort to control the lives of lower-class urban adolescents and to maintain their dependent status. For him, the child-saving movement was highly instrumental for the implementation of authoritarian, paternalistic and class-motivated policies, as apparent in the contributions of politically conservative, socially prominent, middle-class women in the movement.

A contemporary paternalist position on children's rights is upheld by religious conservative movements. The *American Christian Rights Movement*, for instance, strongly advocates against the CRC, because it would contain a direct attack to natural rights of the family and would undermine the parent's authority (Butler, 2000; Herman, 2001). Children are parents' propriety and have no more rights than the rights to love and protection they receive from their parents. The *Concerned Women for America*, a conservative Christian political action group which promotes Biblical values and family traditions, for instance, explains how, in its view, the UN Convention on the Rights of the Child 'usurps parental authority by embracing the view that children are autonomous agents who are capable, in all areas, of making adult decisions and dealing with adult situations. This radical legal doctrine stands in stark contrast to the traditional concept, upheld in America, that children are "minors" in need of parental protection' (1997).

A distinctive form of paternalism is defended by the philosopher Thomas W. Simon (2000), who takes as a starting point the universal moral obligation for all individuals not to inflict the gravest harms upon children. Simon does not reject the CRC, which he paraphrases as the 'United Nations Convention on the Wrongs to the Child', but he considers it as a guiding framework because for him the 'harm provisions' constitute its core. Children's protection rights and the obligation to avoid the gravest harms being inflicted on children form, according to the author, the central part of the CRC, much more than participation rights. Simon acknowledges that the protection of children against serious physical and mental harm is not only paternalistic, but can even be contrary to the respect of children's right to autonomy, which he finds only a small price to be paid in the light of the gravest harms inflicted upon children, such as malnutrition or child abuse.

Liberation

Liberation takes the opposite stance of paternalism on all issues discussed and therefore can also be labelled as anti-paternalism. Liberationists consider children as independent actual citizens (beings) who are competent to make well-founded, rational decisions. They have the right to autonomy and to full participation in society, in the same way as adults. Child liberationists consider the liberation of children as part of a broader movement for the emancipation of all mankind. They take as a starting point the claims to autonomy of children and emphasize the importance of their rights to self-determination. This movement struggled for the recognition of equality of children, rather then stressing children's differences compared to adults. Children are, can be and deserve to be exactly what adults are, can be and deserve to be. Therefore, liberationists are not confronted with a dilemma needing to balance general and special rights; the recognition of children's equal rights is the only justifiable approach.

The works of Richard Farson (1974) and John Holt (1975), which hold a passionate plea to granting children autonomy rights, are emblematic of the liberationist approach to children's rights. Their basic claims are 'that the modern separation of the child's and adult's worlds is an unwarranted and oppressive discrimination; that this segregation is accompanied and reinforced by a false ideology of "childishness"; and that children are entitled to all the rights and privileges possessed by adults' (Archard, 2004: 71). Some of the issues put forward by the child liberationists are still on the children's rights agenda, such as the claim for granting children political rights, and in particular the right to vote, which is not mentioned in the CRC. Bob Franklin (1998: 173), a scholar who has worked on children's voting rights, argues that giving children the right to vote 'would place the responsibility for protecting children's rights where it properly belongs. Not in the hands of well meaning but potentially paternalistic adults, but with those who have the greatest interest in ensuring that those rights are not infringed; children themselves'. Another autonomy right advocated by the children's liberationists, and which continues to receive support, is the claim for recognizing children's right to work. Manfred Liebel (1997: 81), who has worked for years on working children's movements, for instance, states that 'legislation should establish the children's right to work, without any age limitation. Society and the State must guarantee the same labour rights enjoyed by adult workers, including equal pay for equal work, social security coverage, trade union organisation and collective bargaining rights'.

Welfare

The childhood image defended by welfarists is more nuanced compared to the position defended by paternalists and liberationists, as they consider children *both* becoming and being. In the debate on competence, they consider children mainly as incompetent, but accept that proof can be given of the contrary; from a welfare perspective, the burden of proof lies on those who would argue in favour of recognizing children's competence. In line with its embracing of the CRC, the welfare approach to children's rights acknowledges the three series of rights, stressing, in order of importance, children's protection rights, provision rights and participation rights. To determine their position in the difference dilemma, the welfare approach, albeit to a certain extent acknowledging children's equal rights, starts from children's particularity and mainly defends children's special rights.

Today, the welfare approach to children's rights is largely dominant in the child welfare sector, both on the national levels as well as in international cooperation. UNICEF, the United Nations' leading organization for providing long-term humanitarian and developmental assistance to children in developing countries, for instance, states in its mission statement that the organization's basic aim is to advocate for the protection of children's rights, to help meet their basic needs and to expand their opportunities to reach their full potential. Although recognizing children's actual citizenship, UNICEF's main focus is to advocate for measures to give children the best start in life; arguing that proper care at the youngest age forms the strongest foundation for a person's future. UNICEF claims to be guided by the Convention on the Rights of the Child and hence embraces the full range of the protection, provision and participation rights. The organization's major focus, however, is on children's survival and protection rights. It is only in addition to the aim of meeting children's basic needs that attention is given to their participation rights.

The welfare approach is also present in the work of philosopher Laura Purdy (1992), who refutes the liberationist thesis and argues against granting children equal rights which would undermine parental authority. In her view, children first and foremost need to be protected, because of the position's immediate advantages. Protecting children and limiting their rights to freedom encourages their future options. One classical example is the justification for compulsory schooling. Denying children the right to choose to go to school or not is justified from the future possibilities that are offered by the educational system. The absence of compulsory schooling would push too many children into the labour market, where, without any training, they would be compelled to accept the least attractive jobs. In Purdy's view, granting children an equal right to work would be unfair, because this would deepen the gap between the rich and the poor. However, her refusal of the radical liberationist approach does not turn the author into a paternalist. She does, for instance, recognize the adolescents' right to sexual activity and emphasizes the necessity to expand young girls' access to abortion without parental consent.

Michael Freeman (1997) discusses tensions between equal and different rights by stressing the importance of taking seriously both welfare and autonomy of children. For him, '[i]t is not a question of whether child-savers or liberationists are right, for they are both correct in emphasizing part of what needs to be recognized, and both wrong in failing to address the claims of the other side' (ibid.: 40). Freeman describes his position as 'liberal paternalism' and balances children's rights to 'present autonomy' with their 'capacity for future autonomy', which in some instances can be invoked to limit their present autonomy. As a justification for his liberal paternalism,

Freeman refers to future-oriented consent. Treating individuals paternalistically is only justified when they agree with the limitations. In the case of children, who lack certain capacities to give their consent to these limitations here and now, it is their (hypothetical) future consent that will justify paternalism. Will the child, once he or she becomes a capable adult, agree with the imposed limitations to its autonomy as a child? 'We have to treat [children] as persons entitled to equal concern and respect and entitled to have both their present autonomy recognized and their capacity for future autonomy safeguarded. And this is to recognize that children, particularly younger children, need nurture, care and protection' (ibid.: 37).

Emancipation

From an emancipation perspective, children are also seen as both being and becoming, however reversing the order of the welfare approach. Regarding the competence debate, emancipationists shift the burden of proof to those who would deny children the exercise of their own rights; children are competent unless it can be shown that they are not. In listing the importance of rights, emancipationists start with children's participation rights and further acknowledge the importance of rights to provision and protection. Confronted with the difference dilemma, emancipationists start their analysis from children's equal rights, but also acknowledging children's special rights that, in some instances (depending on the outcome of the assessment) might have stronger emancipatory effects.

Working children's organizations that have emerged in various regions of the world since the beginning of the 1990s (Swift, 1999) illustrate this emancipation approach towards children's rights. In their statements and declarations issued at national and international meetings, working children's organizations have made two different claims. They want to participate in the discussions on child labour, and they want their right to work in dignity to be recognized. As their main focus, the working children's organizations consider children as competent beings whose basic human rights should be acknowledged. Translated to the difference dilemma, they do not, however, refute the idea that there can be significant differences between working adults and working children that justify a different treatment. But what they do contest is the idea that these differences must always lead to a one-dimensional response that treats working children differently from working adults. There are probably cases where working children's particular position (for instance, as an apprentice or domestic worker) might best be addressed by a legal framework completely different from the existing adult labour legislation. Conversely, there might be instances when working children's rights are best supported by relying on general labour law principles and legislation, of which their claim for recognition of their right to work in dignity forms an integral part (Hanson & Vandaele, 2003).

Eugeen Verhellen (2000) and Miek de Langen (1992) also write on children's rights from an emancipatory perspective. They explicitly situate the debate on the recognition of children's rights, and the discussion between the general human rights of children as well as their special or preferential human rights, within the framework of human rights. They refer, for instance, to the comprehensiveness of the CRC, which contains a broad range of rights, including civil and political rights as well as social, economic and cultural rights, and stress that the convention's core message is that children are no longer to be seen as mere passive objects of intervention but should be recognized as bearers of rights. Children therefore have the right, in accordance with their evolving capacities, to actively take part in shaping their own lives and environments.

Implications for child research

Since the adoption of the CRC in 1989, the children's rights concept has become a mainstream advocacy tool in a vast array of fields directly and indirectly relating to children's lives. Various interest groups formulate their claims within the existing framework of human rights, using the CRC as well as the provisions in general human rights treaties to sustain their demands. The growing consensus on the strategic importance of the recognition of children's rights as human rights does not, however, solve the possible contrasts between the different approaches towards children's rights. We therefore propose to categorise the different perspectives and stances in four schools of thought in children's rights, namely Paternalism, Liberation, Welfare and Empowerment.

We contend that not only action in favour of children's rights but also the choice of themes and methods in child research are, to a great extent, influenced by the researchers' views on childhood image, children's competence, children's rights and the difference dilemma. The proposed subdivision might thus contribute to a better understanding not only of the rich diversity of the existent children's rights field, but also might be of use as an analytical frame which can help to better situate the wide diversity of contemporary child research. However, we are also aware that, in practice, people rarely adhere to fixed positions and that the boundaries between the approaches will very often be imprecise. The proposed schools of thought should therefore be considered as ideal-typical stances. Our aim is not to evaluative the degree of conformity of the position of child researchers with a particular school of thought or to dictate what they ought to think or study. On the contrary, we propose these schools of thought as a heuristic second-level construct (Tamanaha, 2000) which can serve as a roadmap on children's rights for researchers engaged in child research.

Notes

1. As of 1 January 2008, only Somalia and the United States did not ratify the CRC.
2. See, for instance, the Masters in children's rights offered at IUKB in Sion, Switzerland (www.iukb.ch) as well as the academic teaching programmes offered by the member institutions of the European Network of Masters in Children's Rights (www.enmcr.net) and of the Latin American Network of Masters in Childhood and Children's Rights (www.redmaestriasinfancia.net).

5

Localizing the Human Rights of Children

Wouter Vandenhole

Standard-setting on children's rights and, by extension, on human rights, has traditionally been a top-down exercise. States conclude treaties, which are then to be implemented on the ground. Monitoring bodies at the UN or the regional level offer an authoritative interpretation or settle disputes.

In recent years, this approach has been questioned and challenged. A range of approaches and methodologies has been proposed to draw attention to daily realities and the way human rights are received by ordinary people on the ground. A bottom-up approach would allow a response to culturally or otherwise specific challenges and local issues. Usually, the substance of the norms concerned is not questioned though; the concern is more with implementation or realization of already codified rights.

In my view, real localization of human rights, including the human rights of children, covers at least two dimensions: that of cultural acceptance of the *idea* of children's rights (i.e. that children as human beings are entitled to human rights) and that of strategic local mobilization of children's rights in order to further the cause of children. Both dimensions require a perspective from below.

There has been a growing body of scholarship on human rights from below. At least one proposal has been made to also allow for a reverse *standard-setting* process, so as to have it based on realities on the ground, i.e. that of localizing human rights, as coined by De Feyter and methodologically developed by Oré (De Feyter, 2007; Oré, 2011). This chapter explores how localizing human rights relates to similar attempts to bring in a bottom-up perspective, what it would mean for children's rights in particular and whether evidence can be found in practice of a growing readiness to localize children's rights (i.e. to take practices and experiences on the ground as the starting point). It hones in on two cases in particular: that of harmful traditional practices and that of community-based para-legal advice offices.

It goes without saying that a localizing human rights perspective challenges the understanding of children's and human rights as a legal regime. In a localizing perspective, human rights are rather seen as normative references that form part of a struggle for social justice (Merry, 2006b: 16). This understanding, in turn, necessitates power and change analysis.

Before we define what a localizing children's rights approach would mean, and whether evidence of such an approach can already be found in practice, we briefly situate the localizing human rights project in a growing strand of research that is concerned with human rights from below.

Human rights from below

The universality of human rights is a central principle to the mainstream and politically correct approach to human rights, as confirmed, *inter alia*, by the 1993 Vienna World Conference on Human Rights. However, the universality of human rights has been contested, mainly by states and governments. Human rights have been fundamentally questioned, for they are often believed to promote an excessive individualism. The cultural relativist debate, often but not exclusively in terms of Asian or African values, has resulted, *inter alia*, in a competing discourse on human responsibilities and duties. The cultural relativist critique of human rights aims to be, *in principle*, of a qualitatively different order (Bauer & Bell, 1999; Ghai, 1999; Freeman, 1998; Ibhawoh, 2001).

It is difficult to assess how authentic these claims for cultural diversity or relativism are, given that they are, more often than not, made by governments and states with dubious track records in the field of human rights. Apolitical claims for cultural relativism emphasize the equal value of all cultures:

> According to the cultural relativist position, children's rights cannot be assessed globally using a priori standards, for there would exist no way of establishing such standards 'outside' the scope of a specific cultural context, of which the 'western' is also one. Attempts at doing so would not only be pointless, but potentially harmful: they would stifle other cultures and instill in those who belong to them a sense of inferiority for failing to live up to standards set by outsiders who happen to be more powerful. (Nieuwenhuys, 2008: 5)

More recently, there has been a growing interest in the local or grassroots level. Most scholarship within this strand focuses on the contestation or appropriation of human rights language by social movements and people on the ground. Different notions have been coined to denote this interest in how human rights work out on the ground, how they are appropriated and possibly reinterpreted in the mobilization by social justice movements.

Merry uses the term 'localisation of women's human rights' to refer to the process whereby global human rights are appropriated and translated by local women's organizations (Merry, 2006b: 8). She concludes that the 'rights framework does not displace other frameworks but adds a new dimension to the way individuals think about problems' (Merry, 2006a: 180, compare Merry, 2006b: 8). While she shows a clear interest in how human rights are received on the ground, she still seems to start from a top-down perspective in standard-setting, in the sense that she suggests that 'transnational knowledge of rights' needs to be localized (Merry, 2006a: 179). She does not seem to contest or question that the human rights norms, as defined and codified at the international level, are what they are, and are good as they are; the emphasis is on how 'grassroots individuals take on human rights ideas' (Merry, 2006a: 180).

De Gaay Fortman has coined the notion of 'downstream and upstream human rights'. Downstream approaches are associated with international human rights law, while upstream approaches are said to 'arise from people's own convictions on concrete freedoms and entitlements relating to their human dignity' (de Gaay Fortman, 2011).

De Feyter has made a case for the localization of human rights, i.e. 'taking the human rights needs as formulated by local people (in response to the impact of economic globalization on their lives) as the starting point both for the further interpretation and elaboration of human rights norms, and for the development of human rights action, at all levels ranging from the domestic to the global' (De Feyter, 2007: 68). His interest is in allowing human rights to survive and develop into 'a global protection tool', as well as with equalizing the relationship between the victims and the human rights movement (De Feyter, 2007: 76–7).

De Feyter has identified a chain of actors that needs to be in place in order to allow local human rights realities to impact on the further elaboration of human rights norms. A key role is assigned to the community-based organizations as the first link in the chain: 'If the experience of local communities is to inspire the further development of human rights, community-based organisations will have to be the starting point' (De Feyter, 2007: 77). The second link is local (in the sense of domestic) human rights NGOs. Their role is very much that of transmission: transmission of specific human rights expertise and knowledge to the community-based organizations; and transmission of lesson learnt at the grassroots to the third link in the chain, i.e. international non-governmental human rights organizations. The fourth link is allies in governmental and intergovernmental institutions.

Whether human rights experiences at the grassroots inspire and guide the whole chain depends, in De Feyter's (2007: 83) view, on the relationships between the links of the chain:

A bottom-up approach requires that the human rights experiences of communities set the agenda for the entire network. Whether this will happen depends upon the relationships between the actors in the network, which are ideally based on an egalitarian 'Habermas like' discourse, resulting in a common understanding of human rights and of the strategy to be pursued. In reality, resources may be divided unequally among the actors, and a top-down hierarchy may set in, unless power balances are negotiated very carefully.

In essence, De Feyter's concern is with improving the universal relevance and legitimacy of human rights, by grounding human rights standard-setting and interpretation in grassroots experiences.

In a subsequent paper on sites of rights resistance, which has meanwhile been published in an edited volume on the local relevance of human rights, the emphasis on local practice remains, but the grassroots actor is much more closely defined than in the 2007 chapter: reference is made to the affected group, which can be 'any form of open organisation based on the identification of a common need or interest. They may, and often will be geographically located [footnote omitted], but could also be rooted in a common experience [footnote omitted], such as the sharing of a similar status within society (e.g., the exercise of an occupation that is culturally considered as impure)' (De Feyter, 2011: 15). The approach is less normative and prescriptive (the four links of the chain have disappeared), and there is more emphasis on local accommodation of human rights claims, while the added value of framing claims in human rights language is also treated more explicitly. So implicitly, the emphasis seems to have shifted from standard-setting to human rights action and from the globally oriented action to the local as a site of struggle.

Oré has developed a methodological backgrounder to the localizing human rights approach, on 'concepts and approaches to "learning from experience" in order to advance social transformation' (Oré, 2011: 12). In her view, different research methodologies may prove useful, including case study, systematization of experiences and participatory impact assessment. While a case study combines quantitative and qualitative methods, systematization of experiences is a participatory approach, whereby those who participated in the experience, together with the beneficiary local population, reconstruct and analytically reflect upon experiences of social promotion in order to generate knowledge from practice (Oré, 2011: 125).

One key hypothesis of the localizing human rights approach is that it depends on cooperation amongst actors at different levels, such as local communities, community-based organizations, local and international NGOs. (Oré, 2011: 115). The existence of a network of human rights actors is an essential criterion, therefore. A research team should consist of scholars from Western and local universities along with the local actors involved in the situation (Oré, 2011: 129).

A case typically focuses on 'experiences in which claims were either framed using human rights language or argued under a principle contained in international human rights law, without necessarily having resorted to specific treaty norms in the first place' (Oré, 2011: 115). Nevertheless, interaction with international human rights norms, institutions or structures is inherently part of the paradigm, as the following figure illustrates (Oré, 2011: 131):

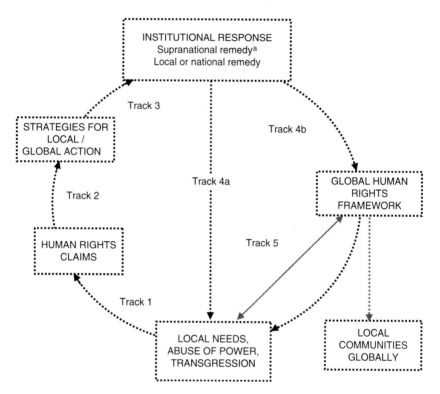

Figure 5.1   The process of localising human rights

Note: [a] Regional court, UN monitoring body, decisions by international organizations, universal jurisdiction judgements.

The starting point is people's local experiences of disempowerment, deprivation, social exclusion, marginalization (Oré, 2011: 111, 130). A network of actors uses the global human rights framework to frame their claims and to take action. The action typically meets an institutional response at different levels, which ideally informs and transforms the global human rights framework, thereby enhancing its potential to respond better to local communities' needs (Oré, 2011: 130–40).

Let us know turn from general human rights to children's rights in particular, and explore whether this approach and methodology require adaptation in order to work out well for children's rights in particular.

Localizing children's rights

In the field of children's rights, too, there has been a growing interest in the local level. Some of the interest, though, seems to have been informed primarily by a concern with the legitimacy of the UN machinery that has been established to monitor implementation of the Convention on the Rights of the Child, in particular the UN Committee on the Rights of the Child. Typically, the focus is then on narrowing or bridging the gap between 'Geneva' and the grassroots (see, e.g., Veerman & Levine, 2000). But other strands have been concerned with a need to localize children's rights, i.e. to take children's local needs and issues as a point of departure. In the Introduction of this book, consistent with his earlier work, Liebel argues that such a need exists indeed:

> In order to ensure that children embrace rights and make use of them for themselves, they must be conceptualized in a context specific way and give answers to the children's life experiences. The task cannot be only to 'implement' formally existing children's rights, but they must rather be reflected according to their cultural, political and structural coherence and weighed against the possible consequences for the children's lives. In doing so, the large differences amongst living situations of children across the globe, between girls and boys, between privileged and marginalized, must be considered and can lead to different meanings of the same rights. If need be, the rights must be specified and extended with children significantly participating.

Here, we want to address the question of whether De Feyter's localizing human rights approach and Oré's methodology could also be applied to children's rights, and whether they hold potential for children's rights. The question of whether the approach can also be transposed to children's rights may seem superfluous, as children's rights are the *human rights* of children. However, as the approach was developed with no particular category of rights-holders in mind, and as the children's rights community often claims that children's rights are somehow special, it may be worth raising that question nevertheless.

In light of De Feyter's *Localising Human Rights* piece, the emphasis would be on how local realities of children may impact on the global norm-setting concerning children's rights. Four links in a chain would play a role: community-based organizations, national children's rights NGOs, international children's rights NGOs, and governmental and intergovernmental institutions. One critical factor is whether the relationships amongst all actors in the chain are egalitarian. In the *Sites of Rights Resistance* paper, the first link does not need to be a community-based organization but can also be a loosely defined organization that is rooted in a common experience or status in society. Children, or particular categories of children, may all quite easily fit this definition of a common status in society.

From a children's rights perspective – but most likely also from a more general human rights perspective, what is missing in the *Localising Human Rights* approach is profound attention to power relations at the grassroots level. The assumption seems to be that power is only relevant in the relations amongst the four links, not *within* the links. In particular, the paper seems to ignore power dynamics at the local level. When applied to children's rights, one crucial question is whether and how children, and which children, are involved in the community-based organization or the more loosely defined open organization. Given the pivotal importance of participation in the children's rights domain, further development of the analysis of power relations at the local level is warranted.

Secondly, one may wonder what the ultimate goal is and who the ultimate beneficiary of the whole exercise is. Is this about making children's rights more relevant for a particular local group of children or about increasing the legitimacy of the global children's rights regime? Why would a local group of children be interested in changing the global children's rights norms, and how could they benefit from it?

The shifts in De Feyter's thinking between 2007 and 2011 – from standard-setting to action and from an almost exclusive focus on the global to the local level when it comes to impact – are welcome developments, I believe. They allow focusing on what the localizing approach may have on offer for the local groups or communities concerned. More often than not, they will not be concerned with influencing standard-setting at the global level in order to possibly have beneficial effects for them, but with much more immediate and tangible change on the ground.

We will now proceed to testing the localizing human rights approach with regard to a substantive norm, i.e. on harmful traditional practices, and a particular institution, i.e. that of community-based para-legal advice offices in South Africa.

Harmful traditional practices

Probably the most straightforward example of how children's rights standards have been questioned on the ground, by the alleged beneficiaries, is that of the prohibition of child labour. As documented by Liebel and others, movements of working children have not only rejected the internationally codified prohibition of child labour but also have claimed that they have a right to work (Hanson, 2006; 2012; Liebel, Overwien & Recknagel, 2001; Liebel, 2004; van den Berge, 2007). While a localizing children's rights approach could be applied here, it may have relatively little added-value to frame the issue also as a localizing children's rights approach, as it has already been very well documented in its own right. Moreover, resorting to the working children's movements might also suggest that child labour is the only issue for which a localizing children's rights approach is potentially relevant or needed.

So, let us leave the trodden paths and go for a harder case, for instance, child soldiering or the prohibition of harmful traditional practices. As child soldiering has been examined from a 'refraction' approach (Hanson, 2011), the choice has been made to focus here on the case of harmful traditional practices. Lest there be any doubt, the purpose here is not to provide an in-depth discussion of harmful traditional practices. Nor have I been working on this topic in the past so that I could claim a particular expertise. This is simply a first exploratory attempt to test the localizing children's rights approach to an issue that has often caused charges of Western imperialism or neo-colonialism.

Harmful traditional practices have been addressed in two core children's rights instruments, i.e. the CRC and the African Charter on the Rights and Welfare of the Child. Article 24(3) CRC reads:

> States Parties shall take all effective and appropriate measures with a view to abolishing traditional practices prejudicial to the health of children.

The African Charter on the Rights and Welfare of the Child (ACRWC) originated because the member states of the then-Organization for African Unity (currently the African Union) believed that the CRC missed important socio-cultural and economic realities unique to Africa. In many respects, the Charter attempts to address the real or alleged peculiarities of Africa by introducing rights and obligations that do not legitimize these peculiarities but rather challenge them. It firmly establishes the supremacy of the rights in the Charter over any custom, tradition, cultural or religious practice that is inconsistent with the Charter. Article 21 of the ACRWC on the protection against harmful social and cultural practices reads:

1. States Parties to the present Charter shall take all appropriate measures to eliminate harmful social and cultural practices affecting the welfare, dignity, normal growth and development of the child and in particular:
   (a) those customs and practices prejudicial to the health or life of the child; and
   (b) those customs and practices discriminatory to the child on the grounds of sex or other status.

2. Child marriage and the betrothal of girls and boys shall be prohibited and effective action, including legislation, shall be taken to specify the minimum age of marriage to be 18 years and make registration of all marriages in an official registry compulsory.

The best-known, and possibly most challenging, example of 'cultural and social harmful practices' or 'harmful traditional practices' are undoubtedly initiation rites that include circumcision, i.e. female genital mutilation (FGM) or female genital cutting (FGC). There is a quasi-consensus that female genital cutting is harmful and there is an urgent need to stop female genital mutilation. Concern has been raised by Ahmadu, who has pointed out the 'unjustified conflation of varied practices of female genital cutting' (Ahmadu, 2000: 284). Others have pointed out the paradox that 'those who emphasize female "circumcision" as a public health issue at the same time oppose any medical intervention designed to minimize health risks and pain for women being cut', for fear that it would institutionalize the practice and counteract efforts to eliminate it (Shell-Duncan, Obungu Obiero & Auko Moruli, 2000: 110–11).

From the perspective of the lived experiences on the ground, there is a certain ambiguity towards FGM. While FGM is only exceptionally considered not to be harmful, physically and psychologically, it often (though not always) is part of a rite that marks the transition to womanhood and/or marriageability. Chinkin (1998: 99) has captured that ambiguity and tension well when arguing that 'categorization of female genital surgery as torture is complex':

> Unlike other forms of gender-specific violence ... , female genital surgery is performed by women on their daughters and grand-daughters who may view it as a prerequisite for womanhood within their society. One of the defining characteristics of torture is the obliteration of the victim's identity or personality. Identity and membership are precisely what the ritual brings to a girl, who may become an outsider in her own community if she has not undergone the surgery.

Human and children's rights campaigns on FGM tend to focus on legislative action (i.e. criminalization) and awareness-raising. Criminalization of FGM may have paradoxical outcomes, as it may force the practice to go underground and become secretive, thereby depriving girls of any protection whatsoever. In addition, the announcement in some countries of a legislative ban to be introduced, has led to FGM being practised on much younger girls than usual.

At least one 'local' practice in Kenya has been documented of dealing with FGM in a way other than through criminalization and legislation based on international and/or regional human rights instruments. Maendeleo ya Wanawake Organization (MYWO), the national women's organization, believes less in outlawing the practice as an effective strategy, as it fears that it will simply be driven underground. The organization rather focuses on awareness-raising and the introduction of alternative initiation rites. These rites are said to maintain the cultural and social significance of female circumcision while doing away with the practice itself (Mohamud et al., 2002; Reaves, 1997); they therefore represent an appreciation of local communities' traditions and values. Viewed from the LHR perspective, the local group concerned is the girls who may have to undergo FGM. Admittedly, this local practice is more related to the implementation strategy to be followed than to the creation of new norms or standards, the more so since the treaty provisions mentioned higher (i.e. Art. 24(3) CRC and Art. 21 ACRWC) do not impose an obligation of criminalization of harmful traditional practices, but refer in general wording to 'all appropriate measures'. Nevertheless, it does present a break with the standard international approach, which tends to focus on legislative initiatives to prohibit FGM.

For the alternative initiation rites, MYWO has had a partnership with the Programme for Appropriate Technology in Health (PATH), a US-based global health organization. While PATH is not a human rights organization but rather a health organization, it has adopted a rights approach in some of its work and publications (see, in particular, PATH, 2002). PATH has found 'a number of FGM abandonment approaches...to be insufficient or ineffective when implemented alone', such as laws criminalizing FGM (Muteshi & Sass, 2005: 45). This submission echoes an earlier finding of Packer, who has examined the limits and potential of a human rights approach to, *inter alia*, harmful traditional practices and, in particular, female genital mutilation. She points out that legislation should come after change of attitudes; 'adopting and seeking to enforce legislation banning traditional practices in the absence of widespread popular support for such a ban is likely to be futile' (Packer, 2002: 204).

One weak point in this local practice of alternative initiation rites is that cooperation with and participation of children/girls themselves in developing and implementing the alternative initiation rites is unclear. PATH publications refer to the involvement of girls but contain no specific indications of how, and to what extent, that has been done. A second criticism could be that not calling into question the need for initiation rites, but only some of its aspects (e.g. the cutting), reflects the acceptance of power relations in local communities unless girls themselves are also strongly committed to initiation rites per se.

The impact on international (human rights) practice of this alternative strategy of dealing with harmful traditional practices seems to have been quite limited so far. The United Nations Division for the Advancement of Women's efforts tend to be geared towards legislation. In 2009, an expert group meeting co-organized by the United Nations Economic Commission for Africa produced a report on good practices in legislation on harmful practices against women. The report consists mainly of recommendations for legislation on harmful practices, although it does not focus on criminalization to the exclusion of prevention, support and protection of victims, and of mechanisms for effective implementation of legislation (UN Division for the Advancement of Women, 2009). In its 2003 general comment on adolescent health, the UN Committee on the Rights of the Child explicitly addressed harmful traditional practices, including female genital mutilation. It has used fairly general wording, focusing on the obligations of states to protect adolescents against harmful traditional practices, through awareness-raising, education and legislation (UN Committee on the Rights of the Child, 2003: §§ 24 and 39[g]). Punishment and awareness-raising are also key in the UN Study on Violence against Children (UNGA, 2006: §§ 98 and 100). The alternative initiation rites developed in Kenya have been mentioned by some donors (US Department of State, 2001; GTZ, 2007), although it is unclear whether there has been much impact beyond recognition.

In sum, alternative initiation rites as an alternative approach to female genital mutilation can be considered an example of a localizing human rights approach, some weaknesses notwithstanding. While the impact in local communities seems to have been quite high and sustainable (PATH, 2002: 77), impact on international human rights practice has been marginal or non-existent.

Community-based paralegal advisory offices

A second example involves a local human rights institution, i.e. community-based paralegal advice offices in South Africa. Again, this deviates from the assumption underlying the localizing human rights approach that tends to focus on new substantive standards. However, 'children's rights from below' has to do with not only the meaning of rights but also with institutions and tools that have evolved on the ground in order to make these rights a reality. Although the LHR methodology paper shows a clear bias towards a kind of litigation – a human rights claim needs to be presented to an institution, of which a response (in the sense of a remedy) is expected – it does not exclude local practices or institutions.

Community-based paralegal advice offices have been labelled a 'contextually appropriate response to the dire needs of … people for legal services' (Meyer, 2006: 7). Paralegal advice offices in South Africa originate quite frequently from resident associations and are often situated in community centres. Advice offices have grown organically, when a real need for advice has been felt within a community, by taking action by the community and establishing an advice office (Bodenstein, 2007: 17). They are therefore truly community-based initiatives. Quite often, they can be found under the same roof with community centres, church halls, HIV testing and counselling centres or rape-crisis centres. They do not take a strictly, or even primarily, legal approach but are more often embedded in social and community development work. Community actions such as home-based care, social economy or tertiary-sector service activities have been developed as well, for instance, community communication centres[1] (Bodenstein, 2007: 80). Interestingly, there is an almost natural superseding of the human rights-development divide, given the intrinsically interwoven nature of human rights work and social and community development activities.

Paralegals themselves – in particular, the more politically activist older generation – define their work not so much in terms of children's or human rights, as in terms of justice, tolerance and equity (ibid.: 25). Participatory observers and national structures refer to 'supporting constitutional values', 'protection of socio-economic rights' (ibid.), 'social justice' (NADCAO), and 'strengthening democracy and upholding South Africa's Constitution' (ibid.: 49).

'Human rights', 'rights of woman and child' and 'domestic violence' are key topics in community education, and widely covered in workshops offered by advice offices, but it is unclear to what extent the topics of the workshops are informed by the priorities of fund providers rather than by community demand. Bodenstein has suggested that there might be a gap between the socio-economic problems experienced by communities (as reflected in the categories in which advice was mostly sought) and the categories of workshops offered (ibid.: 33).

Research on the role of community-based paralegal advice offices in the realization of children' rights in South Africa shares with the LHR approach the starting point of experiences of social injustice, the translation of these experiences into human rights claims, and subsequent human rights action. There is also a network of actors, which corresponds, to a large extent, to the four links of the chain: community-based paralegal advice offices, university-based legal clinics (as back-up offices), and a National Alliance for the Development of Community Advice Offices that is composed of national organizations and international NGOs and donors. There has been no attempt, so far, to get an international institutional response, so that a potential impact of the global institutional response on the global human rights framework is lacking, but that does not seem to be so central anymore either, in the more recent conceptual underpinning of the LHR approach, now that much more attention goes to the local as a site of struggle and resistance.

In line with the localizing human rights methodology, I have set up a case study with a local research team, i.e. the Centre for Community Law and Development, based at Northwest University. In four sample areas of Mpumalanga Province in the North East of South Africa, household questionnaires were used to find out whether people knew of the services of community-based paralegal advice offices, and which children's rights problems people considered important. In those sample areas which housed mainly lower-income families as well as informal settlements, about half of the households interviewed knew about the advice office. In the two more affluent areas, knowledge was as low as 10 to 20 percent. As to the most prevalent children's rights issues in the area, households were asked to rank the following eight issues from most prevalent to least prevalent: access to government services; access to social grants; acquisition of identification documents; child trafficking; child-headed households; children suffering from, or influenced by, HIV/AIDS; family violence and infrastructure (e.g. sports facilities). The two more affluent sample areas flagged up in common, the acquisition of identification documents and the impact of HIV/ AIDS as particularly prevalent problems. The two poorest areas expressed a common concern about access to government services and infrastructure. These issues were also among the topics that had been taken to the community-based paralegal advice offices. Interviews with non-governmental and community-based organizations learnt that awareness of socio-economic rights of children and of a paralegal advice office was extremely low to non-existent, although these same non-governmental and community-based organizations were the main points of access for socio-economic needs (van Rooyen, 2009). Unfortunately, no resources were available to involve children themselves in the research undertaken, which is a major weakness both from a children's rights and a localizing human rights methodology perspective.

What do these findings teach us, keeping in mind that they are limited to one province in South Africa and therefore not open to generalization? First, children's rights issues that were identified as particularly prevalent have indeed been taken up by the community-based paralegal advice offices, such as access to identification documents, the impact of HIV/AIDS and access to services and infrastructure. Second, children's rights awareness seems to be particularly low. Awareness of community-based paralegal advice offices is not too bad in the least affluent areas but is very low to non-existent in the more affluent areas and with local non-governmental, community-based and faith-based organizations. Third, while some of the needs of children may be sometimes taken up by community-based paralegal advice offices, children themselves do not seem to have much of a voice. This brings us to the critical question of whether and how (power) relations *within* grassroots organizations or groups are accounted for in the localizing human rights approach. While that question was initially by and large ignored, it has been flagged in the most recent account of the approach's methodology (Oré, 2011: 118–120).

A critical approach to children's rights

In essence, the attention currently paid to children's and human rights 'from below', of which the localizing human rights approach coined by De Feyter is one example, goes back to the question of how we understand human rights, including those of children. Different strands exist. Goodale (2006: 6) has identified three main views, which he places on a 'spectrum of degrees of expansiveness': human rights as referring to the body of international law; to the concept of human rights; and to a discursive or critical approach.

A discursive or critical approach is characterized by a radical decentralization of international human rights law; a focus on human rights normativity itself, and on the aspirational or visionary capacity of human rights; and the assumption that social practice itself is constitutive of human rights (Goodale, 2006: 6–10). Clearly, what discursive or critical approaches share is an 'understanding of "human rights" beyond the narrow confines of international law' (Goodale, 2006: 9). As Goodale has argued, 'the most important consequence to re-conceptualizing human rights as discourse is the fact that the *idea* of human rights is re-inscribed back into all the many social practices in which it emerges' (Goodale, 2006: 9–10).

The localizing human rights approach (as refined in the 2011 chapter), and its children's rights variation explored here, clearly falls within the category of critical or discursive approaches, for they clearly relocate the human and children's rights idea in social practices. Human and children's rights thus clearly go beyond codified rights; they rather represent a 'moral-political force' (de Gaay Fortman, 2006: 23). This shift from an emphasis on codified rights to practices goes hand in hand with the introduction of a power and change dimension, which also requires 'power and change' analyses (de Gaay Fortman, 2008: 55). This interest in power struggles and resistance, rather than in norms and their implementation (see De Feyter, 2011; Nieuwenhuys, 2008: 7; Merry, 2006b: 5), also implies that attention is shifted from courts to additional actors as the champions of human rights. As de Gaay Fortman has put it: 'the struggle for the implementation of human rights cannot be restricted to the courts. It is fortunate indeed that these rights play a part not just as sources of law, but also as political instruments' (2006: 38, footnote omitted). These two basic tenets of a critical or discursive approach are clearly present in the 2011 chapter on sites of rights resistance, where power, struggle and resistance are central to the analysis, and where litigation has moved much more to the background than in the 2007 framework.

In sum, I conclude that, conceptually, the localizing human rights approach may also be applied to children's rights. A children's rights take on the approach has highlighted the need for the LHR approach to reflect upon and analyse the power and change dynamics *within* the local setting. It provides an additional stepping stone to an understanding of children's rights beyond the legal instrument of the CRC. It also invites us to take the *practices* in which the idea of children's rights is mobilized as the starting point and to reconsider some of the current practices or prevailing norms.

Note

1. A community communication centre offers the community access to phones, the Internet and personal computers and generates funding for the advice office at the same time.

6

Discriminated against Being Children: A Blind spot in the Human Rights Arena

Manfred Liebel

> We rang an ambulance, and we thought an ambulance was going to come, and then suddenly, because I sound like a child on the phone, so suddenly he said, how old is the person involved, and I said 14, and he said, well you have to get an adult to ring us up then ...
>
> (12-year-old, quoted in Young Equals, 2009: 9)

> I walk into a shop, and security guards follow me around. I'm not allowed to have my hood up or hands in my pockets without someone coming up and asking me questions.
>
> (16-year-old, quoted in Young Equals, 2009: 16)

Not to be discriminated against and to be protected from discrimination belong to inalienable human rights, also for children. The criteria by which discrimination is measured (for instance, to be disadvantaged because of skin colour, sex or social background) are defined in international human rights treaties and in the same way found their way into the UN Convention on the Rights of the Child (CRC). The fact that humans can experience discrimination on grounds of their age has only been recognized very recently and here and there has led to corresponding requirements and legal policies. However, thus far, elderly people were almost exclusively envisaged. The following chapter intends to explore reasons and ways in which persons can also be discriminated against in specific ways for *not yet* being of age, that is, as children or 'minors', and how this is to be confronted.

What is to be understood by discrimination?

Often, a distinction is made between direct and indirect discrimination. The term *direct discrimination* applies when a person or a group of persons

is deliberately disadvantaged because of certain visible or attributed characteristics and is thereby prevented from having equal status, equal access
to resources, equal access to decision-making, exercising rights in an equal
manner or various other advantages. *Indirect discrimination* applies when,
for instance, certain laws, regulations, measures and social norms appear
to be neutral and applicable to all persons equally but in fact have detrimental consequences to a person or group of people, or such consequences
are accepted in their implementation. Furthermore, *harassment* counts as
discrimination, when the dignity of a person is damaged and an environment is created that is characterized by intimidation, hostility, humiliation,
degradation or insult.

The discrimination ban, as a *prohibition of arbitrariness*, is mainly applied
to government action but can also apply to the non-governmental domain
and dealings between persons. The latter depends on the significance a society places on the controversial principle of private autonomy and other basic
rights. The discrimination ban, which was initially conceived as a *defence
right*, has since also been understood as a *provision* or *participation right*,
for example, when it is expected that the state or a local authority spends
money to tackle discrimination, i.e. to promote legal and social equality.
In Germany, the duty to the corresponding implementation is, according
to the jurisdiction of the German Federal Constitutional Court, subject to
the 'reservation of the possible, in terms of what the individual can sensibly
claim from society'.[1]

The characteristics defined in international human rights treaties[2] that
are not allowed to lead to a disadvantage, apply to all humans irrespective of their age. Until now, it has not been expressly contemplated in
these treaties that discrimination can have as a primary reason the age of
a person or a social group.[3] Where since recently in national legislation
reference is made to age as a possible reason for discrimination, consistently older people are thought of, whose full participation in social life is
intended to be protected and guaranteed. Corresponding provisions have
found their way into, for instance, the anti-discrimination directives of the
European Union or the German General Equal Treatment Law (Allgemeines
Gleichbehandlungsgesetz: AGG, 2006). Nevertheless, what is receiving little
consideration is the fact that persons or social groups may suffer discrimination or find themselves in a situation of dependency because of either a low
social or legal status in connection to their state of being a minor.

Age-based discrimination of children

Although in some countries, laws and regulations protecting elderly adults
from age-based discrimination[4] have recently come into force, in hardly any
country is the age or status of children officially recognized as a reason or
cause for discrimination. On the contrary, many countries have regulations

and legal practices that sustain age-based discrimination of children. In the German AGG, for instance, which does consider age-based discrimination, there are provisions that explicitly allow different treatment in relation to age, mainly with regard to young persons. In this way, minimum age limits and special requirements for entering a job and professional education, as well as setting working and job requirements, including the terms of payment and for termination of the working relationship, are considered 'objective and befitting and justified by a legitimate cause'. This is justified by claims that it aids the integration of young people in the work force and ensures their protection (according to paragraph 10, 'Justifiable differential treatment due to age').

Another case in point is the legal sanctioning of wage differentials depending on the age of the worker. In Australia, so-called junior wage rates are currently exempt from anti-discrimination legislation.[5] Such practice is sometimes also explicitly established in minimum-wage regulations. In the Netherlands, the minimum wage is scaled according to age; there is no minimum wage at all for workers below the age of 15 (although various kinds of employment are permitted from age 13), and a 15-year-old is entitled to only a third of the full adult minimum wage, gradually increasing to the full adult minimum wage at the age of 23. Similarly, in Britain, the National Minimum Wage Act (1998, chapter 39, 1, 2, c) does not apply to those below the age of compulsory schooling (16); in 2009, the hourly minimum wage was £5.73 for an adult, £4.77 for those under 22, and £3.53 for those under 18. In these countries, therefore, age-based discrimination in wages is sanctioned and regulated. In the Netherlands, this is explicitly justified by the Ministry of Social Affairs with assumed productivity differences, increasing young people's chances in the labour market, the lower needs of young people compared to adults, and the need not to make work more attractive than school to young people (Bourdillon et al., 2010: 177). Some international conventions (e.g. the Convention 138 of the International Labour Organization, in which minimum ages for different types of employment are set) may also have similar discriminatory effects on children.

The lack of consideration for the child-specific aspect of discrimination in human rights treaties has occasionally led to the question of whether human rights are considered only as 'adults' rights' (see Wintersberger, 1994). Notably, age-based reasons for discrimination are not mentioned explicitly in the UN Convention on the Rights of the Child. Article 2 reads as follows:

1. States Parties shall respect and ensure the rights set forth in the present Convention to each child within their jurisdiction without discrimination of any kind, irrespective of the child's or his or her parent's or legal guardians race, colour, sex, language, religion, political or other opinion, national, ethnic or social origin, property, disability, birth or other status.

2. States Parties shall take all appropriate measures to ensure that the child is protected against all forms of discrimination or punishment on the basis of the status, activities, expressed opinions, or beliefs of the child's parents, legal guardians, or family members.

This article is often understood as a prohibition on discriminatory treatment based on difference attributes amongst children, i.e. in comparison to other children, however not in relation to adults.

Although the CRC does not expressly name age as a possible motive for discrimination, the UN Committee on the Rights of the Child,[6] in its various Concluding Observations, alluded to the age-based discrimination of children and calls for its termination. In particular, it anticipated a continuous checking of age limits according to their supposed protection purposes and their appropriateness. Here the Committee is guided by two notions: regulations concerning aspects related to the protection and development of children and young people (for instance, juvenile criminal law) should set higher age limits, while the age limits in regulations that are connected to children gaining independence (for instance, participation rights) should be checked as to whether and how they could be lowered or whether age limits should apply at all.[7]

Thus far, age discrimination against children has been neglected in debates and research on children's rights. The formation of the corresponding theory is also only in its infancy.[8] Therefore, a typological differentiation between several variations of this kind of discrimination should be undertaken initially. In our opinion, four categories of discrimination can be distinguished, which relate to children as individuals or as a social group constituted by generational orders:

1. Measures against and punishment of undesired attitudes of children, which are tolerated or seen as normal in adults;
2. Measures that are justified by real or assumed children's special needs for protection, but which in the end lead to a further disadvantaging of children, be it as their scope of activity is limited, and be it that they are excluded from specific practices and spaces of social life;
3. The limited access, in comparison to adults, to rights, goods, institutions and services;
4. The lack of consideration of the social group of children in political decision-making that might have negative consequences in the later lives of the children and the following generations.

The above-named types of age-based discrimination of children are found almost all over the world. But they do not affect all children equally. The first three, at least, are particularly common for children who live in great poverty or who count as particularly 'endangered' or as 'difficult', whether it be because their social behaviour is not in line with the prevalent perception of behaviour appropriate for a child or because they have comparatively few opportunities to know their rights and insist on their application. Age-specific discrimination is often accompanied by discrimination on other grounds and strengthens it.

In this regard, one should look out for discrimination that remains concealed behind, or combined with, other kinds of discrimination ('hidden' or 'intersectional' discrimination) and which is particularly suffered by children who are already disadvantaged and who can not draw attention to themselves or can only do so in 'conspicuous' ways. Conversely, reference to age can serve as an 'unsuspicious' reason to conceal, for example, racist or sexist motives.

Forms of discrimination that are age-based or legitimized by (young) age may be the expression of an understanding of childhood under which children are, in principle, inferior to adults and have a lower status or fewer competences. It is a (not always consciously used) means, of conserving the vantage of adults and to prevent or put off the equality of children. On the one hand, the children's need for protection must be served; on the other hand, the supposed need to 'civilize' children through education or rules of conduct.

Discrimination owing to undesired behaviour

One common form of age-based discrimination of children is policies against, and the punishment of, behaviour that is not desired of children, whilst it is tolerated or seen as adequate in adults. These types of behaviour are rejected and persecuted not for being in breach of criminal laws nor because they imply danger to other persons, but solely because they involve a 'minor'. Amongst these so-called status offences (CRIN, 2009c) are measures such as curfews and prohibitions to be in public places limited to persons of particular ages, and punishment in the event that these are not respected. In a broader sense, it can also include repressive measures due to, or to avoid, undesired or 'insubordinate' behaviour, 'roaming the streets', 'vagabondage', creating cliques, running away, 'truancy from school',[9] disobedience, collecting rubbish or other types of behaviour that are seen as 'anti-social' or inadequate for children.[10] 'Anti-social' is understood to possibly even include types of behaviour in children that are usually understood as 'normal' for children, but that adults find disturbing. This can be seen, for instance, in that the 'noise of children' is taken to be a disturbance of the peace and therefore is the reason for prohibiting children from playing and 'rampaging' in yards and public places, or to prevent child facilities from being built in residential areas.[11]

Measures against children and young people using public places often happen in the context of privatization and commercialization of these spaces. Young people, who do not conform to consumption-orientated behaviour, be it because they do not have sufficient financial means or because they want to use it for their own enjoyment or for communication appropriate for them, are expelled and even hunted by the police. One example from Germany is a police regulation, which came into force in Chemnitz on 26 March 2009. Under the aim of protecting citizens from harassment, and of ensuring the protection of young people, young people in specific are banned from meeting in groups of more than two persons in public places, to, for instance, consume alcohol or other drugs, beg 'aggressively' or behave in any other 'uncontrolled' fashion. Football fields and playgrounds may 'only be used for their purposes', not with 'dangerous objects', and may not be entered at all after 10 pm.

Social practices that damage the physical and mental integrity of children and young people, or put their health or even their lives in danger, can also be added to this category of age-based discrimination, for instance, corporal punishment as a form of correction against undesired behaviour.[12] Another form of damage to physical and mental integrity, which in particular pervades affluent societies, is the electronic monitoring of the living space and behaviour of children and young people, who use the streets for themselves, particularly if they are in groups.

In many countries, minors whose behaviour is deemed to be undesirable are threatened with arrest and other forms of imprisonment, although they did not infringe generally applicable criminal legislation.[13] Once they have come into contact with the police or the justice system, they are often denied legal aid, and they fall into a spiral of growing depreciation, stigmatization and disrespect to the point of forms of lasting exclusion from social life.[14] This can also be the case for children who aggravate their own parents or new step-parents and are therefore denounced to the authorities as 'asocial' or as 'rebellious' in order to be banished.[15] Particularly affected are children who linger 'on the streets' and who particularly easily come under suspicion for being criminal and a danger to other people because of their dissentient or 'disturbing' way of life. In extreme cases, the persecution goes as far as children becoming the targets of so-called death squads, which – occasionally upon the request of rich businessmen – dedicate themselves to 'social cleaning' of whole city districts and put at risk the lives of children.[16] Such practices are sometimes even abetted by state legislation, for instance, by laws for 'combating gangs' which brand children and young people, based on their outfit alone, as a danger to public security and order. As mainly those from poor districts are targeted, one can speak of a criminalization of poverty or of 'hidden discrimination'.

When in this regard 'children with difficulties' are mentioned, the problems of children are not usually addressed; rather, the children are regarded as the problem itself. 'Conspicuous' behaviour of children is exaggerated, removed from its causes and used as a reason to justify certain measures, be it to guard against undesired behaviour or to nip it in the bud.

They are usually justified by the argument that children are notably in need of education and that one must 'set limits' for them. In fact, young people are thereby considered as human beings, who (still) lack 'civilization' and from whom one can therefore fear particular disturbances or dangers. Their behaviour is measured against benchmarks erected by adults and projected onto children and young people. They are typical of an adultist and paternalistic society. This also represents the second form of age-based discrimination, which is justified by the necessity of protecting children.

Discrimination in the wake of child protection

Age-based discrimination does not always take place due to an intention to harm children but can be an unintended consequence of protection that is deemed necessary. Children are undoubtedly dependent on the care and protection by adults, and more so the younger they are. In some cases, certain regulations are absolutely essential for the protection of children, which are different to regulations for adults, for instance, to keep children out of armed conflicts or to prescribe particular seats and safety belts in motor vehicles. Usually – particularly in legal theory – it is presumed that age limits are the best way to achieve such protection for children. However, setting age limits can have ambivalent consequences, as can be seen in many examples.

Children are confronted with a perplexing array of age limits from the time they are allowed to make their own decisions – many of them with grave consequences on their lives. The ages at which they have a say in medical treatment, can get married, can vote or can decide which religious beliefs they follow are regulated differently in each culture and at times even within the same culture. In some societies, children already take on responsibility for actions, for which they do not in other societies as they are considered to be unsuitable for children; in the latter societies, the protection of children can go as far as excluding children's own decisions almost completely.

The examples of age limits for child labour and the exclusion of working children from minimum-wage laws show the extent to which these regulations can lead to the discrimination of children. It denies a whole age group the decision to earn money for themselves or to contribute to the maintenance of their family with their income, regardless of the conditions this occurs in. Children who work and are younger than this age limit move among the shadows of illegality, must conceal their work and cannot enforce any rights at work. This not only makes working children defenceless against exploitation and maltreatment or even subject to police persecution, but also impairs their self-respect. Regardless of the reasons that prompt them to work, they receive the message that they are doing something wrong and that they should be ashamed of it.[17]

Another example is the treatment of so-called disabled children. In many countries, children with mental health difficulties can be locked up on grounds which would not apply to adults. In some places, children are committed to mental health institutions without their views being taken into account, whereas this is not the case for adults. For instance, several US states allow parents to commit their children to mental health institutions voluntarily.

Limitations of children's scope of activity due to their age are generally justified in two ways. First, in some societies or communities it is thought necessary to protect children from themselves as it is deemed that they do not have the necessary skills to foresee the consequences of their decisions. In other societies or communities, it *is* admitted, that children of the same age may have varying skills, and setting a minimum age is therefore a rough measure, but it is simply deemed effective, as it is easy to control and implement. These arguments are based on the thought that decisions about children are generally the adult's domain, that adults are superior to children in all issues. They also have a paternalistic understanding of protection because it seems better implemented when in the hands of adults, who best know what is in the 'best interest of the child'.

The protection of children becomes age-based discrimination where the relative lack of experience or competence serves to justify particular regulations in order to extend the children's dependency beyond the necessary measure or to limit their freedom or their scope of activity. In this way, the status of children is subordinated, and the inequality between adults and children is solidified, thereby hindering children from trusting in their own competences and making use of their rights independently. In order to confront this, at least the competencies of children must be taken seriously, and they must be given opportunities to participate in decisions about how and from what they are protected or how they want to mould their lives.

Age-based restriction of access to rights and services

The types of age-based discrimination mentioned above represent a violation of rights that were allocated to children under the CRC. They violate their human dignity as well as the specific rights to gather peacefully and to express their opinion. They are, however, also an expression of the fact that the rights of children, in particular those rights that are meant to be for their protection, are often construed arbitrarily by adults or state institutions, and children themselves have little hope of influencing this or of exercising them as per their understanding.

One of the main intentions of the CRC is, without a doubt, to stop the arbitrary treatment and thereby also the discrimination against children. It ensures the protection, advancement and participation of children as a matter of entitlement. Yet in its treatment thereof, it hardly grants the children any real opportunities to exercise their rights by themselves or to protect themselves from violations of their rights.[18] The fact that children can be discriminated against purely on grounds of their age is not explicitly considered in the CRC. The children are guaranteed that their 'best interests' shall be of primary consideration (Art. 3) and that their views must be considered 'in accordance with the age and maturity of the child' in all matters concerning them (Art. 12). But as the discretion and decision about this is still in the hands of adults, the floodgates of age-based discrimination remain open.

In most societies, decisions that have an impact on children's lives are taken in courts, families, schools and other spheres, in which they are not consulted where adults would be. (Examples from UK are reported in Young Equals, 2009). Children's rights are violated in justice systems around the world as a result of indirect discrimination that comes about because of unequal access to courts and therefore to justice as compared with adults. Children's right to be heard in judicial proceedings are often very limited, either because they are expressly barred from initiating court procedures until they reach the age of majority or because the procedures are complex and not child-friendly. In many countries, children are not heard by courts and are not allowed to participate in decisions which affect them in family courts.

Research shows that child poverty is linked to policy decisions and resource allocations made by states rather than the overall wealth of states, and yet children are rarely considered in the development of macro-economic policies where adults are. The effect of this failure is discriminatory because children's material needs and interests are subsumed in those of the household or family when they may be very different. Even in so-called welfare states, children's services are often allocated a smaller portion of the budget than the equivalent services catering to adults. For instance, in the UK, funding available for child and adolescent mental health services is only 5 per cent of the mental health budget even though children represent 25 per cent of the population. In other countries, children are not permitted to use the 'child allowance' afforded to them by the state or the income from their own work. Children are 'the only group in modern society that can not enforce any legally guaranteed claims to available political and social resources. Even today, children in most welfare states have hardly any direct individually enforceable rights to social services and to their share in society's resources' (Kränzl-Nagl; Mierendorff & Olk, 2003: 11).

This also applies when children are denied civil and political rights, for instance (some examples are reported in CRIN, 2009d):

- When children are prevented from participating in organized associations simply because of their age (e.g. trade unions);
- When children are excluded from consultative procedures with policy makers for developing economic and social policy which are open to adults, or when they are denied the general right to vote;

- When children are not formally granted nationality until they turn 18, or children's citizenship is dependent on that of their parents;
- When only parents can request that children be removed from religious education classes, but children have no right to make such a choice (as, e.g., is the case in UK);
- When unmarried 'minors' are not recognized as the parents of their children (as, e.g., is the case in Colombia).

The reference to age and maturity as conditional factors for the exercise of individual rights, and the consideration of the opinion of children, is a double-edged sword. It can be used to legitimize age-based discrimination against children – and until now, this has been the dominating practice. It can, however, also be used to fight against age-based discrimination. What is required for this is not – as has been common so far – to concentrate on what children *can not* do, but rather to look out for what they *can* do, and that the criteria by which the competences of children were, to date, commonly measured, are challenged. This is requested time and again by children's rights activists and by the UN Committee on the Rights of the Child under reference to the principle of 'evolving capacities' set out in CRC Art. 5. According to it, age limits that build a particularly popular gateway for age-based discrimination should no longer be set; rather, children should be entrusted and given the opportunity to exercise their rights as early as possible and to the extent possible.[19]

Generational discrimination

Age-based discrimination can affect individual children or children as a social group or as a generation. In the latter case, one can speak of generational discrimination, which also is occasionally described as a lack of intergenerational justice. One example of this is the lack of consideration for children as a social group in political decisions, which have negative consequences on the later lives of children and even for following generations, such as the long-term consequences of nuclear energy or the impact of fossil energy production on the environment and the climate. Moreover, decisions on fiscal policy, for instance, national debt, can have important negative consequences on future generations. Children and young people can thereby – according to the experts of the Austrian *National Action Plan for Implementing the Rights of the Child* (Austria, 2004: 110–1) – 'be seen in the same way as a minority group, which experiences a particular, multiple discriminatory treatment at the hands of the ruling majority of adults. This form of (generational) discrimination can apply to almost all areas of law (such as economic, social, cultural, civil and political rights) as well as the child's living environment (family, school, free-time etc.).'

The discrimination against subsequent generations can be understood as a form of social inequality. It arises out of the circumstance that 'minors', due to their lower legal and social status, have fewer opportunities to affect political decisions, even where they themselves are affected by them. They also hardly have any opportunities to take care of the implementation of the economic and social rights themselves. This is further highlighted by the fact that children, even in research, are conceived 'as part of a collective unit which comprises adults (parents) and children and not as autonomous claims makers themselves with respect to societal resources (e.g. income)' (Olk, 2009: 188).

In order to fight generational discrimination, the Austrian federal government aimed at a 'Generation Mainstreaming' in its Action Plan (Austria, 2004). Under this, all political decisions should be checked for their impact on the various generations. Like with 'Gender Mainstreaming', with which gender perspectives were drawn into state actions, the question as to what a particular action would mean for children and young people shall also be questioned when planned, at least in principle. Along with measures of 'positive discrimination' that are meant to speed up the equalization in status and life chances of particular disadvantaged groups – namely, children with disabilities and of minorities – the Action Plan argues for the 'equal opportunities and equal rights for all children as a main political aim and issue for awareness-building measures'. This could be achieved by vetting all intended political measures for their impact on subsequent generations, by considering generational discrimination in the reports on social circumstances in childhood and by encouraging the participation of children and young people.

While it is certainly true that taking generational discrimination and inequality as main conceptual frames carries the danger of interpreting socioeconomic conflicts as conflicts between generations and to '[distract] from the dramatically increasing inequality *within* all generations' (Butterwegge & Klundt, 2003: 8), in view of the importance that generational differentiation retains in relation to the lives of individuals this does not make such an approach useless. Therefore, it is necessary to place generational discrimination in the context of socio-economic conditions and to pay heed to the ways and extent to which the neo-liberal transformation process of fiscal and social policies that can be noticed in recent years aggravates the inequality and justice deficit, both between and within generations and leads to complex patterns of discrimination. The same stands for other policy areas in which age-based discrimination is generated, for instance, in environmental policies.

Conclusion

The issue of age-based discrimination has long been sidelined in the debate about human and children's rights and has hardly been researched to date. Likewise, the CRC itself concedes it little prominence.

The fact that age-based discrimination has attracted more interest in recent times could be due to the fact that, until now, normal separation and subordination of childhood have come into question, as a phase as well as an age group. The boundaries between childhood and the adult world are becoming largely indefinite and more questionable, as children (must) take on responsibilities earlier and by this are encouraged to achieve competences for life and maybe get even a competitive advantage with new communication technology, as well as acquire and draw on socio-cultural maturity. All of this is accompanied by the fact that the sequence of learning, working and consuming is subject to decreasingly defined life phases and that activities that until now were understood as typical of children or adults are increasingly intertwined.

Such processes not only find expression in that children are more clearly perceived as subjects and agents, but that also reveal that they are hindered from obtaining a corresponding social status with further opportunities to act and exert influence. This is reflected in a new sensitivity towards age-based discrimination, not least among children themselves, and for the debate and research on children's rights, this represents a new challenge.

Notes

1. BVerfG, 1 BvR 2320/98 of 10.12.2004, paragraph no. 21; online: http://www. bverfg.de/entscheidungen/rk20041210_1bvr232098.html.
2. Within the framework of the UN, this includes the Universal Declaration of Human Rights (1948), the agreements on civil and political rights (International Covenant on Civil and Political Rights, 1966), as on economic, social and cultural rights (International Covenant on Economic, Social and Cultural Rights, 1966), in addition to the specific conventions that refer to particularly vulnerable groups of persons (i.e. the UN Convention on the Rights of the Child) as well as optional protocols (i.e. on children in armed conflict).
3. The UN Human Rights Committee, which has since been replaced by the UN Human Rights Council, recognizes age as a motive for discrimination by reference to the unspecific characteristic 'other status', which in all human rights treaties follows the naming of specific discrimination motives.
4. One of the few examples of laws dedicated to age-based discrimination is the Australian *Age Discrimination Act* of 2004; see Hemingway, 2004.
5. Junior wage rates contravene Article 27 CRC as well as Article 7 of the International Covenant on Economic, Social and Cultural Rights, which obliges State parties to ensure that everyone has the right to 'fair wages and equal remuneration for work of equal value without distinction of any kind' (Human Rights and Equal Opportunity Commission, 2000: 61).
6. This Committee, which is currently made up of 18 independent personalities elected by the UN General Assembly, evaluates the state reports required by the UN Convention on the Rights of the Child on implementation of children's rights and issues recommendations in the form of the so-called Concluding Observations. In addition, it gives its views in so-called General Comments, on fundamental issues of the praxis of children's rights.

7. See *General Comment* No. 12 (*The right to be heard*, 2009).
8. Age-based discrimination was a central issue for protest of the anti-authoritarian movement already in the 1960s and 1970s, but it was not related to human rights and did not lead to any explicit theory on age-based discrimination.
9. In this regard, it is not a question of a violation of legal school attendance but of the moral degradation, lack of consideration for the motives and repressive treatment of children who do not attend school.
10. For examples from different parts of the world, see CRIN (2009b), for instance the Antisocial Behaviours Orders (ASBO) in the UK and Ireland or the dusk-to-dawn curfews that are differentiated according to age in Russia. Virginia Morrow (2002) sought out the perspectives and reactions of 12- to 15-year-old children in England on the curfew. See also on this General Comment No.10 of the UN Committee on the Rights of the Child ('Children's Rights in Juvenile Justice'): 'It is quite common that criminal codes contain provisions criminalizing behavioural problems of children, such as vagrancy, truancy, runaways and other acts, which often are the result of psychological or socio-economic problems. It is particularly a matter of concern that girls and street children are often victims of the criminalization.... The Committee recommends that the State parties abolish the provisions on status offences in order to establish an equal treatment under the law for children and adults.'
11. In January 2010, Berlin was the first German Federal State to put 'the noise of children' under state protection. In paragraph 6 of the law on protection against noise pollution, the following paragraph has been newly introduced: 'Disturbing noises that come from children, as an expression of natural child development and the preservation of development opportunities suitable for children, are in principle socially appropriate and therefore acceptable.' The necessity for modifying the law was seen in a series of legal cases in which the establishment of childcare centres in residential areas was objected to on grounds of anticipated increases in noise pollution. In the meantime, a corresponding law was adopted by the German parliament for Germany as a whole.
12. Countless examples can be found in the UN-Report on Violence against Children (UN, 2006). In one of the Manuals (CRIN, 2009b) handed out by the *Child Rights Information Network,* it is noted: 'Most countries' laws fail to protect children from violence in the same way that adults are protected.' All over the world, only 24 states have so far prohibited all forms of corporal punishment against children (CRIN, 2009d).
13. In the case of younger children, they can even be directed against adults or mentors, who are seen as culpable by negligence.
14. Even in the guidelines of the United Nations on the Prevention of Youth Crime, 'status offences' are expressly opposed due to their consequences of stigmatization, victimization and criminalization (United Nations Guidelines for the Prevention of Juvenile Delinquency, 1990; online: http://www.unhchr.ch/html/menu3/b/h comp47.htm).
15. Accounts of growing up in children's asylums in post-war West Germany contain many examples of this mechanism. Although already scandalized in the 1970s in the context of a campaign by the student and youth movement denouncing repression and violence against children living there, it has 'officially' been admitted only in recent years.
16. Examples can be found in particular in the Latin American countries of Brazil, Colombia, Guatemala and El Salvador.

17. This and further arguments against the ILO-Convention 138, in which the mini-mum age for engaging in paid work is set, can be found in Bourdillon, White & Myers (2009). For reasons of self-protection and self-esteem, organizations of working children in Latin America and Africa therefore expressly call for a 'right to work' (see Chapter 9). The socio-legal scholar Karl Hanson (2006; 2012), who – in view of different interpretations of children's rights – sees working children exposed to a 'difference dilemma', discusses different legal possibilities to confront the discrimination and disadvantage of working children (see also Chapter 4).

18. To this end, it has been requested for years that children, for instance, have an individual right to a legal remedy for violations of their rights, which they can exercise in national and international courts (see Chapter 7).

19. See, e.g., Lansdown (2005) as well as *General Comment* No. 12 (2009) of the UN Committee on the Rights of the Child.

7
Children's Rights and the Responsibilities of States: Thoughts on Understanding Children's Rights as Subjective Rights

Manfred Liebel and Iven Saadi

> The biggest challenge for the realisation of children's rights is still societal attitude, and how people view children. The status of children is simply not as high as other human beings. People are recognising the human rights treaties, but there are still many stumbling blocks.
>
> (Yanghee Lee, Chairperson of the UN Committee on the Rights of the Child, Interview with the Child Rights Information Network, 2008)

The human rights system of the United Nations is based on the principle that sovereign states bind themselves to internally implement the human rights treaties they ratify. Accordingly, most of the articles in the UN Convention on the Rights of the Child (CRC) define state obligations and start with the phrase: 'State Parties recognize..., shall respect and ensure..., shall take effective and appropriate measures..., shall use their best efforts...' etc. This legal system, which assumes the supreme authority of the state over any aspect of social, economic and political life within its territory, is the basis for current international human rights treaties. However, as we will discuss in this chapter, this specific link between human rights and states is characterized by significant weaknesses. This chapter aims to identify the shortcomings of this legal system with a view to children's rights, and to conceive of possible alternatives. The key questions are how rights are to be understood as subjective rights and how they could possibly be enforced by children themselves.

Children's rights and state sovereignty

The UN Convention on the Rights of the Child is, to date, the strongest and most binding expression of children's rights, although it would be constricting to equate children's rights with the convention. As we delineated in Chapter 1, we consider children's rights to be, like other human rights, an extensive project that reaches beyond only inter-state agreements and their implementation and enforcement through legal means. If we understand children's rights as rights held by children, that is to say, rights that can be used by the children themselves and that protect their 'best interests', then it is indispensable to ask ourselves what meaning they have for children and in what ways children understand them and (could) use them. For many children, children's rights are still an alien concept. Not only were the content and significance of the CRC not adequately conveyed to them, but the fact that children can only understand their rights as meaningful if they are interlinked with their lives and if they can actually take advantage of them, has also not been considered carefully enough.

In this regard, one serious defect of the CRC is that it is the output of what Upendra Baxi (2006: 186) refers to as *'collective diplomatic authorship*, that is, the variety of modes of international production of negotiated drafts and final texts of international instruments concerning human rights' and was developed without any children being involved. It does not 'answer' the problems, questions and demands of children but expresses the specific idea of children's needs the governments and experts drafting the CRC during the 1980s could reach a consensus on. The result is not to be underestimated; it expresses a surprisingly great shift towards taking children seriously and conceptualizing their well-being and welfare not as being at the arbitrary discretion of parents and the state or dependent on the goodwill and benevolence of 'child-saving' charities anymore, but as a question of entitlements. For the first time, children became rights-bearing subjects of international law.

Another innovation was that, in addition to rights to provision and to protection, encompassing civil, social and cultural rights, for the first time rights to participation were accorded to children. Although this was done only in a limited way, the stated intention was to endorse the idea of consulting with children and promoting their participation in decision-making, thus codifying the child's right to be heard and consulted. Along this line of thinking, the UN Committee on the Rights of the Child (2009) has tried to advance a reading of the child's rights to participation based on a notion of evolving capacities and competencies of the child. However, it is evident that there is a critical tension between this notion of children as at least partially competent subjects and the fact that in the CRC rights are codified in a way that they must be exercised by actors other than children. As with any international human rights treaty, the Convention on the Rights of the Child relies on the idea of the sovereign nation state as the primary actor for the implementation and realization of children's rights.

The fundamental conceptual problem in children's rights arises in the separation of the rights-holder and the moral agent, that is who is empowered to act by the institutionalisation of the children's rights. Although the child is treated as a rights-holder under the convention, the child is not regarded as the moral agent who determines those rights. That children are considered incapable of exercising rights themselves is apparent in a reading of Articles 3 and 12 of the convention. Under Article 3, it is 'the best interests of the child', not the child's views, that 'are to be of primary consideration'. So while Article 12 provides a right to express views and the opportunity to be heard, this cannot be read as a right to determine one's affairs. But if it is not the child, who then is the moral agent in the children's rights who determines the interests of the child? (Pupavac, 2001: 99)

Accordingly, the wording of the CRC itself gives rise to the assessment that under it the 'child does not exercise any rights; the state does' (Lewis 1998: 93). To date the paternalistic notion that children's rights are a matter of rights exercised by adults for the benefit of children, with 'parents, guardians and families ... predominantly seen as mediating the state's relationship to the child' (White, 2002: 1097) but not by the children themselves, is widespread among both state and non-governmental organizations. This notion even transpires from practice evolving around participatory rights, as the participation of children is for the most part reduced to projects that are conceived by adults and whose framework and scope are defined by adults. Until now, children have had few opportunities to influence the interpretation of their rights and to take their realization into their own hands.

If children's rights are conceptualized as responsibilities of states, what expectations can we realistically have that these obligations are met? In contrast to some regional human rights agreements, the CRC does not, by itself, provide any mechanism that permits *enforcement* of compliance by, e.g., allowing an international court to impose sanctions or penalties against states in cases of non-compliance. As already noted, implementation and enforcement of the CRC is almost completely dependent on national legal means, that is, its conversion into national laws and legal processes. The principal 'enforcement' mechanism currently at the international level available in relation to the CRC, limited to *monitoring* compliance, is the UN Committee on the Rights of the Child established in CRC Article 42, and the instruments at its disposal. The committee, currently comprising 18 independent experts suggested by the states and elected by the General Assembly of the UN, receives, discusses and issues formal comments on reports on the progress of implementation of the CRC states have to submit every five years. As is characteristic for most recommendations under human rights monitoring mechanisms lacking enforcement authority, the comments on the state reports issued by the committee are predominantly phrased in careful and diplomatic language and do not establish formally binding legal obligations. To date, the efficacy of the recommendations has not been researched empirically, but it is evident that they are frequently ignored, arbitrarily interpreted or, at best, selectively acted upon.

Currently, neither adult non-governmental organizations nor children themselves have any avenue to a legally binding mechanism for insisting on the implementation of commitments made by states under the framework of the CRC. To at least allow for their participation in the limited monitoring instruments at hand at the international level, the UN Committee on the Rights of the Child invites non-governmental organizations, and of late also children and their organizations, to issue alternative reports on the state of children's rights and to participate in the debates of the committee. These reports and opinions, above all, shed light on states' failures to comply with their commitments and are important documents for public-opinion formation. However, not being binding, they are only translated into states' actions to the extent that the respective governments are willing and able to pay heed to them.

At the national level, the realization of children's rights requires resources. The implementation of the right to education and the right to health, for example, depend on well-funded and functioning education and health systems, whereas participatory rights depend on well-funded and functioning instruments enabling children to have a voice in mostly adult-oriented systems of democratic governance. The resources available to governments, however, are not unlimited and can be used in alternative ways. As is evident from the fact that children's rights do not figure prominently in the expenditure priorities set by governments throughout the world, the decisions on governmental budgets are sensitive to a large number of other goals, values and pressures not related to the subject of children's rights. The opportunity for children to be of influence on priority-setting in relation to public expenditures is particularly small, given that, in addition to their exclusion from voting, other social and legal obstacles are in place that make it difficult for them to self-organize effectively and gain political and social leverage.

Many violations of children's rights are caused indirectly, for instance, by policies geared at liberalizing labour markets and reforming welfare architecture. While in the view of many, interventions and reforms in these policy fields do not seem to explicitly affect children and their rights (as would, for instance, educational reforms), indirectly, they can, for instance, be linked to, as the German case shows, increases in the scale and depth of child poverty (Olk & Hübenthal, 2009). Another example of significant impacts on children's rights caused by measures in policy areas not usually related to children is described by Cindi Katz (2004), who shows how agricultural policies aimed at reorienting primarily subsistence-oriented rural economies towards market production can fundamentally weaken the capacities of families, local communities and young people themselves to provide basic necessities of life. As one possible coping strategy, parents or children themselves take on the perilous project of migrating to more affluent regions or countries in the hope of a better life, and in the course of this possibly face even more detrimental effects on their rights.

When in such contexts governments verbally assure their support for children's rights, it can appear as an alibi that is meant to deflect attention from the actual consequences of policies resulting in the social and economic exclusion of a growing number of children (see Cussiánovich, 2010b: 16).

Often, the promotion of children's rights by governments also tends to obfuscate children's rights violations caused by their own actions, both internally and externally, and focuses the blame for children's rights violations on other, mostly southern governments and societies. Here, western discourse on children's rights strongly reminds us of Makau Mutua's (2002: 10–38) savior-victim-savage-imagery of human rights, in which the noble savior (the civilized western state) rescues the victim (children oppressed by traditional and backward cultural and social relations) from the savage (the southern state's elites refusing the civilizing mission of liberalization and children's rights).

Rule of law and accountable governmental institutions are other factors that heavily impact on the implementation of children's rights: 'To have an entitlement implies access to an accountable process in which the discretion of the decision-makers is limited' (Elson, 2002: 102). However, in a large part of the world, rule of law and institutional accountability are only limited or totally absent. In many countries, positions in branches of government, including the judiciary, are seen as providing opportunities for self-enrichment (Hauck, 2004; Bayart, Ellis & Hibou, 1999), and accordingly corruption has an important influence on actions and decisions of state personnel. In some cases, appropriation of resources through access to positions in the state goes as far as directly tapping into funds provided for advancing human and children's rights, as exemplified by the recent exposure of large-scale fraud in connection with the Global Fund to Fight AIDS, Tuberculosis and Malaria (Heilprin, 2011). Then again, state personnel in many regions of the world, especially police forces and the military, are known to regularly cause direct violations of children's rights, including the right to live, particularly affecting poor children. Not only can the perpetrators regularly avoid prosecution, but sometimes governments explicitly justify their actions (OMCT, 2006).

Summing this up, the relative material and institutional capacities that states are equipped with have a significant influence on the realization of children's rights: 'States that are too weak or too poor to guarantee rights for adults are unlikely to be in a strong position to be able to guarantee them for children' (Grugel & Piper, 2007: 118). The implementation of children's rights by means of voluntary state commitments therefore is not the least called into question by the enormous chasm between states in terms of power potentials and economic resources. Children who live in poor and dependent countries will much more likely be deprived of their rights than children living in economically prosperous and politically powerful countries.[1]

The violation of the rights of children is, however, not a negative privilege of States that are perceived as 'failed' or 'failing'[2] or that lack the institutional and material capacities for their implementation. Evidence shows that, at first glance, in well-regulated and prosperous countries, governments do not fulfil, for example, the duty under CRC Art. 27 to take appropriate measures to realize 'the right of every child to a standard of living adequate for physical, mental, spiritual, moral and social development'. In Europe, this is exemplified in the fact that millions of children live in poverty or are hindered from taking advantage of their right to education, both guaranteed under the CRC. One recent example is given by the treatment of children from minority groups, for instance, Romany and Ashkali, by the German government. While in Germany, in relation to their social, legal and financial status these approximately 5,000 children already experience severe discrimination in comparison with children of German nationality (UNICEF, 2010), their situation risks to drastically worsen in the context of deportations to Kosovo currently enforced by the German government. These deportations take place despite the research done by UNICEF (ibid.) on the situation of minority group children in Kosovo,` which reveals that social and economic exclusion and denial of education and health provision awaits the deported children, of whom many were even born in Germany.

The weakness of the international children's rights framework becomes even more apparent when it is related to changes and transformations in the wider, global context, adding explanations to the widespread inconsistencies between the obligations of states to comply with children's rights (and human rights in general) and factual domestic policies often accompanied by direct or indirect violations of children's rights. Exacerbating the problematic posed by the weak institutionalization of the international children's rights framework in relation to enforcement power vis-à-vis signatory states, shortly after the ratification of the CRC, several agreements regulating international trade and property rights have come into force under the newly formed World Trade Organization (WTO). These agreements directly and indirectly weaken states' capacities and willingness to fulfil their obligations under human rights agreements. From a legal perspective on formal international law, trade agreements under the WTO are not more binding for governments than human rights treaties they have committed to (Hernández-Truyol & Powell, 2009: 66–73). But due to the different degrees of institutionalization of international trade law on the one hand, and international children's and human rights law on the other, the reality looks quite different. Because, unlike the human and children's rights systems, the WTO is equipped with a court-like dispute-settlement system capable of imposing significant fines and other sanctions on governments, trade and private property rights regularly trump human rights when both conflict. For instance, the Trade Related Aspects of Intellectual Property Rights agreement (TRIPS), aimed at the worldwide strengthening of intellectual property rights, is widely debated for significantly undermining states' abilities to realize human and children's rights, such as the rights to adequate medical treatment in case of illness.[3]

Similar pressures altering state capacities and willingness to deliver on their children's rights obligations derive from international financial institutions such as the International Monetary Fund and the World Bank (Dohnal, 1994). Conditionality frameworks like the Poverty Reduction Strategy Papers impose economic restructuring, including budgetary restraint and cutbacks in social spending on health, education and other social provisioning systems, in the process significantly weakening the very same structures currently essential to the fulfilment of children's (and other peoples' of all ages) provision rights (Oloka-Onyango & Udagama, 2000), thereby especially affecting the rights of poorer and marginalized groups in society. For example, analysing the Poverty Reduction Strategy Papers of highly indebted poor countries (HIPC), the former UN Special Rapporteur on the Right to Education, Katarina Tomasevski (2005), argues that poor countries are pressed by the World Bank to pass the cost of schooling from the public to the private budget by introducing user fees in order to free resources for the servicing of debts and thereby maintaining access to future World Bank loans.

A system of voluntary, rather than enforceable, state obligations gets an even less sustainable character when seen against the backdrop of the fact that in the context of processes often summarized as 'economic globalization', states in general face increasing pressure to align their domestic policies with the economic and political priorities of the global market, that is, among others, potential foreign investors like transnational corporations and large hedge funds. Generally, as is convincingly argued in literature on the state and globalization, the character of states and state sovereignty have undergone significant alterations in recent decades (see Santos, 2005; Camilleri & Falk, 1992; Sassen, 1996; Linklater, 1998), with 'issues of democracy and human rights [being] displaced by concerns to achieve ever-greater market efficiency' (Evans, 2011: 122) as primary consideration for state decisions, thereby severely undermining democratic debate and decision-making at the national level, for instance, on the appropriate social, political and economic paths to take. Alongside the problem of legitimacy and non-accountability of governments vis-à-vis the governed (including children), adjusting to 'market discipline' among others includes downsizing and privatization of public services, cutting down of subsidies, introducing user-fees and other cost-recovery-charges for access to social provisioning systems, the deregulation of labour markets, and deflationary macro-economic policies, all of which can significantly reduce the capacity of states to fulfil their human and children's rights obligations (Hart, 2008a; Oloka-Onyango & Udagama, 2000). And considering, for example, the evidence provided on the effect of such market- and competition-oriented policies on women's livelihoods and rights in the course of the 1980s and 1990s (see Elson, 2002: 87–99), it is rather doubtful whether children's rights can be realized by means of economic growth and market mechanisms alone.

The direct collision between the aforementioned transformations and human and children's rights sometimes come to the fore when governments refer to the obligations imposed by the global market to justify using police, military and other state institutions against explicit human and children's rights claims by domestic communities and groups. However, the fundamental alterations of states and the international system we are currently witnessing have yet to be comprehensively investigated in relation to their visible and less visible impacts on local childhoods and children's rights, including how different dimensions of social inequality like ethnicity, class/caste, gender and nationality interrelate with age/generation and mediate the impact of these transformations.

Children's rights as subjective rights

Going beyond the codification of rights

The problems described above do not make it meaningless to appeal to internationally warranted children's rights and the state as important actor in their realization. But they call for, in our opinion, an understanding of children's rights that acknowledges the fragility, maybe even obsolescence, of a children's rights project based only or primarily on state obligations. Considering the general weakness of the formal international children's rights system, as well as the fundamental transformations of the state and national sovereignty witnessed in recent decades of which we have only touched the surface, it is increasingly doubtful that the realization of children's rights can be successful if it is made dependent solely on the actions of states and their institutions:

> While the state has been assigned primary responsibility for the protection of human rights under international law, new socioeconomic networks and relations limit the power of the state, whether acting singly or in cooperation with others, to carry out the task. (Evans, 2011: 116)

Such considerations call for, in our opinion, an understanding of children's rights that does not focus only on state obligations but conceptualizes them both in a broader, more encompassing and also subject-oriented way, as rights that lay in the hands of the subjects (the rights holders) and the communities and associations constituted by them.[4] This requires an understanding of politics and law that is not fixed on states and the legal system, but that regards human rights and law as the constantly alterable result of social struggles and movements.[5]

> None of this is to say that the state is unimportant, nor that the state should not seek to protect economic and social rights. Rather it is simply to say that states should not be regarded as the endpoint in terms of duties to respect human rights, rather as part of a broader social dynamic. (Stammers, 2009: 233)

This necessity also arises from the fact that a focus on state obligations brings with it the danger of reducing human rights to being administered in a bureaucratic and instrumental way,

> [...] whereby law and politics are brought together in institutional structures that operate procedurally, technocratically and in other ways that rend to hollow out the emancipatory and expressive dimensions of human rights. Without dismissing the positive benefits of the international human rights system, there is clearly a major problem with a reduction of human rights praxis that is organised through and orientates towards institutionalised structures of power. (Ibid.: 225)

According to Neil Stammers, the institutionalization of human rights has a tendency 'to remove them from social contestation – sedimenting them within positive law and its supposed timeless majesty' (ibid.: 229; with particular reference to children's rights see also Stammers, 2012). Similar considerations are expressed by Vanessa Pupavac (2001: 200):

> The prescription of higher law beyond the reach of political contestation undermines the right of the people to determine both the good and the political process by which the good is determined, hence is antidemocratic. As a consequence, instead of law deriving from and being contingent upon the will of subjects, law takes on the form of decree.

Taking up a suggestion for conceptualizing human rights offered by VeneKlasen et al. (2005), we suggest going beyond a legalist interpretation of rights focussing on 'rights on paper' and to understand children's rights as work in progress and as the result of an ongoing process in which, among others, actors from below translate their needs and aspirations for a better life into demands for enforceable commitments by governments (see Chapter 9 for more details). This understanding of rights as a process draws attention to the contingency and dynamic development of rights: rights are not fixed or predetermined, but the constantly changing outcome of conflicting needs, ideas or interests and ensuing social and political action of different social actors. This dynamic has at least two dimensions. In the case of already existing and codified children's rights whose legal wording can be very vague, it is a question of interpretation and specification of their concrete meanings and of their implementation: How is the concept of 'best interests' to be filled with meaning, how to balance protective and participatory rights, how to implement children's rights to participation in policy arenas? But equally important, albeit much less investigated in the literature on children's rights, are the efforts of different actors to translate their specific perspectives and interests into rights not yet codified, thereby possibly expanding or otherwise modifying the existing children's rights regime.

Such an approach to rights as work in progress requires reflecting on the actors involved in invoking and interpreting existing rights and trying to create new rights, on the social struggles surrounding the creation and/or preservation of rights and on the power potentials and resources the different actors can bring into these struggles. With this, the widespread tendency to see human rights as 'a process of "top-down" elite construction' (Stammers 2009: 231) can be contested. Instead, 'the processes of "bottom-up" agency in the historical and social construction of human rights' (ibid.) come to the fore.

Children's rights and agency of children

Partly related to the perspective equating children's rights with state obligations, in a large part of the literature a blind spot remains on how children themselves relate to their rights, how they perceive, make use of, enact or aspire to transform them. This neglect towards rights holders is not limited to the domain of children's rights, but is certainly also traceable in other human rights discourses. But while concerning the latter, part of the social-scientific literature realizes the necessity to inquire into rights-oriented aspirations and agency of rights holders, it appears as if in the case of children, such perspectives are significantly less common. Until now, research about the history of children's rights consistently traced their development back to changes in adult social representations of childhood (in Europe) that were given (concerned) expression in laws, memoranda and pedagogic texts (see Veerman, 1992; Verhellen, 2000). In contrast to general human rights, which were originally dominated by emancipatory demands for more freedom and equality, in children's rights the emphasis used to be exclusively on the necessity for protection. It is certainly not farfetched to presume that children were not an impelling force behind this focus. However, to the extent that children's rights were linked to the emancipation of children and understood as agency rights meant to increase the scope of activities and decision-making by children, it must be assumed that children and young people did appear on the scene as actors and that they at least indirectly influenced the process of the development of children's rights.

Indeed until relatively recently, children only very seldom expressed their needs and demands, developed in the context of social movements, in a legal language or specifically framed as rights (see Chapter 8). Therefore, it is not a coincidence that children's rights were long understood not so much as rights of children, but rather as obligations of adults or states. Both refer to each other, but to date the latter has been overemphasized.

To this day, children are structurally excluded from decisions about their rights, at least as far as they are to be understood as codified, official rights. No autonomous and influential role for children is foreseen in either the law-making processes of states or the UN human rights system. This also stands for the decision-making processes in the International Labour Organization (ILO), the only UN-organization in which not only states, but also non-governmental entities in the form of trade unions and employers' organizations participate directly. In this organization, children to date are also refused direct participation in elaborations and decisions on policies and conventions on child labour.

There are only occasional attempts to compensate for this paternalistic imbalance in the UN human rights system, through the late 'involvement' of children in the concretion and implementation of children's rights, for instance, by calling children's summits, child-friendly websites, or, as alluded to above, in the practice of the UN Committee on the Rights of the Child to encourage children to give their opinions and inviting them to its meetings. By laying out the following thoughts, we hope to identify possible ways in which the paternalistic imbalance in the debate about children's rights and the respective practices could be further confronted and are partially already being confronted with farther-reaching perspectives.

In the following we are looking for innovative lines of engagement that could provide alternative, possibly more viable, avenues for the realization of children's rights. Doing this, we consider it important to distinguish between immanent and transformative innovations of the children's rights project: Immanent innovations mostly focus on existing legal instruments, practices and institutions of the international human rights system in terms of attempts to strengthen the influence and decision-making powers of the rights subjects within the existing system. With a different focus, transformative innovations have the potential to achieve a more fundamental reordering of the social and economic relations that condition the situation of children's rights, including the relationship between children and adults.

Innovations against the paternalistic imbalance

Immanent innovations

One currently debated immanent alternative is to introduce, by way of an optional protocol to the CRC, an individual complaints mechanism into the international children's rights framework. By this instrument, the position of children as subjects of rights is supposed to be strengthened and their chances of taking part in controlling the implementation of their rights increased. Thus, according to the advocates, the CRC would 'be lifted to the same level as other human rights agreements, which already have such a control procedure. A lack of credibility would be addressed and children would no longer be discriminated against' (Dünnweller, 2009: 123). By the same token, it is hoped that 'the position of children as fully entitled holders of rights will experience increasing recognition' (ibid.) and it aims to provide them with more effective tools against violations of rights for obtaining remedy when necessary.

A further immanent alternative can be seen in the attempt to widen children's opportunities for participation and exerting influence in existing national institutions. This is partially carried out by pressuring for legal changes, with the aim to strengthening the legal position of children in these institutions (for instance, reform of laws on students' participation in public schools or of statutes governing municipalities), or by exerting pressure on governments and public authorities to establish more independent ombudspersons on children's rights (at all political levels) and provide funding for participatory projects with decision-making competences in all questions affecting children, which would eventually provide children with better opportunities to stand up for their rights and interests.

While these attempts are certainly laudable, it is necessary to point out their inherent limitations. Individual complaint procedures under other international human rights conventions, such as the Convention on the Elimination of All Forms of Discrimination Against Women (CEDAW), do provide opportunities for limited individual redress against rights violations, but they fall short of opening up avenues to binding and enforceable rulings against states violating their human rights obligations. Experience with already existing individual complaints mechanisms under other human rights treaties causes a prominent human rights scholar to claim that '[although] these [individual complaints] procedures have brought about a few demonstrable changes in state practice and occasional remedies for individual victims, to call their impact negligible would be extremely charitable' (Donely, 2006: 73). Adding to the general weakness of these instruments, they are incapable of resolving the obstacles to the realization of human and children's rights posed by the much stronger global institutional entrenchment of, for instance, property rights and trade agreements described above.

Similarly, the possible reach of interventions attempting to improve the political clout of children on decision-making processes, for instance, in educational institutions or local and national elections, is limited by the ongoing transfer of political and economic power towards actors and institutions beyond democratic control. Thus, both lines of intervention, aimed on the one hand at complementing the existing international children's rights system, and on the other at increasing children's influence in existing institutions at the local or national level, raise the spectre of resulting in only improving the participation of children in arenas that either from the beginning have only limited influence or that currently face important decreases in influence.

A similar line of reasoning is found in attempts to call upon, with reference to and trusting their independence, national and international courts for the implementation of children's rights even when these rights are violated by the states themselves (see Save the Children Alliance, 2009).

Transformative innovations

In view of the current inefficacy of states and their institutions to advance children's rights and, in some cases, the open violations of children's rights caused by states themselves, the emergence of children's rights-related practices and strategies independent of (or even avoiding contact with) the state should come as no surprise. When, for example, because of their social and political status of being 'non-adults', they keep being effectively shut off from decision-making processes at the local and national levels despite their rights-based claims to participation, or when they constantly experience the state and its institutions as rights violators, children and youth are left with few other choices than relying on self-help through individual or collective action beyond the state, for instance, in the form of social movements acting as substitutes to, or sometimes as protection against, a state perceived as delegitimized and oppressive. This is particularly the case in countries where state apparatuses (for instance, police forces, the military) directly and continuously violate the rights of children, factually leaving young people no choice other than to try to devise strategies to improve their lives that lie beyond the state.

It is in such contexts that children and youth begin to formulate their own rights and through collective organization strive for the realization of these rights in their local communities and beyond. Some of these activities may rest upon the rights codified in the CRC or on resembling rights, or also involve claims to the national authorities. One well-known example of such collective inventions and interventions by children and youth is the '12 Rights', a list of rights formulated in 1994 by the then nascent African Movement of Working Children and Youth. Since then, the ever-growing number of grassroots groups constituting the base of the movement on the basis of these '12 Rights' advocate and act for their implementation and, arguably, have achieved significant improvements of children's lives (see Liebel, 2004: 21 and Chapters 8 and 9). Some alternative critiques of the existing generational order by children, that, based on categorizations as 'minor' and 'adult', marginalizes children and youth politically, economically and legally, can take the form of demands for a repeal of age limits for voting, for children themselves having control over child allowances or other child-related income, or replacing compulsory education with a right of children to choose, themselves, whether to attend school or not.

Other strategies may be driven more by need or survival considerations, for instance, when HIV/AIDS or war orphans take the responsibility for their lives into their own hands along with siblings and other affected children ('child-headed households', see Chapter 3), or when children and youth, experiencing oppression and exploitation in their labour relations, by means of cooperatives formed and run by themselves try to create alternatives for earning a living, alternatives more compatible with their conceptions of dignity. While not wanting to romanticize such responses to marginalization and oppressive social relations, we would still warn against reducing them to mere coping strategies. As is similarly the case with the 'everyday forms of resistance' amongst marginalized groups in rural and urban Africa (Cheru, 1997: 153) or the informal provisioning practices of economic 'castaways' in the globalizing cities of the Majority World (Latouche, 1993), such strategies also can include the potential for emancipatory transgressions of dominant political, social and economic structures and modes of thought.

Even in contexts of dire poverty and exclusion important transformative instances of collective organization and self-help initiatives formed by children and young people can be identified. Examples are when children organize collectively without first being invited to do so by adults, develop alternative aspirations and ideas of social relations among peers, including generational relations that are more suitable to their ideas of justice and dignity, make claims to rights based on their own experiences, and take the realization of these rights partially or fully into their own hands. Here, children do not primarily wait for amelioration through the state or adults but try to realize their ideas of entitlements and rights independently and insist on their own responsibility and agency. Often, these processes are accompanied by the development of more self-determined ways of social interaction both among children and between children and adults.

One question certainly is how the individually and collectively formed and enacted aspirations for more generational justice and equality can find recognition and endorsement in their local communities and societies (and, where appropriate, also by national bodies and international organizations). Related to this, another necessary inquiry is how they are mediated with other social struggles, for instance, of indigenous people, for gender equality or for more cooperative and sustainable ways of production and reproduction. But, either way, the 'transformative core' of the described strategies is that, in the course of such practices, children can 'forget' or 'un-know' the marginalization and impotence that society attributes to the position of 'child', and they can through their own actions contribute to improvements in their lives (and sometimes also the lives of their communities).

Conclusion

In this chapter, we have aimed at identifying the weaknesses and growing fragility of a children's rights project primarily focused on the state and the existing mechanisms of the international children's rights system. With this, we do not propose to entirely dismiss the state and solely impose the responsibility for the realization of children's rights on the (rights-bearing) individual in the sense of the neoliberal narrative. Continuing to pressure states to fulfil their responsibilities is indispensable, at least as long as the state, in the conventional sense of nation state, is placed at the core of the organization of the political. But for the children's rights project to have a future, it first must be acknowledged that rights-oriented, but non-legal, practices and strategies that take place in social and political spaces relatively unrelated to the state are essential and that, secondly, in these practices children themselves have an eminently important role to play and are capable of doing so.

Notes

1. However, one must note that the intensification of extreme socio-economic inequality within countries witnessed in recent decades (Gill, 2003: 191) lays the ground for an increasingly more complex picture, in which rich children in poor countries can have considerably more chances to see their rights realized than poor children in rich countries.
2. Increasing doubt is cast on the analytic and descriptive adequacy of the use of attributes like 'failed', 'failing' or 'weak' for characterizing states (see, e.g., Bilgin & Morton, 2002; Hauck, 2006; Jones, 2008).
3. The case of patent protection of anti-retroviral treatment against HIV/AIDS is particularly illustrative of the conflict that can link property and trade rights on the one hand, and human and children's rights on the other (see Cohen-Kohler et al., 2008; Correa, 2002; Orsi & d'Almeida, 2010; Orsi et al., 2007). For an overview of the long chain of possible impacts of HIV/AIDS on children and their rights, see Foster & Williamson, 2000.
4. This idea was applied to children's rights in the jurisprudence research by the Mexican jurist Mónica González-Contró (2008), where it is substantiated in detail.
5. In a critical legal study, the German rights philosopher Sonja Buckel (2008) shows the ways in which the 'social relations of forces' condense in legal systems and that 'legal concepts' are 'sedimented strategic-selective products of past conflicts'.

Part III
Practical Perspectives

8
Grassroots Children's Rights
Manfred Liebel

> *Only children know what children want.*
> (Hannah, 12 years old, 'Child Mayor' in Moers, Germany)

Generally, when speaking of children's rights, reference is made to the UN Convention on the Rights of the Child (CRC), which was adopted by the General Assembly of the United Nations on 20 November 1989. The CRC is a formally binding international treaty by which the signatory states commit to adapt their laws and administrative regulation to match the provisions of the convention. The CRC is, without a doubt, 'a mile-stone in the history of children's rights' (UNICEF), as for the first time it has made children the subjects of their own rights. It has also intensified the debate on children's rights worldwide and, in many countries, has led to initiatives and legal measures that have brought about improvements in the legal status of children. Manifold initiatives to promulgate the CRC have led to children taking on an increased interest in their rights.

The Convention is a treaty amongst states, whereby they commit themselves to act in the 'best interest' of the children. It *gives* children rights, which, according to the concepts held by state representatives and their advisors participating in the decade-long deliberations on the CRC, best correspond to special needs and interests of children. The views and demands of children themselves played no role worth mentioning in the drafting of the CRC, nor were children involved in the adoption of the convention. It was only afterwards that attempts were made to involve children in the further development and implementation of the CRC; e.g. in the course of 'children's summits' and 'children's forums' or at meetings of the UN Committee on the Rights of the Child.

The children's rights set out in the CRC are codified legal norms, whose legitimacy arises out of inter-state agreements. Almost no child or adult who advocates for children would disagree with them. However, they are not all-embracing and are not perceived and understood by all people in the same way. With the rights in the CRC intended to apply to childhoods globally and, in comparison with the entitlements contained in other human rights conventions, being characterized by very broad and comprehensive concepts and formulations (Grugel & Piper, 2007: 113), the tasks of interpreting, specifying and putting them into practice is outstandingly challenging and prone to conflict. But for all the comprehensiveness embodied in the CRC, it does not provide answers to each and every question arising out of the lives of children and on how to deal with them adequately. Moreover, the CRC is the result of a long process in which different conceptions of and knowledge on childhoods rooted in historically and culturally specific social configurations had to be negotiated, and it is evident that in the light of permanent social change, the CRC cannot be eternally valid and appropriate.

It would fully correspond to the underlying principles of the CRC to take the views and perspectives of children more into account in the future. Corresponding attempts have already been undertaken. However, children's rights are far from being understood as what the children themselves 'consider to be fundamental for their current lives' (Funes, 2007: 61). A situation in which children can exercise all of the rights assigned to them themselves is far from being achieved, although the CRC states that children are subjects of their own rights from the moment of birth.

Children's rights that come from children

When children express their ideas and wishes, they usually do not do so in the language of the law. The process of thinking in categories of codified rights is alien to them. They are often sceptical of anything that has to do with law and legislation, or show little interest for it. One reason for this is that the legal sphere is predominantly an adult domain. Children (to date) can neither make law nor administer justice, because to date they have been denied the political rights of 'citizens' which are prerequisites to be able to undertake such activities. For the most part, laws bring with them rather uncomfortable experiences for children: they primarily limit their freedom of action, either because, being 'minors', children are forbidden to carry out specific actions or because some laws providing entitlements only apply to adults.

Since the CRC exists, this relation between children and rights has partially been modified. One vague idea of children's rights is gradually seeping into the consciousness of children. On the one hand, children come into contact with the children's rights discourse through media such as the Internet, through the activities of organizations that assist or educate adolescents and children, during mediatized, symbolic days such as the Universal Children's Day, or at school. In these contexts, children are often also encouraged to show an interest in children's rights and to make them their own. On the other hand, politically engaged groups and organizations of children and youth start framing their demands in the children's rights discourse in order to gain legitimacy and to increase acceptance of their demands. In the process, either the rights contained in the CRC are related to particular situations and are reformulated in more precise ways, or rights that are not part of the CRC are requested or demanded.

In many countries, initiatives and projects aiming at the participation of children and young people inspire an interest in children's rights. Youth associations and youth centres organize reality-related project days or weeks, during which the use of children's rights is encouraged. Children are invited to summer camps or to 'children's summits', at which certain rights take the centre stage. Some governments and children's rights organizations maintain special websites for children, which present children's rights in an entertaining way and call for participation. Or UNICEF, children's agencies, child representatives and similar services organize 'children's rights polls' at which children can express which rights in the CRC are most important to them. The aim of all of these projects and events is to familiarize children with their codified rights and to arouse their interest. While the children participating in such events are invited to do so, thereby fulfilling an expectation placed on them rather than using children's rights by their own initiative in order to achieve something, occasionally initiatives emerge through which children can directly deal with specific facets of their reality and stand up for the implementation of their rights.

This is the case for a number of child and youth groups that raise specific issues and in doing so refer to the rights of children. These groups do not primarily have codified children's rights and campaigning for them as their main *raison d'être* but arise out of discontentment with particular situations, which they eventually frame as violations of children's rights. They do not only refer to the CRC but also 'invent' and demand rights that, to date, have not been officially granted to children. For instance, a group from Berlin calls for the general right to vote for children without age limits and opposes paternalistic ideas and laws on child protection. This group also campaigns against compulsory school attendance, which the members see less as an expression of the right to education than as a violation of the right to freedom and participation of children. Other groups campaign for the right to residence and education of child refugees, or act against racist and discriminatory treatment of minorities, against the sexual abuse of children or for the legal and social recognition of organizations of working children in countries in the majority world.

In many majority world countries, social movements and self-help groups of children living and working in dire poverty or having to fight an everyday battle for survival on the streets have appeared. Nowadays, they, too, invoke the fact that they have rights and struggle for their realization. Many of these groups have gone beyond the CRC and formulated their own rights which they consider to be more adequate to their situations. The African

Movement of Working Children and Youth, for instance, has established a catalogue of 12 rights whose implementation is continually reviewed by its grassroots groups. In the catalogue, one can find, for instance, the right to stay in the village and to be able to live there in a dignified manner or the right to be able to exercise a light job appropriate to their age. The children demand that these rights, as well as the rights enshrined in the CRC, be respected and applied.

When children formulate their own rights or reformulate already existing rights, they usually do not express them as general and encompassing principles but often rather refer directly to specific situations the children involved have experienced. These claims for rights are often accompanied by campaigns, solidarity appeals or other activities in order to increase the momentum for their recognition and implementation. When children express themselves on their rights or even formulate their own rights, they usually do so in a direct language free of legal clauses. At least when they refer to themselves, their own interests and perspectives as children under particular circumstances find expression in the formulations. In the following, we will present various examples of self-formulated children's rights, differentiating between individual and collective expressions.

Individually formulated rights

For an example of individually formulated rights, we will look back at a children's rights vote that was organized in 2005 by the children's commissioner of Munich, Germany, as well as at the results of public surveys of children in Spain and Serbia.

At children's rights votes, children are presented with a set of rights chosen by adults, which usually are drawn from the CRC and translated into a language suitable for children. At the vote in Munich, children between the ages of six and 17 had a year to choose which of 10 convention rights, chosen beforehand for being considered the most important fundamental rights, are most important for them personally and that, in their view, are in most need of action in Munich. During that time, they were requested to decide on three rights they viewed as particularly important for themselves and for children in other countries. Around 3,000 boys and girls took part in the vote, which took place at schools, children's events and some mobile and stationary voting stations.

With reference to themselves, the *right to health* had the most votes (14.6 per cent), followed by the *right to play, leisure and rest* (14.3 per cent) and the right to *parental care* (12.3 per cent). Jana Frädrich, the children's commissioner of Munich, explicates the high number of votes for the third right with reference to how children in discussions often expressed 'that they suffer from the fact that their parents only have little time for them, that some of them have no or little contact with one of their parents. Usually it is the father that is absent. Or that, in situations of parental separation, children find themselves between their parents and do not know where they can turn to get support and help in crises' (Press release of 9 December 2005).

The other listed rights were voted for in the following order: The *right to special protection and assistance when affected by war and when being a refugee* (11.1 per cent), the *right to protection from exploitation and violence* (10.2 per cent), the *right to equality* (9.1 per cent), the *right to education* (8.7 per cent), the *right to private sphere and personal dignity* (8.4 per cent), the *right to express opinions, to information and to be heard* (5.7 per cent), and the *right to special care in case of disability* (5.6 per cent).

Breaking this down by age and gender leads to some differences. For instance, boys from the age of six to 14 saw particular room for improvement in relation to the rights to play, leisure and rest. Amongst girls, there was a greater variation. Primary school girls saw the right to health and the right to play, leisure and rest as the most needed improvement, whilst older girls wanted to see improvements in particular concerning the right to education and the right to equality. Boys, as they grew older, considered it particularly important to enhance the rights to freedom of expression, to information and to be heard. And amongst children from both genders, the right to a private sphere as well as to protection from exploitation and violence took on an increasingly important role the older the children were.

In relation to children in other countries, the children held the following rights as particularly important: The *right to special protection and assistance when affected by war and when being a refugee* (20.5 per cent), the *right to health* (17.6 per cent) and the *right to education* (13.2 per cent) as well as the *right to protection from exploitation and violence* (11.1 per cent).

One shortcoming of such children's rights votes is that children are given predefined rights to choose from, which in addition have been phrased in a particular way. At the Munich vote, the children at least had the right to name additional rights they regarded as important. The most frequently named were: the right to have one's own friends and to choose them oneself; the right to participate in political debates; the right to self-determination and to taking decisions; a right to pocket money as well as a right to good and clean food and drinks.

Furthermore, the children's comments were documented in their original wording. Some examples thereof are:

- I would find the right to longer holidays very important. During the holidays, adults always look at towns, and one has little time to play. (Boy, 10 years old)
- I wish I had the right to freedom to play. The grass of our yard should be mowed to play football. (Boy, 10 years old)

- I wish I had the right to my own money. Because children should learn how to deal with money. (Boy, 11 years old)
- I find the right to parental care the most important. Because I think that it is not only important for children, but it also shows parents that children have a right to it. I also find that the right to trust should be introduced. Because I have many problems [...] and it is very important that you can trust somebody. (Girl, 11 years old)
- There should be a right that the teachers don't always shout. [...] You can go deaf from shouting, and it is not cool when others then laugh about it. (Boy, 10 years old)
- There should be that to friendship. Because when parents have a fight, then their children can stay friends. (Girl, 10 years old)
- I would like a right to have friends. Because some children don't have any friends. They have to work. (Boy, 10 years old)
- Parents have to be nice to their children, they have to be fair with them, and most importantly, they have to show them love. (Girl, 10 years old)
- I chose the rights to equality, to parental care and the right to be cared for. Because I have exactly as many rights as anyone else. If somebody is ill, he can not do anything about it. I want my parents to have time for me. (Boy, 12 years old)

The Spanish example comes from a primary school in Barcelona. In this example, five- and six-year-old girls and boys were asked which rights they would like to have. During a group discussion, they had the opportunity to freely their ideas express. In doing so, the following list (in no particular order of precedence) was created (quoted in Funes, 2007: 61):

- The right to have friends
- The right to have a house
- The right to play
- The right to get angry
- The right to go to school
- The right to rest
- The right to eat
- The right to be happy
- The right to sing
- The right to cry
- The right to decide
- The right to have a family
- The right to kiss or not to kiss
- The right to grow up well
- The right to be different
- The right to be respected

- The right to make mistakes
- The right to be free

The rights listed above express wishes and aspirations, partially in a specific and partially in a general way, about what a 'good' and satisfying life should look like, and what must be changed in order to attain that life. The extent to which the children relate the rights they put forward to their own lives is not clearly identifiable, but it is to be presumed that they had them in mind.

Older children who are going through puberty, often wish for other rights. In a workshop about sexual and reproductive health, for instance, which also took place in Spain, such children defended their right 'to decide, to protect oneself and to make love' (quoted in Funes, 2007: 61). The children understand these rights not only as rights to 'sexual freedom' but also as rights to treat each other in a humane, emotional and caring manner and to have access to the corresponding conditions and means. The desired freedom is accompanied by a desire for responsibility.

When children – younger and older alike – have the opportunity to think up rights that are important to them, they usually do not have privileges in mind that give them advantages over adults. They see themselves as subjects who can do something that corresponds to their specific situation as a relatively powerless group, and their changing needs and interests as they grow older. This usually revolves around 'small rights of everyday life' (Funes, 2007: 61). Occasionally, children also express their wish to take on responsibilities (e.g. in the local government) or show themselves to be 'responsible' for others, for instance relatives. This fits with the finding of a study on children in Germany, that, when questioning eight- to 11-year-old children, among the most frequently named activities was to participate in relief operations for persons in need (21 per cent) or for children in other countries (23 per cent) (World Vision Deutschland, 2007: 213).

When adolescents are interviewed, it is, rather, the differences with regard to adults that are stressed, and to a certain extent they want to distinguish themselves. However, it is not about demanding to absolutely always do 'one's own thing'. The youth 'call for the right to make decisions, to discover and to experiment, to make mistakes, but they don't claim uniqueness for doing so. They ask for the right to be adequately considered by adults and to have the necessary security' (Funes, 2007: 61).

One example from the South East of Europe is the research a children's rights coalition from Serbia, carried out in 2007 amongst 1,132 children. The coalition comprised 25 children from various youth organizations and representatives of children without parental care, children with disabilities and children who live and work on the street. This group developed a questionnaire in which a catalogue of rights was presented, and the children were to estimate the importance of each right for them. The group collected data on the children's views of the most important rights to them.[1] The data were analysed in view of differences between boys and girls, where the ten most important rights for boys were in the following ranking:

- Health care protection
- Life and physical safety
- Protection from human trafficking
- Family life
- Protection from narcotics abuse
- Protection from physical violence
- Protection from sexual violence
- Free time
- Privacy and protection of intimacy
- Protection from psychological violence

And the 10 most important rights for girls were:

- Protection from sexual violence
- Protection from physical violence
- Protection from psychological violence
- Protection from human trafficking
- Protection from narcotics abuse
- Health care protection
- Life and physical safety
- Family life
- Privacy and protection of intimacy
- Protection from participation in war

It is not surprising that girls name protection from violence and human trafficking more frequently than boys. Interestingly, the protection of privacy and intimacy is rated relatively low in both boys and girls, and the right to free time does not even rank in the most important 10 rights for girls.

The results, which focused on violence against children, were shared with the UN Committee on the Rights of the Child, which met with the children from Serbia. In its recommendations to Serbia, the Committee emphasized the problem of violence in families, schools, institutions and the community (Vučković Šahović, 2010: 18).

Collectively devised rights

We speak of collectively formulated rights when they are the result of shared reflection and decisions and are collectively articulated by a group of children. They usually come about within groups, organizations or social movements in which children create their own norms, align their views and objectives and collectively make decisions on their own authority. They partially also get formulated during events in which children themselves organize the communication on issues that are of interest to them and reach common conclusions. Such groups, movements and events can be understood as social spaces in which children become aware of shared interests and which they use to achieve specific aims or to raise awareness about problems and challenges in an organized way. Occasionally, this happens in the form of rights that are self-defined, and represented or claimed collectively. In contrast to individually formulated rights, the rights devised in these ways are more than just select or situation-dependent expressions of opinion. This implies that they are usually embedded in comprehensive declarations, and the underlying reasoning is explicated.

As examples of collectively elaborated rights, we will now turn towards a children's charter devised by children from townships in South Africa, then to the already mentioned rights catalogue of the African Movement of Working Children and Youth, and eventually to a proposed law on the rights of working children drafted recently by the Bolivian Union of Working Children and Adolescents (UNATSBO). Thereafter, we will look at elements of a rights-based initiative of young immigrants in Germany and the children and youth reports addressed to the UN Committee on the Rights of the Child.

At a meeting of children from South African townships that took place from 27 May to 1 June 1992 – two years before the end of apartheid – a *Children's Charter* was adopted (archive of *terre des hommes*, Germany), which states amongst other things:

- *All children have the right to be protected against political violence and violence in townships, and to find a 'safe place', and they have a right to institutions to which they may turn for assistance and protection from violence.*
- *Children have the right to say 'no' to violence [...and...] to found youth groups to protect themselves from abuse.*
- *All children have the right to demand health and medical care, without obtaining permission from their parents or mentors.*
- *All teachers should be qualified and should treat the children with patience, respect and dignity. All teachers should be trained and prepared, in order to guarantee that they will protect the children's rights.*

- *All children that have no family should be given a proper and clear place within the community in which they live, where they are accommodated and receive food and clothing.*
- *All children have the right to protection from slavery and from obligations to work inherited as a duty from their parents or relatives.*
- *All children have the right to participate in governing the country, and particular attention should be paid to negotiations with children on their rights and their situation.*

At the founding meeting of the African Movement of Working Children and Youth, which took place from 18 to 23 July 1994 in Bouaké (Ivory Coast), the delegates formulated *12 Rights*, detailing them as follows (quoted in Liebel, Overwien & Recknagel 2001: 208–9):

- *The right to be taught a trade*

  Organise ourselves so that we can take part in our own training schemes, and those set up by the government or others. Get sponsors for this training, work for the realisation to training even for those that work during the day.

- *The right to stay in our village and not move away*

  We the Working Children work a lot in the cities and earn very little. We are not respected, we are exploited and we are afflicted by many sicknesses for which we get no treatment. We want to remain in our villages to develop the activities that allow us to be responsible for our own future. To do this, we must organise ourselves in our villages.

- *The right to security when working*

  To work without being harassed by the authorities and people in general (not to be man-handled, to be trusted).

- *The right to access to fair justice (in case of trouble)*

  Children never win against employers, authorities and those who have the money even though everyone is supposed to be equal in the eyes of the law. We demand the equality and the possibility to be given aid to establish the truth if we are not satisfied with the official version.

- *The right to rest when sick*

  We should be given rest when we are sick to allow us to fight the illness and recover.

- *The right to be respected*

  Recognise our jobs, our contribution to the economy. Recognise that we are human beings, children and full actors in the development of our country.

- *The right to be listened to*

  Respect us and pay attention to what we say. Adults and authorities should consult us when making decisions that affect us.

- *The right to light and appropriate work (adapted to our ages and abilities)*

  When we take up the work, we negotiate the type of work which is appropriate to our age, but this agreement is never respected. There are no fixed hours, we start early and finish late. We ask that we not be given hours of work and tasks that you would not ask your own children to do.

- *The right to health care*

  We should be able to take care of ourselves if we do not have enough money to get professional help. We should have access to cheaper health services, just like school-children do.

- *The right to learn to read and write*

  To learn how to read and write in French or Portuguese…, and then in our own languages. Lend support to the training schools that we create in our neighbourhoods.

- *The right to play*

  There should be both recreation time and space available to children, house workers should be allowed to watch the television. We should be allowed to play with our friends on Saturdays and Sundays.

- *The right to express ourselves and organise ourselves*

  To assemble, unite, speak as one and defend our group interests. Speak without gags, to say what we think, to be listened to and to give our opinion.

The rights catalogue ends with the following commitment by the children:

> *We must respect and love our work, respect ourselves, listen to our elders, be diligent, be honest, and not sell ourselves out. We have to show ourselves to be, in a sense, model youths. We have to believe in what we are doing, believe that our strength lies in our unity, organise ourselves and set up legally recognized associations.* (Quoted by Liebel, Overwien & Reckagel, 2001: 208–9; with partly differing wording, also to be found in *Voice of African Children*, 2001)

This commitment clarifies that the children regard their 12 rights not as a mere piece of paper but as a vision and project that need to be put into practice. This view is held not only by children who originally decided on the declaration of 12 rights but also by the many children who, in the course of time, have joined the African Movement of Working Children and

Adolescents. To what extent the African Movement of Children and Youth has taken the 12 rights seriously until today can be seen in that the grass-roots groups in various countries hold a meeting every year only to determine how far they have come with the implementation of the 12 rights and what hindrances have arisen, and for instance, in that the dissemination of awareness about the 12 rights among children and youth on the whole continent has a central place in the movement's activities.

The South African children's charter, described above, is presumably less binding. It sprung from specific, now partially overcome, conditions in South Africa during apartheid. And it was not embedded in a similarly coherent organization as the 12 rights are, which could have guaranteed the continuity of succeeding generations of children. However, it is still a document that shows the vision that children in a particular historical context had of a better future, and that they wanted to achieve it by means of their own rights.

The rights set out in both documents partially overlap in content with the children's rights of the CRC. However, some also go further, are more specifically phrased and particularly relate to specific situations and problems experienced by the children involved. In the South African charter, this is, for instance, the case for the right to demand health and medical care without first having to obtain permission from parents or guardians, or for the right to take part in governing the country. Out of the 12 rights of the working children and youth, the right to stay in their village and to undertake light and appropriate work transcends the rights set out in the CRC in terms of form and purpose. It is worth noting that, with a different contextualization and phrasing, a similar right to work is claimed by the movements and organizations of working children in Latin America and Asia. In Latin America, this is with an explicit emphasis on the human dignity of children and a vision on forms of economic and social organization based on solidarity.

One recent example for this is the draft for a law on the rights of working children and adolescents which is currently being elaborated by the Bolivian Union of Working Children and Adolescents with the support of Bolivian and international NGOs (UNATSBO, 2010; on the union's history see Sainz Prestel, 2008). In contrast to the ILO conventions on child labour and the current Bolivian legislation, no minimum age is set for children's paid economic participation. The rights and regulations set forth in the current draft legislation are meant to apply to all children from birth until they reach 18 years of age. Only some regulations differentiate between working children (below 12 years) and working youth (from 12 to 17 years). Working children and youth are understood as 'social subjects by their own right', who in equal measure have the rights and the capacity to 'actively take part in the productive dynamic and the servicing of society'. The state has the duty to recognize and value the economic, social and cultural contributions that children and youth provide through their work. Included in this recognition and valuation is the acknowledgement that the work of children and youth is a constituting element of their identities and a form of their participation, as well as forming a context of their socialization and of their acquisition of values and norms. Every child and youth is entitled to be protected in work, as well as to obtain an integral and vocational education that corresponds to their wishes, features and capabilities useful for life in general as well as for working. The state is obliged to protect children against any form of exploitation and against types of work that are dangerous, harm their education or threaten their health and mental and social development.

In view of the implementation of the rights, the children and youth are ensured equality before the law and are entitled to the same protection and guarantees as adults. No child may be excluded, discriminated against or favoured for reasons of age, gender, colour, sexual orientation or identity, origin, culture, nationality, language, religious beliefs, political opinions, affiliations to political parties, civil status, economic and social situation, profession, degree of education, attributes perceived as disabilities, pregnancy or any other reasons. Beyond equal rights and the general prohibition of any discrimination, working children and youth are entitled to special rights in relation to their work. Seven groups of rights are explicitly named: the rights to health, education, sports and leisure time; the rights to freedom, rights and dignity inside and outside of work and school as well as in society in general; the rights linked to the expression of one's culture, as manifested in language, clothing, world view (cosmology) and values; the rights to organize in the workplace, to join trade unions and to conclude collective agreements; the rights to social, psychological and legal assistance, especially in cases of work-related conflicts; the rights to special assistance and protection in work for children with 'other' abilities[2] and the right to generally accessible vocational education provided by the state. In relation to the more specific regulation of the rights of working children and youth, different types of work are differentiated in the draft legislation: a) dependent, monetarily remunerated work; b) apprenticeship; c) self-employment; d) work within one's own family and household; e) work in the context of indigenous communities.

This legislative drafting process is a novelty both in terms of the history of children's rights and in relation to labour and social law making. While it is true that in the last two decades children and youth have sometimes been consulted in drafting processes for children's and youth laws, but never has a drafting process been predominantly in their hands. Another innovative aspect is that it embodies the perspective of working children's organizations on the topic of children's work and is based on the notion that children and youth also have a right to work. As currently drafted, the legislation is intended to enable children themselves to take action against exploitation and abuse, to preserve their dignity and to exercise their rights.

The mere existence of such a drafting process involving working children and youth is owed to a uniquely conducive historical situation. For several years now, Bolivia has been experiencing sizeable social and political transformations, in the course of which a heterogeneous alliance of formerly marginalized groups is trying to overcome a past characterized by racism and extreme socio-economic inequality. The new constitution developed in this context acknowledges the existence and legitimacy of children's work and, with implicit reference to indigenous traditions, entitles children and youth to work in familial and social contexts (see Chapter 9). With the legislative draft, the working children's organization UNATSBO invokes this new constitution. But in view of the local and international resistance against this specific vision of the work of children and youth, it is uncertain whether the draft will eventually be enacted into state-sanctioned legislation.

Another recent example for collectively envisioned rights can be found in Germany. An organization of young immigrants and refugees active throughout the country, *Jugendliche ohne Grenzen* (Youths without Borders), compiled a catalogue of rights for young refugees and other immigrants requesting that the national and local governments comply with it.

- *All children and adolescents that go to schools or nurseries in Germany, that live here, have fled to come here or who were born here, should still obtain the right to live in the Federal Republic of Germany with their parents and relatives. Their parents should be allowed to work so that they can care of their children. The children should later be allowed to learn a trade. They, too, should be allowed to work, to travel and to continue to live here.*
- *Sick persons, elderly persons and persons that need care, as well as persons harmed by war and other events, must be assisted. They should also be permitted to stay here! Families should be allowed to live together.*
- *The meeting of the German State Ministers of the Interior[3] should at last pass a law for a right of residence for the 200 000 only 'tolerated' refugees and it should also stand up for the full recognition of the UNO children's rights.[4]*

What is noteworthy about the catalogue is that it not only refers to the age group of children and adolescents but also includes people of all ages. Together with other organizations, the initiative continues to assert pressure for the implementation of their demands through demonstrations, postcard campaigns and other public manifestations.

Another form of collectively devised rights can be found in the reports of child- and youth-led groups and associations submitted to the UN Committee on the Rights of the Child. These so-called alternative reports become increasing practised all over the world. The first two such reports were submitted in 1998 by organizations of working children from India (Heesterman, 2005). Only between 2007 and 2009, the UN Committee received reports from children from more than 20 countries, including Australia, Austria, China, Denmark, India, Ireland, Japan, Kenya, Latvia, Lesotho, Mali, Moldova, Netherlands, Norway, Peru, Senegal, Serbia, Sierra Leone, Sweden, Thailand, Uganda, the United Kingdom and Uzbekistan. Children sometimes raise issues or provide evidence on subjects raised neither in the official states' reports nor in the alternative reports submitted by adult child-focused NGOs (Vučković Šahović, 2010). Though the reports are mostly written for the Committee and decision makers, they are a valuable source of children's perspectives on their rights and might also be used to understand children's priorities better. By their reports, the children want to draw attention to their usually neglected perspectives (Dimmock, 2009; Simeunovic Frick, 2011).

As an example for neglected perspectives, we will to take up some reports from European children in which they refer directly to their own working experiences and corresponding measures of child protection, usually not taken into account in the case of children living in wealthy regions of the world. For instance, demands for the improvement of working conditions, against age discrimination in the labour market and for the right to work are voiced in three reports from the United Kingdom (Report UK, 1999; Report Northern Ireland, 2002; Report UK, 2002; see also Leonard, 2004) and one from Belgium (Report Belgium, 2001; see also Willemot, 2003).

In the British reports, employment is highly valued because of its financial, social, educational and identity dimensions. In general, the children claim for fewer restrictions on their participation in the labour market as well as for extension of minimum-wage provision to persons under 18. Relating to discrimination, one particular criticism is that young people of colour have much more difficulty finding a job. In one report (Report UK, 1999), there is also a rather cautiously phrased demand to abolish the minimum working age. Most of the children and youth participating in the report agreed that young people should be allowed to work from the age of 13 or 14. In general, the young people, taking into consideration their performance at work and whether they can work as well as adults, consider their usually arbitrary payments a form of discrimination and economic exploitation. On the other hand, the existing measures aimed at protecting young workers are not considered efficient enough and are seen as morally questionable.

In the report from Belgium, the children distinguish amongst different types of work, understanding 'decent work' (without further explanations) as the desirable opposite of exploitative child labour. The main demand documented in the report is the recognition by society of children's work and their right to work. Legislators and policy makers are asked not to consider the thematic in the light of how to protect working children and youth, but instead to think about how to promote their right to work and how to create more working opportunities for children and youth. Decent work is considered as having to be voluntarily chosen by children and young people; working conditions are expected to be not only protective in an adequate way but also empowering. Work offered to children and young people should be suitable for them and should correspond with their interest. The report expresses the overall demand that working children and their work be respected by their co-workers and by society in general.

When children claim rights, they sometimes embed these claims in campaigns for specific actions that they would like to see implemented by adults or by 'politics'. For instance, in Germany, at 'children's summits' of the youth organization *Naturfreundejugend,* which the children and youth have carried out since the year 2000, they want to convince politicians to do more to ensure the natural means of livelihood of today's and tomorrow's generations. At the 2008 children's summit, which took place under the heading 'Do we buy the next earth?', around 120 children aged eight to 12 formulated a 'future contract' in which they established many demands and commitments. In this contract, they describe, amongst other things, how they want to achieve 'fair global economy', how they want to protect endangered species or how 'biodiversity' should be better researched and how they themselves can contribute to this.[5]

In November 2007 the 3rd World Congress on the Rights of Children and Adolescents was held in Barcelona. While the congress series was originally initiated by (and mostly for) adults who aspired to create a worldwide social movement for children's rights, in the course of the first two congresses (2004 in Caracas/Venezuela and 2005 in Lima/Peru) it turned out that children and adolescents demanded a more central role in the congresses. In Barcelona, children and adolescents from 20 countries who attended phrased their own declaration, in which they condemned poverty and violence against children as a serious violation of human rights, underlined their right to quality and cost-free health care and education and demanded living conditions that would permit them to 'achieve our dreams without external pressure'. In order to achieve these aims, 'every policy that does not favour participation should be ended' and in every country and on an international level, child councils should be constituted.[6]

Children's rights seen from the perspective of children

What children think about their rights is important, as it is their lives which are supposed to be ameliorated by children's rights. Their views and opinions are therefore essential for testing the validity and appropriateness of existing rights in relation to their benefits for concrete children's lives on the ground. Then, as has become evident, for instance, in relation to the rights claimed by the African Movement of Working Children and Youth, and through the specific manner in which the alternative reports from Great Britain and Belgium have framed the problematic of children's work, we must acknowledge that children's and youth's perspectives on what is amiss in their lives, on the particular improvements that are necessary and on how these could possibly be best achieved, can differ from the conceptions and assumptions held by adults. Dismissals of the perceptions and visions held by children on the ground of arguments of irrelevance or lacking competences are not an option anymore, as the CRC itself and the competences and capacities of children 'unveiled' by the newer social childhood studies have largely deprived these arguments of their persuasiveness. The rights activism by children must have an essential place in any children's rights project aiming at a substantive and meaningful improvement of the lives and social positions of children, and therefore children have to have the opportunity to express their perspectives and aspirations in relation to rights and to bring them to bear in a wider context. This also holds true when children have rights in mind that have not yet been foreseen for them, or when they judge and weigh rights differently from adults. In this chapter, we have given several examples of children individually and collectively making claims in a rights language. But for the reasons we have mentioned, the rights discourse is not the only terminology in which children identify problems, demand improvements to their lives, make claims or express wants that re relevant to a rights project appropriate for the heterogeneity of children's lives. In view of the way rights are the gradually evolving product of complex social processes of learning, forming of opinions and values, the views and expectations of children must be given consideration irrespective of whether they are explicit rights claims or not. They embody what the British social researcher Judith Ennew (2002) calls the 'unwritten rights' of children, in order to highlight the fact that codified laws never provide a sufficient response to the particular and specific problems and life situations of children. We further should not forget that rights talk may currently be the dominant discourse for morality and ethics, but is not the only meaningful (and not even necessarily the best) mode to frame aspirations for a better and more just life (Twining, 2009: 427).

Notes

1. Adapted from Child Rights Centre Serbia, *Child Rights in Serbia, the Children's Perspective*, Belgrade 2007, http://www.crin.org/resources/infoDetail.asp?ID=16483&flag=legal, date accessed on 23 March 2010.
2. To be understood in the sense of abilities that are considered abnormal or as disabilities.

3. The states federated in the Federal Republic of Germany have partial sovereignty over their affairs, including over aspects relating to migration and refugee politics. Many important decisions in this domain can only be taken in accordance with all German State Ministers of the Interior who hold meetings twice per year.
4. Quoted from http://www.jogspace.net.
5. See: http://www.kindergipfel.de.
6. see http://www.iiicongresomundialdeinfancia.org.

9
Children's Rights as 'Work in Progress': The Conceptual and Practical Contributions of Working Children's Movements

Iven Saadi

> Do you understand how you insult me, when you talk of 'combating' and 'abolishing' the work that I do? I have worked as a domestic servant since I was eight. Because of doing this work, I have been able to go to school (which my parents in the village could not afford); I help my parents with the money I earn. I am very proud of the work I do! I joined the movement of working children, and I know the Convention says about children's rights: the Convention also says that you should listen to me!
>
> (13-year-old girl from Senegal at the 1997
> Urban Childhood Conference, Trondheim, Norway,
> quoted in Bourdillon et al., 2010: 9)

Dominant social representations of children mostly imagine children as incapable of meaningfully and significantly engaging with their rights. Accordingly, even when taking a 'broader' view on children's rights, outside of the children's work debate, a large part of the literature seems to be based on the assumption that children first need to be enabled and offered spaces by adults to do so, or are simply dependent on the advocacy of adults understood as a speaking and acting on behalf of children and their rights. Grugel and Piper (2007), who in their monograph about the rights of migrants and children and their relation with newly emerging global governance regimes repeatedly refer to the necessity of inquiring into the rights-related practices of the rights holders themselves, and explicitly highlight the value of 'introducing a social movement or activist perspective into the academic debate about rights' (ibid.: 32), still largely confine their description of social and political struggles revolving around children's rights to the actions of NGOs and other adult actors. While we agree with the assessment that 'poor

143

children and migrants [...] are among the most marginalized and invisible groups in all societies' (ibid.: 152) and face 'considerable obstacles to their self-organization into effective social movements' (ibid.), from our own empirically based studies and practical experience with children and youth we know that the invisibility of children's organizations and social movements in dominant discourses on children does not equate with their inexistence. Instead, as the example of working children's movements to which we want to turn shows in more detail, children do find ways to form their own movements and organizations, and collectively act and articulate demands in the children's rights arena despite the significant obstacles they face.

Since the 1970s, rising numbers of working children in various regions of the majority world have collectively organized themselves. In some places their organizations developed from various forms of peer and informal self-help groups constituted by children themselves, while some others were initiated by youth and adults encouraging working children to take the realization of their rights into their own hands. While no exact numbers on their membership base are available, a rough, but conservative, calculation points to hundreds of thousands of working children and adolescents throughout the world being members. Through their unfamiliar views on children's work, a variety of social activities, and interventions into and beyond the different polities relevant to children's work, they have managed to raise quite a lot of attention in the realms of academics, civil society organizations, and sometimes even policy-making bodies interested in the subject of children's work.

In this chapter, we attempt to describe main elements of these children's movements and organizations in Latin America, Africa and Asia, where the most active of them are located, and of their regional and global cooperation. We will try to give some insights into their respective origins, the views they take on children and their work and the wide and diverse spectrum of activities they are engaged in. Additionally, we want to touch on some of the criticisms and challenges they face, especially in the course of their efforts to gain access to and increase their momentum in national and international labour law making. As in this book we are interested in a providing a view of 'children's rights from below', evidently a core interrogation will be on how the organizations and movements of working children and youth do or do not engage with the children's rights project.

But before starting into this endeavour, we will briefly delineate a conceptual framework on children's and human rights through which, we argue, an exploration of working children's movements can meaningfully contribute to the wider debate on, and practice of, children's rights.

Children's rights as work in progress

As it was repeatedly alluded to in preceding chapters, much of the literature frames children's rights as related to questions about state obligations and the legal implementation of the rights codified in the UN Convention on the Rights of the Child (CRC). Some authors inquire into the degree of implementation of specific rights, for instance, the state (or lack) of translation of participatory rights into national legal systems and practice. Others investigate possible options to strengthen the existing international legal framework through better monitoring and/or the introduction of an optional protocol to the CRC establishing a mechanism for an individual complaints procedure. Most of these and other angles have in common that they at least implicitly impart the impression that with the CRC, a final and definite consensus has been reached on the rights that are important and necessary for children, and all that is left to explore are how exactly to interpret and how best to implement the content of the CRC.

Reference was also made to newer approaches to the study of human and children's rights taking a broader view on rights and their (lack of) realization. From the perspective of a rights-based approach to development, VeneKlasen et al. (2005: 7) argue for a conceptualization of human rights as a process,

> [...] in which people translate their needs and aspirations for a better life into demands and enforceable commitments by governments. Going beyond 'what the law says', this understanding builds on a notion of rights as a *work in progress that is forged and refined through social struggles.* (Emphasis added)

Concerning the production of codified rights, rights cannot be understood as predetermined or definite, but as the open-ended outcome of conflicting needs, ideas and interests and ensuing social and political action on the background of changing socio-economic and cultural configurations. Accordingly, it is necessary to investigate sites of struggle in which rights, including alternative or complementary rights to those already codified, are claimed and interpreted, of looking at the actors involved in voicing or resisting these claims, and the ideas, social relations and the distribution of power and resources forming the background of the different aspirations and the strategies these actors are involved in.

While in relation to the realization of rights, 'working with laws and legal systems is critical, it has become clear that narrow legal approaches usually fail to expand the scope of rights or appreciably strengthen accountability and capacity to deliver resources and justice' (ibid.). One necessary ingredient in the explanation of the gap between rights on paper and rights situations on the ground can be identified if we remind ourselves of the difference between human rights-related legal events and social events that have a potential human rights content, and of the large disproportion between both types of events (Woodiwiss, 2006: 34).

We must assume that an encompassing realization of rights in the lives of the rights holders is only possible if the norms or behavioural expectations contained within rights (or overlapping norms part of other imageries of social justice and good life, for instance, distributive justice, recognition or solidarity) also widely inform the non-legal social events with a potential rights content. Given the sheer amount of non-legal rights-related events happening every day, we cannot reasonably expect (or want) law and law enforcement alone to guarantee the respect of the behavioural expectations established by rights. Rights and law in general are important but form only one part of 'a larger set of social relations that produce and enforce behavioural expectations' (ibid.: 37). Thus, when looking into the intended and unintended contributions of organizations and movements of working children to the children's rights project, we also must pay attention into their practices advancing the acceptance of the behavioural expectations and norms conducive to the realization of children's rights.

It is in this conceptual framing that we will try to shed light on how organized working children and youth engage with the rights project, with a focus on how they translate their perceptions and aspirations into small-scale activities directly and practically dealing with their working and living conditions, and into political interventions on different levels of policy making.

The origins of contemporary working children's movements

When looking at the beginnings of working children's and adolescents' movements, one can very broadly differentiate between two origins. Some are stemming from spontaneously formed and self-initiated groups of working children and youth who already knew each other, for instance, because of shared working or residential locations both in cities and in the countryside. Such peer and informal self-help groups allowed for respite and solidarity in a wider context characterized by everyday social and economic struggle. In some cases, the children took the initiative to transform their groups into more formal interest groups, which was sometimes linked to their experience that already existing adult's organizations offered no room for the articulation of working children's concerns.

Other working children's movements have emerged in the course of activities provided for by adult organizations motivated by children's rights. In the context of such activities, which were not necessarily targeting the specific concerns of working children, and encouraged by the use of participatory approaches to project development and implementation, groups of children would sometimes direct the space and resources available towards activities concerning their realities and needs as workers. Over time, the activities would then be formalized and transferred into working children's own organizations.

Not all spontaneous groups of working children and adolescents formalize, while others have done so only over a short time before disbanding again. In the following, we will mainly focus on the working children's organizations that explicitly regard themselves as interest groups of working children.

The Latin American movements

Contemporary, more formal organizations of working children first emerged in Peru. The first stable and more structured one was founded in the capital Lima in the late 1970s: the Movement of Working Children and Youth Sons and Daughters of Christian Workers (MANTHOC). MANTHOC originated from an informal group of working children and adolescents facing outrageous working conditions and loosely connected with the Peruvian branch of the *Young Christian Workers*. They were working and struggling alongside adults in a context of rapidly deteriorating working and living conditions affecting both adults and children. However, while participating in the struggle against social and political measures initiated by the military government, the children had the impression of being mere appendages to the existing adult organization, and of not being sufficiently recognized as independent and competent subjects with specific experiences stemming from their status as children. This resulted in the children taking the initiative to create their own organizational basis, which would provide them with the space for specifically addressing their needs and rights as both workers and children, and were supported in doing so by young adult Christian trade unionists. Since then, MANTHOC has sought to advance the rights of children as workers and to foster a collective social and political agency based on the idea of children as actors of social change (see Nieuwenhuys, 2009; van den Berge, 2007; Liebel, 2004; Swift, 1999).

Within a very short time, MANTHOC started to attract close attention from working children and adult individuals and organizations working with children in similar conditions in other Latin American countries. Other localized organizations and then national movements of self-organized working children (some of them with thousands of members) began to develop in the majority of Latin American countries, leading to a series of regional meetings and, in 1988, to the creation of the continent-wide movement, which is today called MOLACNATs (Movement of Working Children and Adolescents from Latin America and the Caribbean) (Liebel, 2004; Swift, 1999).

The African movement

The African Movement of Working Children and Youth developed differently. Inspired by the CRC, the West African adult civil society organization Enda Tiers Monde, based in Dakar, Senegal, decided to refocus its child- and youth-oriented projects from acting and speaking on behalf of children towards a more participatory approach aimed at strengthening children's own agency. This led to contacts to already existing, albeit very informal groups of girl domestic workers and other children, who, gradually, gained more and more ownership of the activities offered by Enda. At the initiative of a group of child domestic workers supported by Enda, working children participated in the May Day celebrations in Dakar in 1994, where they were met with a lot of enthusiasm by the adult marchers. A few months later, during an Enda-supported, but child-initiated, meeting of working children from a number of West African countries held in Bouaké (Cote d'Ivoire), the African Movement of Working Children and Youth (AMWCY) was founded (see Nieuwenhuys, 2009; Liebel, 2001; Swift, 1999). While the foundational meeting was attended by only 12 delegates of working children's groups, the African movement has spread quickly. Through wide grassroots dissemination of the '12 rights', the specific interpretation of working children's rights discussed in Chapter 8, and by reaching out to loosely organized groups of working children, the African movement has quickly developed a substantial membership base, especially in western parts of Africa. According to the results of a census presented at the 8th African Meeting of Working Children and Youth in Cotonou (Benin) in November 2009 (Terenzio, 2009), over the years almost 200 associations of working children and youth (as the chapters at city or regional level are called) from 21 different countries have joined the African movement, now with more than 90,000 members organized in *groupes de bases* at the grassroots level. About 72 per cent of the members are children and youth below 18, and 54 per cent are girls or young women.

The Indian and Asian movement

When in the early 1980s, two young adult trade union activists in the southern Indian state of Karnataka made attempts to reach out to and organize adults working in the urban informal economy, they were confronted with the unanticipated fact that their meetings were regularly attended by large numbers of working children, who constituted up to 40 per cent of the participants. Child labour being prohibited by law, and working children therefore not officially existing as workers, the children were barred from becoming members of the trade union as a way of improving their working situations. To address this situation, some trade union activists decided to create an organizational platform (Concerned for Working Children) allowing them to lawfully address some of the children's work-related needs and demands. The organization started providing non-formal education and vocational training for working children. In the early 1990s, these activities eventually led to the creation of the children's union Bhima Sangha (see Nieuwenhuys, 2009; Swift, 1999; 2001), in which about 25,000 children and youth were organized at the beginning of the millennium.

In the 1990s, except for Bhima Sangha in Karnataka and Bal Mazdoor Union, another Indian working children's organization located in the Delhi region, the independent working children's movements in Asia had only sparse continuity and were most often constituted by working children with no independent organizations, and often having to rely on support of adult organizations in favour of an abolitionist approach to child labour. But in 1996, in the course of Bhima Sangha's and Bal Mazdoor Union's ongoing efforts to strengthen international cooperation between working children and their organizations, the International Movement of Working Children and Youth, later called World Movement, was founded (see Nieuwenhuys, 2009). And in 2004, after the wider mainstreaming of participatory approaches amongst the adult organizations, working children and adolescents from India, Bangladesh, Afghanistan, Mongolia and Nepal took advantage of the second World Meeting of Working Children and Youth and finally launched the Asian Movement. They held their second meeting in Kathmandu (Nepal) in 2005 with a more extended membership.

The world movement of working children

The World Movement of Working Children was launched in 1996, when, at the invitation of Bhima Sangha and CWC, children representing movements and organizations from 33 countries and three continents met in Kundapur (India) for a ten-day conference. Despite difficulties, they regularly met in 'World Meetings' and 'Mini Summits', took part in ILO conferences in 1997 and 1998, had representatives at the Urban Childhood Conference in Trondheim in 1997, and were involved in informal talks with high representatives from the ILO, UNICEF and international NGOs active in the field of children's rights. To date, the most important expressions of the emerging World Movement were the second World Meeting in 2004 in Berlin (Germany) and the third World Meeting in 2006 in Siena (Italy). One important motivation for realizing these meetings in European countries was the intention to bring the voices of organized working children from the majority world into the geographical region they identified as the location of the main international institutions and non-governmental actors resisting the recognition of working children's movements and their positions on children's work and children's rights.

One of the main aims of organizing internationally is to strengthen solidarity among the movements and organizations worldwide, and since the formation of the World Movement, the national and continental movements are in regular contact with each other to network, share information and successful practices, devise and coordinate common strategies to advance the situation of working children worldwide and be more visible in the global discourse on children's work and children's rights. As the final declaration of the Sienna meeting states.

Our World Movement can help us to improve solidarity among us and our strength, and to express ourselves everywhere with a single voice. Through our World Movement, we are committed to promoting our rights, developing actions aimed at reducing poverty, and improving our working conditions; we are committed to fighting against child trafficking and exclusion, and also against violence perpetrated against children – and working children in particular. We promote and defend the dignified work of children. We are the main actors in changing our working and living conditions. We have decided to create a label of protection for the products that we produce. Our Movement is also a way to promote protagonist participation of children.[1]

At the same meeting, the Movement decided to celebrate the 'World Day of Working Children' on each year on 9 December, both to remember the date during the Kundapur meeting in 1996 on which the world movement of working children made its first common Declaration ('Ten points of Kundapur') and to highlight its positions in the international debate on children's work.

Common features and positions of working children's movements

Despite the differences in the origins and forms of organization, and the differing cultural and socio-economic contexts of the organized working children and adolescents, various common features and shared positions can be identified. They predominantly consist of children and youth 12 to 18 years of age working in urban and semi-urban informal economies and as domestic workers in more affluent families (van den Berge, 2007; Liebel, 2004). Many have migrated from the countryside, on their own or with their families, as a result of increasing pressure put on rural livelihoods. The great majority of organized working children live and work under conditions that clearly violate children's rights. As is similarly the case with adult self-help groups aiming at organizing especially marginalized individuals (forinstance, undocumented migrants), they have difficulty reaching children in especially dire working conditions, as the ability to engage in working children's organizations largely depends on having spare time and a minimal control of work relations for attending meetings and other activities (van den Berge, 2007; Liebel, 2004). But as we will later see, with their organizations, working children are increasingly trying to reach out towards children working in other contexts and in creating livelihood alternatives for children confronted with especially exploitative or dangerous working conditions (AMWCY, 2009).

Framing of demands in a rights discourse

Most working children's organizations solidly frame their demands and actions in a discourse based in existing human and children's rights, and especially in the rights set out by the CRC. By doing so, they clarify that they consider themselves holders of these rights to whose application and realization they are entitled. They are particularly assertive in reference to the provisions outlining the right to participation and, while criticizing some of its limitations, demanding the right of children to have a say in matters concerning them. Additionally, they regularly concretize their specific understanding of children's rights, and in their many declarations they rephrase them in accordance with their own living situations, thereby demonstrating that they also consider themselves entitled to interpret and specify the meanings of rights they hold, and not only as passive recipients of a rights-based benevolence of adults. But the children's movements go even further by demanding children's rights not yet codified. Before looking at these, we will turn to the perceptions on which this claiming of new rights is based.

Underlying the working children's movements' understanding of participatory rights is a conception of children that stands in stark contrast to constructs framing them as victims and passive objects of adults' agency and social structures. In the movements' conception, children are considered active and competent participants of their social world who are capable of analysing their surroundings and devising strategies positively contributing not only to their own living situations, but also to a longer term amelioration of social relations in the communities and societies they live in.

Included in this self-conception as social subjects is a specific understanding of the relation of children to economic participation (see Liebel, 2003). In contrast to the dominant Western model of childhood (see Chapter 1), they regard children's economic activities to constitute an important element in the making and maintenance of social life, for which they demand recognition. To gain a better understanding of this, one needs to look closer at what exactly they consider to be work or economic activities. Generally, their conception of children's work is both wider and narrower than conventional definitions of children's economic activities. It is wider in the sense that they tend to include reproductive and other unpaid activities which are not included in the United Nations System of National Accounting (Levison, 2007), like helping out in and around the home, working in subsistence agriculture and sometimes even schooling. Therefore, most working children's organizations are open to any child considering himself or herself working.

Their conception of work and economic activity is narrower in relation to the activities enumerated in Article 3(a-c) of the ILO *Convention No. 182 on the Eradication of the Worst Forms of Child Labour,* namely all forms of slavery and practices similar to slavery, child prostitution and pornography, and illicit activities like use of children in drug trafficking. For the working children's movements, it is beyond any doubt that strong and immediate action is necessary against any of these. But whereas international child labour legislation treats these activities as forms of children's work (critically Hanson & Vandaele, 2003), for the working children's organizations this is an unjustified amalgamation. In their perspective, the activities named above should legally be considered and practically treated as crimes with no relation whatsoever to the concept of children's work they endorse. This was already expressed in an international meeting realized 1998 in Dakar (Senegal), attended by delegates from Africa, Asia and Latin America (quoted in Liebel, Overwien & Recknagel, 2001: 354): '*We are against prostitution, slavery and drug trafficking by children. These are crimes and not work. We want the decision-makers to distinguish between work and crime.*'

The movements take partially differing views on the specific value of, and reasons for, the economic participation of children. The working children's organizations in Latin America generally seem to attach an empowering value to economic participation and understand it as a path to autonomy and independence of any social actor, whereas some working children's organizations in Africa and Asia relate it less to choice than to economic necessity that both children and adults are confronted with. This distinction of understandings of the reasons for children's economic participation does not imply that any of the organizations isolates children's work from the wider social setting. In their statements, concerns about poverty, social inequality, injustice or neo-liberal reforms are regularly voiced but are more often linked to the specific conditions children work in than to the existence of children's work in general.

Despite the differences mentioned, the working children's organizations share the demand for acknowledgement, respect and social recognition for the activities they consider children's work (Nieuwenhuys, 2009). They articulate that working to sustain themselves and to help their families does not render them less 'children' than the (supposedly) non-working children in wealthier social strata and countries. Going even further, they demand in their declarations, over and over again, an explicit legal recognition of their work considered a basic human right for adults: they specifically demand *a right to work* (Liebel, 1997; 2004; 2011; Hanson & Vandaele, 2003; Hanson, 2012), also expressed in the Dakar meeting (1998) with the following words (quoted in Liebel, Overwien & Recknagel, 2001: 354): '*We want all the children in the world to have one day the right to choose to work or not to work.*'

Conceptions and qualifications of children's work: adding rights in work to the right to work

When claiming a right to work, the working children's movements usually do so with the qualification that it should be 'dignified', 'in dignity' or 'in good working conditions', and clarify that they distinguish between qualities of children's work.

The organizations are well aware of the fact that children can be, and often are, exploited in work. It would be surprising if they weren't, since most of the working children who organize do so precisely because of the dire working conditions they encounter in their daily lives. But in contrast to the so-called abolitionist position in relation to children's work or child labour, which strongly relates differences in qualities of children's work to the age of the child performing the work, working children's movements strongly reject, first, the underlying idea that this exploitation stems from a supposedly innate and universal vulnerability shared by all children (Nieuwenhuys, 2009), and, second, that it would abruptly cease to pose a threat when children reach specified age limits. (See Bourdillon et al., 2009 for a critical discussion of minimum-age standards in children's work.) This is stressed in the Dakar declaration (1998) with the following words (quoted in Liebel, Overwien & Recknagel, 2001: 354): *'Work should be in accordance with the capacity and development of each and every child, and not depend on his/her age.'* Additionally, while over and over again voicing (and, as we will see, also practically implementing) their resolve to fight such exploitation, they share a view on how this challenge should not be approached. After the experience of many working children with practical implementations of the abolitionist agenda over the course of the last decades, they are very sceptical of the 'protection' provided by prohibition, boycott and compulsory schooling approaches to children's work. In their view, which is now widely corroborated by research (Boyden, Ling & Myers, 1998; Hungerland et al., 2007; White, 2009; Bourdillon et al., 2010), these most often not only fail to improve working children's lives but regularly cause severe harm by excluding children from basic labour regulations, pushing them underground and into worse work contexts, and thereby make them more vulnerable to exploitation.

Working children's movements consider children's exploitation to be the result of specific working conditions, which include a lack of proper wages, long working hours harming their educational opportunities and leisure time, and insufficiently regulated and enforced workplace safety. From this, they infer the necessity to legally regulate these working conditions, thereby postulating necessary rights *in* work. Such an approach to exploitation is not at all novel, since it coincides with the general approach taken by national and international labour law regarding adult workplace exploitation and work-related hazards (Hanson & Vandaele, 2003; Hanson

2012). The persistence and regularity with which the working children's organizations in their declarations and other texts repeat their aspirations to have both a right to work and rights in work reflects the significance this concept has for them. The following excerpt of a declaration by the sixth meeting of the Latin American movement (Asunción, Paraguay, 2001) gives a quite representative summary of it:

> We fight for children's work: 1. dignified and in good conditions; 2. recognized as a right and not as an obligation; 3. respected and protected by the national laws and codes; 4. not discriminated nor exploited for being done by children.[2]

The specifications given by the different organizations on which exact *rights in work* are necessary can differ in their content, which in parts is related to the particular social and work contexts the different groups of working children are engaged in (Hanson & Vandaele, 2003; see the African movement's '12 rights' catalogue quoted in Chapter 8).

Translating aspirations into practice

So how do the working children's movements translate their claims into practice, and what is their impact, especially in relation to the intentional and unintentional realization of written and unwritten rights? To answer this question, it is useful to differentiate between two levels of engagement: first, the more localized activities aimed at disseminating awareness of, and respect for, working children's rights, and directed towards fairly immediate improvements of working and living conditions; second, the organizations' and movements' efforts oriented towards influencing and changing the wider context of children's work, for instance, public policy and labour legislation at national and international levels, but also the global context of poverty and inequality. While the latter constitutes an important goal for organized working children, their everyday operations are more oriented towards pragmatic changes at the local level, to which we will now turn.

Practical activities and their impact

Of very fundamental importance are the results of the social relationships constituted by regularly interacting among peers facing similar difficulties and rights violations in a context of mutual respect, support and trust. Through this, children come out of social isolation and start a process of reciprocal recognition and meet to share and discuss problems and devise strategies to tackle them. The empowering effects can be substantial, of which many organized working children and adolescents as well as unorganized children give an account (see Ratna, 2000; Reddy, 2010). Group membership is also an issue greatly valued by children living without direct family support, since it can fill in this gap and also offer relative protection from abuse by authorities or a generally unsympathetic public (see Liebel, 2004).

These impacts are closely linked to the pedagogic activities and rights awareness-raising they are engaged in. The AMWCY, instance, still considers awareness-raising on the '12 rights' to be at the heart of all of their activities (Imorou, 2009). The instrumental importance of rights education to individual working children lies in the fact that knowledge of these rights can add to their self-esteem and confidence to stand up to abusive employers, customers, police, parents and adults in general, and that it contributes to strengthening their resilience when facing hardships (see Ratna, 2000; Myers, 2009).

When addressing adults and the general public with awareness-raising activities, working children's organizations are concerned with building a constituency of support, or at least reducing the widespread negative perceptions on working children. When effective in mobilizing respect or understanding for working children, they can reduce everyday discrimination and substantially improve working children's and adolescents' daily lives (see Liebel, 2004; Ratna, 2000).

Other immediate and tangible rights-related benefits for working children are those derived from basic and non-formal education programs like alphabetization and vocational training, improving the realization of the children's right to education. Other examples include the provision of health care and health-related education and counselling on reproductive rights. Since the majority of contexts that working children's organizations are engaged in are characterized by the absence of (or only a very limited provision of) such services, or one which is not sufficiently adapted to the specific needs of working children, this can constitute a significant improvement of their members' and other children's living conditions. In some cases, these services are provided not only to working children but also to non-working children and adult members of the communities they live in, thereby raising the social standing of working children and their organizations (AMWCY, 2009; Ratna, 2000).

Worldwide, working children's organizations are also increasingly getting involved in creating cooperative income-generating activities (IGA). By doing so, they establish viable and empowering alternatives to especially hazardous or exploitative working conditions for members and non-members alike. For example, in rural areas of Western Africa, AMWCY grassroots groups engage in animal-breeding projects or in mobile phone or computer and Internet services run cooperatively by children and adolescents. Similarly, movements in Latin America and India have been involved in establishing, amongst others, bakeries, handicraft and soap production and carpentries on a collective basis. Some children's organizations have, with the support of adults, established children's banks and provide micro-credits to working children's cooperatives; others provide vocational and organizational trainings specifically addressing needs of self-help cooperatives. In cooperation with supporting adult organizations from European countries involved in fair trade, some working children's cooperatives from the three continents have found access to some Western markets for their handicraft (AMWCY, 2009; see Chapter 12 for more details).

Through cooperative IGAs, working children's organizations directly increase children's control over their labour relations and working conditions and allow for work that is not to be so easily equated with exploitation and is more compatible with children's rights to education and leisure. Adding to this, it increases outreach towards working children who, because of especially restrictive working situations, are heavily constrained from taking advantage of the movements' activities.

In sum, with these and other interventions at the micro level, the organizations of working children and youth evidently cannot completely alter the working and living conditions of working children. Nor can they change the structural contexts like poverty and inequality that are characteristic of many of their and their communities' lives. But on the ground, the working children's organizations and movements are fundamental in protecting and promoting the written and unwritten rights of working children, both in the sense that they directly advance the realization of specific rights, for instance, to education, health and participation, and indirectly by achieving small, but important, changes in the social relations that organized working children experience in their daily lives that have a potential children's rights content. This was, for instance, expressed in the final declaration of the fifth African meeting held 2000 in Bamako, Mali:

> In those places where we are organized, our 12 rights have considerably progressed for us and for other working children and youth. We can now learn to read and write, we benefit from better healthcare, we can express ourselves, we are respected by everyone as well as by the Judiciary, we are well treated and can work in safer environments, working in a manner in line with our capacities and can rest sometimes.[3]

Working children's organizations impact on policy making

Important for a lasting strengthening of the working children's organizations' perceptions and strategies is the standing they have in relation to the meso- and macro-level polities affecting them. On the background of the direct and practical activities they are engaged in, it can reasonably be argued that most of the working children's organizations have won small victories and have partly advanced the realization of written and unwritten rights they deem necessary for working children. But in relation to policy-and law-making bodies in their respective national contexts and the international arena, their degree of influence is more heterogeneous and harder to trace.

In some Latin American and Western African countries, working children's movements have become partners in the provision of education, giving them the possibility to directly influence curricula and time schedules and adapt them to the needs of working children. Similarly, through their role in the dissemination of health and reproduction-related services and education, they are accepted and acknowledged by health authorities at different levels (see AMWCY, 2009; Liebel, 2004). Where their organizations have succeeded well in establishing themselves as partners of public administrations, working children have sometimes also developed greater negotiating power in relation to political institutions and other important political actors, as well as raised their social standing in their local communities (see Ratna, 2000; Reddy, 2010).

In some countries, they are explicitly acknowledged as representatives of working children and as partners on questions of children's work by governments, local administrations and other socially influential organizations (Liebel, 2004). In parts of Latin America and in India, some working children's organizations are affiliated with, or have been endorsed by, trade unions (Invernizzi & Milne, 2002), thereby opening up avenues for indirect and, rarely, also direct, voice in labour law-making processes.

This influence can even go as far as to some working children's organizations gaining weight in constitutional reform processes,[4] of which developments in Bolivia give a very recent example. Art. 46 of the Bolivian Constitution, approved by popular vote in January 2009, establishes the right of any person working to work in dignity, with no age-related limitation mentioned. More importantly, Article 61, whose first clause bans 'any form of violence against children, either in the family or in society', states in its second clause: 'Forced labour and exploitation of children are prohibited. The activities children and adolescents perform in familial or social settings are oriented towards their formation as citizens and have an educational function. Their rights, guarantees and protection mechanisms will be subject to special regulation' (Republic of Bolivia, 2009; own translation). This final wording is quite remarkable, since a draft of the Constitution proposed in 2007 reflected a decidedly abolitionist perspective by containing a blanket prohibition of children's work ('*se prohíbe todo tipo de trabajo infantil*'). According to civil society commentators (ProNATs, 2009), this change towards a relatively positive constitutional acknowledgement of the value of children's work for society can be at least partially attributed to the vocal protests by the *Bolivian Union of Working Children and Adolescents* (UNATSBO), their success in demanding to be involved in the constitutional drafting process and their subsequent lobbying and partnering with members of the

Bolivian parliament willing to support their cause. As discussed in Chapter 8, this has led to UNATSBO having an important role in the currently ongoing process of drafting legislation on children's work.

Although this example does not constitute the only instance of working children's organizations views directly influencing legislation dealing with children and children's work, such cases are very seldom and, broadly speaking, the organizations of working children and youth do not amount to a power factor that could directly cause influential political and economic actors to take decisions aligned with the positions of working children (Liebel, 2004). Where the movements get such a weight, their effectiveness in being recognized as relevant organizations and having leverage in policy and law making is very closely linked to the existence of social processes and power structures conducive to their political participation (ibid.). Of similar importance, albeit also constituting the backdrop for one of the most regularly voiced challenges against the legitimacy of working children's organizations and their views (Invernizzi & Milne, 2002), is the presence of, and coalition building with, adult initiatives, civil society organizations and institutions engaged in, amongst other social causes, the advancement of human rights and the realization of the CRC.

But it seems that the closer the working children's movements approach the realm of international policy and labour law making, the less the aforementioned preconditions conducive to the perspectives of the movements are realized. At local and national levels the organizations have found their activities eased by the fact that decision-making processes in which children act only as objects are increasingly being called into question. But in the case of the ILO, the most important international institution when it comes to the legal regulation of children's work, the mere existence of working children as active stakeholders of child labour legislation is in fact still not recognized. Even when the working children's organizations and their positions gain access to the international stage, as they have in the preparatory process to ILO Convention No. 182, they find themselves confronted with the allegation of not being authentic representatives of working children, by both the ILO and large NGOs mostly from the minority world (Sanz, 1997; Invernizzi & Milne, 2002). This is why the movements consider having an impact on the child labour-related policies of international organizations and on the perceptions on children held by non-governmental organizations and adult social movements as the biggest challenges they have yet to overcome for gaining recognition of their views on which rights exactly are necessary for working children, that is to say a combination of a right *to* work and specific rights *in* work.

Contested legitimacy: working children's organizations and adult support

As indicated above, this muting of the voice of organized working children and the questioning of the legitimacy of their claims usually targets the relationship they have with adult individuals and organizations supporting them. In its different variations, the argument adds up to stating that the working children's organizations and their vocal engagement in the child labour debate lack any legitimacy because they can only be the outcome of manipulative action by adults (Invernizzi & Milne, 2002). While this is not the place to discuss this suggestion on the wider background of conflicting socio-cultural conceptions of childhood and its relation to economic participation (see Chapters 1 and 10), and in light of a generalized tendency to question the authenticity and legitimacy of uninvited or dissenting political engagement by children and youth (Elshtain, 1996; Milne, 2007), a few comments are in order to shed light on what constitutes the specific relation between working children's organizations and the adult organizations supporting them (see Coly & Terenzio, 2007; Invernizzi & Milne, 2002: 414–22, for more detail).

The fact that the movements represent themselves as being child-led does not mean that adults do not have a role to play. As already mentioned, the adult organization Enda's participatory activities and support were decisive in the formation of the African movement, and together with other organizations it still provides an important support structure, whereas in Latin America, since its early days, the movement has been, and continues to be, actively supported by individuals and organizations constituted by adults and now grown-up, former working children (Liebel, 2007a).

Besides the fact that this allows for organizational continuity in a context of a permanent aging-induced loss of members atypical for adult organizations, the support is more importantly necessitated by the marginalized social and legal status of children in general and of most working children in the majority world in particular. On their own, they generally would have very limited access to the information, education and financial and logistical resources indispensable for organizing and effectively transforming aspirations into collective and socially relevant action. Additionally, they are severely constrained by the fact that, in most countries, children neither are legally allowed to create formal organizations nor have the right to conclude the contracts necessary for logistically sustaining such organizations, for instance for renting spaces or getting telephone lines. Adults therefore have been important and most probably will continue to be so in the organizational life of the working children's movements.

But their roles are clearly defined: adults are 'educators', 'facilitators' or 'collaborators', and valued for their experience, advice, criticism and support. They have no direct role to play in the leadership and decision-making of the working children's organizations. This situation certainly constitutes a balancing act for both children and adults, but adults' compliance with this repartition of roles and responsibilities is usually eagerly monitored by the children themselves, even in relation to adults whose cooperative relation with the organizations already spans a few decades. When adults occasionally do take part in decisionmaking, they have most likely explicitly been invited to do so by the children. Overall, the everyday workings of the organizations reflect that their *raison d'être* lies in that they are run by the children themselves, who translate their own attitudes and ideas resulting from their own living and working situations into specific structures, demands, proceedings and forms of action (see Coly & Terenzio, 2007).

But while at the micro level and in the context of the international networking among the movements this repartition of roles seems to be well established and effective, at the meso and macro policy-making levels, it poses other challenges. For instance, it is not clear how compatible it is with the increasingly high professionalism, the institutional sophistication, the networking capacities and, not least, the power necessary to gain influence within the highly politicized realms of international policy and international lawmaking. As is evidenced in Anna Holzscheiter's (2010) discourse-analytical account of the drafting process of the CRC itself, these preconditions are not easily met, even by most states of the majority world. Adding to this difficulty of an uneven playing field heavily permeated and structured by power relations, at this level, both the minority world representation of children as passive, dependent and incompetent and the actors promoting a fundamentally different vision of how to adequately deal with children's economic participation are institutionally deeply entrenched.

Conclusion

Whether and how the aforementioned obstacles can be overcome is obviously not a matter easily answered. At present, there are both hopeful and worrying signs. On the hopeful side, it appears that in the course of the last decade, the movements of working children and adolescents have achieved an opening of the debate on child labour/children's work and working children's rights at least a bit. Many of their views have been confirmed by findings of academic research, and their originally self-invited political involvement is, in parts, eased by the strengthening of approaches inspired by the child's right to participation.

On the worrying side, however, core actors committed to the eradication of child labour are continuing to actively deny working children's organizations a right to have a say in the matter of how to deal with children's work appropriately. For instance, an international conference organized in May 2011 by the government of the Netherlands and the ILO attended by about 400 delegates from around the world was characterized by a total neglect of the existence of organizations of working children. While in the course of the conference representatives from the ILO, UNICEF and other organizations repeatedly voiced their commitment to the CRC, which in our interpretation necessarily includes a commitment to the participatory right of children to have a say in all matters affecting them, the only children present *in* the conference were a dancing group engaged for the entertainment of the delegates and a young former 'child labourer' whose life story fit well into the agenda of the conference organizers. At the same time, just *outside* of the entrance of the conference premises, a small group of delegates from the Latin American Movement of Working Children protested against the conference, which they a severe violation of their participatory rights. The scene, witnessed by the author, not only offered strong evidence of a discomforting understanding of participation limited to 'decoration' and 'tokenism' (Hart, 1992)[5] on the side of the ILO but was also particularly illustrative of the close relations amongst rights, participation and power.

Even more worrying in relation to the project of realizing both written and unwritten rights of working children is the growing enormity of the task to tackle the global configuration of political, economic and ideological forces that are an important background to the impoverishment and marginalization of children (Hart, 2008b) – the same conditions that make it indispensable for working children to organize as workers in the first place.

Still, the organizations of working children and youth have demonstrated that they refuse to be silenced, and that the impact they have on working children's and other people's lives should not be underestimated. They do not accept the role of incompetent, passive and dependent objects of adult benevolence that dominant social representations of children usually imply. Transgressing these assumptions, they themselves take action to realize lasting improvements for their own and other children's lives. Among the children they reach, they contribute to awareness about having entitlements, of having the right to have rights. They partially modify the perceptions held of children within their local communities and societies, thereby contributing to relatively more respectful and equitable relations between children and adults. Sometimes the movements establish themselves as essential interlocutors for governmental institutions and non-governmental actors. And while they do engage in a children's rights practice aimed at existing, codified rights, their collective actions and interventions also testify to the fact that working children's organizations have their own expectations and visions of necessary rights that go beyond the existing children's rights corpus.

Notes

1. Quoted from http://www.italianats.org
2. Quoted from http://www.pronats.de
3. Quoted from http://www.pronats.de
4. Reflecting experience from Latin America and South Africa made in relation to women's rights, Georgina Waylen (2006) discusses the opportunities and limitations of a constitutional engineering approach for institutionally securing rights and creating an enabling framework for their realization.
5. According to Roger Hart (1992), tokenistic and decorative participation are in fact equivalent to non-participation.

10
Cultural Variations in Constructions of Children's Participation

Manfred Liebel and Iven Saadi

> We are children and adolescents of 34 indigenous peoples. We are creators, bearers and preservers of our cultures whose contributions to humanity are to coexistence, diversity and peace. Nevertheless, we have to live in conditions of exclusion, alienation, racism and discrimination which prevent us from developing like human beings and full citizens with specific rights. We have come together because we want to know and respect each other as different peoples, and to share our desire to take part in the construction of a more just world. That's why we demand our elders and the governments to listen to us and in this way make it possible to solve our problems and to exercise our rights to territory, identity and culture, to health and nutrition, to education, protection and participation, among other fundamental rights.
>
> (Declaration of the Ibero-American Summit of Indigenous Children and Adolescents, Madrid, 7 and 8 July 2005)

Children's participation is globally considered a goal to strive for nowadays. It is viewed as an indicator of whether children are respected as subjects, with their own rights and their own dignity, and whether they get the opportunity to exert influence on events and decisions affecting them in their respective social environments, societies and international contexts. UN organizations like UNICEF and NGOs supporting children's participation most often refer to the so-called participatory rights established in the UN Convention on the Rights of the Child (CRC). When doing so, they sometimes encounter scepticism and resistance in countries outside Europe and Northern America. They are accused of disrespect toward local cultures and the generational relations and age orders based therein and of imposing a 'Western' conception of children and their rights in a manner reminding of colonialism or missionary practices (see examples in Johnson et al., 1998). In this chapter, we will try to disentangle such controversies and to contribute to an awareness of the wide diversity of conceptions and practices related to the participation of children throughout the world. We take two premises as starting points: 1. minority world societies and the organizations and individuals originating in them do not possess a monopoly on defining what constitutes adequate childhoods, children's rights or children's participation; 2. all societies and cultures, both in the minority world and the majority world, offer contact points for, and necessitate changes in, relation to children's participation. In this context, the question of which children's social activities are considered legitimate in the different conceptions of participation is especially relevant to us.

We first consider semantic aspects of the notion of participation, compare different conceptions and objectives, and expound the problems of elements of the minority world discourse on participation. In the second part, focusing more specifically on empirical instances of children's participation, we discuss different variations of participatory practices with and by children and finally concentrate on the question of political participation.

Participation in general

Semantic aspects

Intercultural communication about participation faces a semantic difficulty (which we will only be able to discuss approximately because of our very limited knowledge of the global diversity of languages). Originating from the Latin words *pars* or *partis* and *particeps*, the word *participation* does have similar meanings in contemporary European languages (at least in English, French, Spanish, Italian, Portuguese and German), but it presumably does not have counterparts identical in meaning in non-European languages. Instead of looking for semantic equivalents of the English term *participation* in other languages, we consider it more useful for an intercultural understanding to take an unprejudiced look at different practices of young people of different ages, to search for the designations in the local language (by children and youth as well) and determine their meaning. Any such examination must reflect self-critically on the cultural specificity of any understanding of participation, including that of the CRC.

On the purely semantic level in the sense of the etymologic origins of the term *participation*, no clear statement can be made on its meaning and in ways in which it can be used. The span of the meanings conveyed by its use reaches from 'having an open ear' for other persons' concerns to 'self-organization'. Even if similarly to the use of the term *empowerment, participation* is often understood as having a positive connotation, it would be misguided to simply understand these two terms as 'good', since both provide discursive space for unreflected and/or such goals that, for instance, are contrary to a more democratic society. Participation can be active or passive; invited or uninvited; forced or voluntary; unplanned or used with manipulative aims; morally good, bad or neutral. Whoever listens, loves, is creative or just takes part in his or her life participates. But when ethical standards are set, participation can be morally assessed. Often, the term is understood as being related to positive and desirable goals, but one can also participate in objectionable activities and cooperate in pursuing reprehensible goals.

Because of this vagueness, *participation* is a term providing space to a wide range of different and partially contradictory meanings and interests. Bearing in mind French ethnologist Claude Lévi-Strauss' coining of the term, it can be characterized as *floating signifier* (see Anderson, 1998: 574). The term acquires a more specific meaning only through the targets aimed at, and the conditions under which these targets are set also must be taken into consideration. Finally, participation can happen in different spheres of live and action (for instance, the family, public sphere) and relate to personal, private, social, economic or political ends (that cannot always easily be differentiated in reality).

Different aims and concepts

Concerning the aspect of the aims we consider most useful the differentiation between instrumental or utilitarian notions of participation (participation as a means) and rights-based, transformative or emancipatory concepts of participation (participation as a goal) (see Theis, 2007). Before addressing this difference, we still want to warn against trying to assess the quality of specific instances of participation just by looking at whether they have been initiated with an instrumental or emancipatory aim. As, for instance, Cornwall (2008), Masaki (2004) or White (1996) describe in relation to experiences in development practice, the outcomes of participatory projects can drastically diverge from what the initiators intended.

An instrumental or utilitarian notion of participation is prevailing when it is used with the intention of improving the efficiency of an intervention by involving the persons concerned and enhancing their identification with the measure; or when it serves to increase a performance by making a project more personal. As according to this conception of participation only its 'usefulness' is relevant, it will only be applied as long as it meets the expectations. Nowadays, this type of participation can be found not only in managerial production strategies but also in some reform projects in social work, in urban management or in development assistance. In all of these examples, it is predominantly used to enhance identification with processes and measures and to diminish resistance. Relating to children, instances of this conception of participation are practiced in schools, for instance, where it is meant to reduce truancy rates and bring students to apply themselves more, or to avoid conflict with 'rebellious' children. Another setting of instrumental participation is within municipal projects, where the participatory involvement of children and youth is used for greater efficiency or as an 'innovative' advantage in competing for funds between different municipalities. We can find a similar understanding of participation in cases when adults launch 'children's organizations' to mobilize children and achieve specific, predefined goals through them; the same applies even when only a limited leeway is granted to the children and 'their' organizations.[1]

A fundamentally different understanding of participation comes to the fore when it is considered as a right to which any person is entitled, regardless of whether it is of use to someone or not. According to this conception, which occasionally is undergirded with theories of democratic justice, participation is an inherent part of the acting subject, broadening his or her latitude and keeping him or her from being degraded to a simple object of the actions of others. With the CRC, this right has also been established for children, even though in a restricted measure linked to their respective 'maturity'. A specific view of humans underlies this conception of participation, in which every human is interested and, in principle, capable of making use of this right.

This rights-based understanding of participation usually aims at promoting emancipation and equality and at contributing towards democratizing society and social relations. Consequently, a transformative aim of participation is established, that necessarily engages with issues of political and social (structural) power. For assessing whether this conception of participation really serves emancipation and equality in practice, a look at the underlying interests and concrete conditions of the realization of participation is necessary, since this is the only possible way to establish whether persons can lay claim to their right to participate, and whether doing so makes sense for them. In the case of children, these approaches often confine themselves to invoking the usefulness of experiences with 'democracy' for children and youth as (potential) citizens, or they tend to interpret children's participation as a politico-educational or pedagogical way of 'training' them to become 'real' or 'competent' citizens. Consequently, understandings of children's participation grounded in democratic theory are not any more immune to instrumentalizing children for heteronomous intentions than instrumental understandings are.

Participation is often primarily considered from the perspective of the individual, be it in relation to the widening of his or her wealth of experience and room for manoeuvre, or in respect to instrumentalizing him or her. However, if we maintain the semantic openness of the term, participation could also be thought of from the point of view of a group or a society, without necessarily reducing it to an instrumentalist or utilitarian meaning. In this heretofore uncommon sense, participation would stand for being part of a larger 'whole'. Evidently, this applies to any person living in society. But what would have to be addressed more specifically is the manner in which this relation is regulated and perceived. At any rate, conceived under this angle the term *participation* could be more compatible with non-Western societies and their cultural norms.

Relations between individual and society

If participation is considered as an individual right, the manner in which the relation between individual subject and society is conceived must be addressed. We try to reflect some different approaches to be found in the 'Western' social philosophical thinking.[2] The liberal reasoning developed in the context of the European Enlightenment suggests conceptualizing the subject in an individualistic sense, being total and complete in himself (during the Enlightenment, the subject was predominantly thought of as male) and standing apart from society. Understood in this way, the individual is a non-social being, only afterwards and artificially being united with others on legally regulated terms. The German philosopher Gottfried Wilhelm Leibniz (1646–1716), for instance, conceptualized the individual only in terms of his bare existence (*Monade*) and considered society as the sum of single individuals. 'Under the influence of liberalism, the teaching of free competition has totally got into the habit of thinking of the *monade* as something absolute, a being of its own' (Institut für Sozialforschung, 1956: 42).

But also in the 'Western' world, this liberal-individualistic approach stands vis-à-vis competing concepts of the relationship between the individual and society. Here the individual is not thought of as last entity or in terms of an atom, but as a social being that is not only necessarily always part of society and dependent on it, but also essentially constituted in the relations to other human beings.

> If the human being exists only through corresponding others and is what he is only through them, then he is not in the last instance defined by a primary indivisibility and uniqueness, but through necessarily having a part in the other and being able to communicate himself. He is fellow human being, before also being individual; he acts towards others, before explicitly acting towards himself; he is a moment of circumstances, before maybe one day being capable to self-determination. (Ibid.: 42)

Thus society as a 'whole' is always simultaneously contained in the individual, as well as conversely the whole does not exist and make sense without living human beings. The 'whole', in the sense of the German terms *Gesellschaft* and *Gemeinschaft,* must always be thought of as historical and structured. We are always part of it, but our position within it varies, for instance, powerful or powerless, appreciated or disregarded. We suggest understanding participation as both a mode of individuation (for instance, more liberty and self-realization) and of social integration, with the relationship between both modes being a necessary and constant point of enquiry. With this in mind, participation can be taken as the possibility of the individual to increase room for manoeuvre, to gain power and influence in the context of an inegalitarian or un-free society (liberation, empowerment), as well as the possibility to emerge from a marginalized position and to find social acceptance and a feeling of belonging (inclusion).

Instead of only thinking in categories of either-or, we prefer to assess the interdependencies. Only being autonomous can also mean being alone and isolated and possibly to feeling abandoned and useless. On the other side, participation can include that one has had no option to do otherwise, or that non-participation in one social arena is sanctioned with the exclusion from other social domains, or that participation only comes at the cost of subjugation or compliance with relations of inequality. For instance, working children are regularly proud to be capable of supporting their families (i.e. sense of belonging, being acknowledged, reciprocal solidarity), but they simultaneously insist upon themselves determining the use of the money earned (i.e. sense of autonomy, self-determination, individual freedom).

From our point of view, a cross-cultural examination must not try to evaluate differing concepts and practices of participation in terms of binary oppositions like 'advanced' or 'backward', 'modern' or 'traditional'. Instead, the point at issue is to investigate the prevailing practices and concepts of participation in their immanent content and their specific meanings for the persons living in the societies under consideration – in our case, children.

Children's participation

Age orders

An inquiry into children's participation across cultural systems requires investigations of the specific positions and statuses of children within their respective societies, in relation to adults, in the generational order and in the context of how the social reproduction takes place or is thought about. These specific conceptions and practices of childhood are central in relation to the specific notions of children's participation and in view of which social domains are considered legitimate for children's participatory practices to take place in (see Thomas, 2007: 206–7, 215).

All human societies divide the process of ageing into stages which are normally specifically identified by different terms. But while in the present-day societies of the minority world childhood is considered a distinct and mostly pre-social life stage which is fundamentally differentiated and separated from the one 'inhabited' by adults, children in the majority world are more often understood as being an integral part of the social whole and, accordingly, they take part in activities that in the minority world would be perceived constitutive of 'adult' social domains. Often, there is no such thing as a specific and separated 'childhood' as in the minority world conception, while at the same time there are age groups or age structures that can be more differentiating than only between children (youth) and adults.

Usually, the life stages and persons are classified not by years or by age but by the physical conditions and the capability to assume specified roles and perform certain tasks.

Because children are universally relegated to a position of powerlessness (see Alanen & Mayall, 2001), it can be assumed that the interests and perspectives of children and adults differ regardless of the culturally specific regulation of the generational orders. Accordingly, a reassessment of adults' views on children can be assumed to be necessary in all societies. Thus, concerning participation, the necessity emerges to question any form of participation as to whether the interests and perspectives of children are also taken into account. Children are as much part of society as adults, and they should have the opportunity to contribute to shaping it on their terms.

We consider participation to be a children's entitlement irrespective of its official recognition and legal embodiment as right. There is no contradiction to the *expectation* on children (upheld in some cultures) to participate in social affairs and to take on responsibility. Whether participation is considered a 'right' or a 'duty' depends on the existence and explicit differentiation of pertinent norms in the society under consideration. Applied to children and youth, it also depends on how the respective age stages or groups are understood and what status, tasks, responsibilities or freedoms are considered appropriate for them and how relationships between generational groups are determined. For instance, children can have a large amount of responsibilities and extensively take part in social processes without explicitly having corresponding legal rights. On the other hand, children can have far-reaching rights while, at the same time, their actual participation in social life does not reach any substantive level.

In the following, we will try to demonstrate how, in societies and communities that often are qualified as 'underdeveloped' and 'backward', children's participation can take on other forms and even go further than in so-called advanced or developed societies. As a result, it will emerge that the conception of participation underlying the CRC is only partially suitable for grasping the variety of empirically observable practices of children's social participation. Along the way, we will focus on economic and political instances[3] and inquire into whether the CRC is suited for facilitating and strengthening children's participation.

Variations and ranges of children's participatory practices

The participatory rights codified in the CRC and its Articles 12 to 15 and 17 in particular are based on the idea of a child having individual rights to have a say and to be heard. As already pointed out, underlying this is the conception of the child as a being separated from the adult world in a state of attaining adulthood. Co-determination is restricted to 'all matters affecting the child', which is often interpreted as outside of political and economic responsibility for the society. The participatory rights are limited to

> [...] two main areas: being consulted and making decisions. This narrows participation down from generally *doing* into specifically *talking, thinking and deciding.* [...] So to define participation mainly in terms of children influencing or making decisions is part of the general minority world transfer from doing to talking. (Alderson, 2008a: 79; emphasis by the author)

Just as 'productive' participation as in the form of taking part in vital economic activities, assuming political responsibility for the larger community or polity seems mostly excluded from this conception of participation, at least in relation to its realization (see Wyness et al., 2004).

In many majority world societies, however, children are viewed as integral members of the community who may be endowed with specific capabilities, but that need not be rigidly separated from the adult members and their activities and practices. Depending on their capabilities (which are not necessarily assessed by chronological age), it is either expected of children or at their discretion to take over specific tasks which are important for the community. These tasks can be of a social, economic or political nature, for instance, taking part in fieldwork, carrying out household chores or assuming 'political' responsibility in and for the larger community.[4] Concurrently, specific arrangements can be observed (for instance, in some localities in Western and Eastern Africa or the Andes region in Southern America) through which children are granted specific goods and resources (for instance, arable land, animals), in the form of early inheritances during the lifetime of the parents as well as a collective contribution of the community, that do not have the quality of 'private property', but include having to be put to a use that provides for the needs of the whole community (see Liebel, 2004: 77–111; Dean, 2002: 38–49). These expectations and arrangements can be interpreted both as prerequisites for, and forms of, participation (without explicitly being called that way or being individually obtainable rights). In terms of the social position and influence of children, these arrangements can go well beyond Western concepts and practices of children's participation, especially when these children are considered as full and responsible members in their respective communities or societies.

Also relatively common in the majority world are conceptions requiring children to participate in the provisioning of society and while doing so to be unreservedly obedient towards, and at the disposal of, adult members of the community (above all, in relation to their 'providers'). For instance, Bart Rwezaura (1998: 59) describes the intergenerational relations in Eastern and Southern Africa as largely characterized by an ethic of dominance, through which children's important social and economic contributions are determined:

> [The bond between children and elders] is contained in the notion of fil-
> ial respect and is in turn reinforced by the ethic of dominance. [...] Every
> child was born and raised into this system in which his or her social and
> economic roles and duties were more or less predetermined.

The situation in parts of pre- and post-colonial Western Africa is depicted in similar terms (see Twum-Danso, 2005), and in South and Central Asia children are often thought of 'as the property of adults, passive recipients who should listen to their parents, teachers and elders and respect all that they say' (O'Kane & Karkara, 2007: 136). In a similar line, Lolichen (2009: 135–6) gives an account of observations from India:

> Children participate in numerous arenas, such as the home, school,
> workplace and community in various capacities. As members of these
> units, they are involved in its functions and activities. This is a part of
> the socialization process of children, and each home, school, workplace
> or community – based on its social and cultural setting – defines the
> nature and scope of this participation. Most often these acts of participa-
> tion are not linked to children's evolving capacities to influence and be
> party to decision-making processes. This is also true of several NGO-led/
> initiated processes in which children 'take part'. These, by definition are
> not *rights-based* children's participation.

Borrowing from Alderson's aforementioned differentiation of participation in *doing* and *talking*, such instances of participation could be described as follows: children participate in the doings of society while being excluded from the talking and deciding about the contents and terms of their doings. However, the respect often emphasized and demanded of the young towards senior persons in non-Western societies can have meanings that might elude an easy verdict. Respect does not necessarily mean subordination under other persons but can also allude to the recognition of expertise and traditional knowledge represented by these persons. Respect in this sense is not only directed towards persons but also includes a thoughtful approach towards the natural environment and the livelihood. It could be interpreted as aiming at a more 'harmonic' coexistence, one that is characterized by solidarity, attention and mutual esteem, all of which are also practiced in relation to children (e.g., PRATEC, 2005: 161–2 on the South American Andes). Still, one should not underestimate how such ideas of morality and appropriate behaviour can contribute to, or even reinforce, structures of ine-quality by limiting the exercise of open voice and self-determined agency, transparency in decision-making or the naming of perceived injustices (see Cleaver, 2004).

These partially contradictory norms and practices described in the two preceding paragraphs can coexist within the social reality of a community or society, overlap, only be valid for select spheres or levels of the social (e.g. the family, the 'public' sphere)[5] and be differently applicable, depending on the child's gender, ethnicity, class/caste or other socially attributed characteristics. We also must distinguish between the cultural norms and pretences of societies and the actual practices, with the latter often being much more fluid than the former would suggest. Additionally, the question arises as to what extent specific ideas of participation or its contrary are intertwined with power structures and aspire to change or preserve them. Participation is not transformative per se but can also be put to manipulatively integrative uses or maintain power relations.

To demonstrate how diverse and, in parts, contradictory both the relations between elder and the young and the social position of children in societies and communities in the minority world can be conceptualized and put into practice, we will now turn towards two examples from Sub-Saharan Africa and Asia. Among the Eritrean ethnical groups Tigrinya and Saho, the norm is to keep children away from important, especially complicated, topics.

> The Tigrinya and Saho informants stated that the participation of the child in family and community issues depends on whether the child could be bothered or mentally disturbed after hearing the conversation. [...] The informants believe that if a child listens to family or neighbourhood disputes it could develop feelings of resentment or hostility against one of the parents or neighbours. [...] A child can attend discussions in the local assembly upon reaching adolescence. (Woldeslase et al., 2002: 30, quoted in Fleischhauer, 2008: 77)

In sharp contrast, in the same country, among the ethnical groups Tigre and Hedareb, a child gets

> [...] maximum opportunity to participate in family and community affairs. A child is permitted to listen and contribute ideas in family discussion held between a mother and a father. A child is welcome to suggest choices of pasture and render an opinion which of the livestock could be sold or exchanged. [...] A male child is welcome to attend any discussion held in a local assembly. The purpose is [...] to educate and inform the child in all family and community affairs. (Ibid.)

Our second example deals with refugees from Bhutan living in camps in Nepal (Evans, 2007). In contrast to Western models of childhood that emphasize children's vulnerability, the Bhutanese refugee community views children as competent actors who significantly contribute to their families' and society's well-being. Ethnographic material (see Hinton, 1996; 2000) presents Bhutanese refugee children as active community participants in the private domain, playing essential social and economic roles to support their extended families. Young refugees undertake income-generating activities, vital for the family's economic survival, such as breaking stones to sell, weaving or making chairs. Bhutanese refugees, particularly girls, take on significant household and familial duties from a young age, including collecting water and rations, caring for siblings, cooking and cleaning. Children were recognized by the refugee community as key to maintaining family cohesion. In private spaces, children provided psychological and social support to adults, especially female caregivers. It was in the private spaces where the ideas they brought home were accepted by adults. For example, about health issues they 'were both listened to and acted upon' (Hinton, 1996: 101). However,

> [...] despite this dependence on children's capabilities, the Bhutanese community does not regard children as full social actors and excludes their views from public decision-making processes. Children's participation in public life occurs only at the request of and in a manner authorized by adults. Thus, a distinction is made between children's competencies and responsibilities to contribute to private and family life and their ability to take part in camp or service management. (Evans, 2007: 181)

This situation is increasingly criticized by younger members of the community. They consider that their contributions to everyday life are not acknowledged and demand to have a larger share in 'political' decision making.

Pitfalls of children's participation

The participation of children is especially valued when it is seen as contributing to development and learning. Participatory approaches are meant to help overcome authoritarian or paternalistic modes of intervention and to replace the latter with more egalitarian and democratic forms of professional practice. It is in relation to development practice and educational institutions that we want to now discuss ways in which this often happens and what problems can result.

Development politics

Placing children's rights at the centre of development programmes touching on children's lives is having an increasingly important role. This includes giving special attention to the participation of children. One prominent example that has primarily been designed for application in the majority world is the instrument of Child Rights Programming (CRP). Within this conceptual framework, the responsibility for the realization of children's rights is not considered as only held by the state, but other stakeholders, that is, civil society organizations and other non-governmental actors, are also involved. The duty to respect, protect and fulfil rights still lies with the state, while the role of civil society organizations as agents of accountability is seen in enhancing the capabilities of the state to comply with its duties and thereby increase the accountability of the state as primary duty bearer. Simultaneously, opportunities must be developed with and for children that enable and facilitate the rights-claiming by children as the rights holders.[6]

According to White and Choudhury (2007), three forms of participation can be often identified in projects of Child Rights Programming and other development approaches based on children's rights: *presentation*, *consultation* and *advocacy*. The forms of presentation may range from street theatre, to child survivors' testimonies, to 'cultural programmes' of singing and dancing. The term *consultation* applies when children are involved as interview partners or informers during surveys and in the planning of projects. Advocacy finds an expression when, for instance, videos and newspapers are produced with children, in which they can express their views and intentions, or when children are invited to lobbying activities in national or international events.

All these forms of participation have in common that they consider children as informants and sometimes even as experts. The professional knowledge of the adults involved is seen as only limited and insufficient. The children are imparted the message: 'You understand your situation much better than we do. We must learn from you.' Akin to the reasoning behind participatory approaches to development realized with other target groups, five main arguments are given for this (see White & Choudhury, 2010: 42): First: Only if the addressees of a project are sufficiently involved, there is a guarantee that the project is designed in an adequate and sustainable way (efficiency in the sense of an optimal use of resources). Second: If children speak for themselves, the effect is greatly enhanced in comparison to when the same argument is advanced by adults (efficacy). Third: children have the same rights as adults to speak about, or have a say in, matters affecting them (justice, mostly with reference to the CRC). Fourth: through the means of participation, children gain in self-esteem, and their capabilities and competences are developed (self-realization). And lastly: participation strengthens the position of children and contributes to an overcoming of the reigning hierarchical relations (empowerment).

These arguments, which are not always represented together or by the same people, reflect different intentions. They can be contradictory, and the devil can be in the practical details. One basic contradiction is based in the idea that participation is something that adults offer children. It is the children who are developing or who should play a specific role in the development of societal relations, which adults predefine. Even when ascribed a special authenticity, the mentioned 'voice of children' serves to extend the decision-making power and responsibility of adults. Even the most honourable intentions of adults of wanting to 'learn' from children do not necessarily contribute to changing the unbalanced power relation but can even legitimize it and strengthen it. Participation of children understood in this sense is generally instigated by adults and led by the intention to 'include' children in projects or programmes which adults conceptualize, or to 'activate' children for goals that adults view as being positive and valuable.

Educational institutions

Participation is also considered an antidote for counteracting traditional educational approaches that conceptualize children as the object of adults who claim a monopoly on knowledge and decision-making. While in such approaches children are kept 'small' for them to better be able to 'grow up' with more or less professional guidance, participation-oriented educative practices acknowledge children more in the form of partners with their own skills and abilities. Participation is also meant to ensure that the manipulation of children is avoided and that they are given the opportunity to have ownership over, or at least contribute to, the organization of their educational process.

Two main reasons are given for participatory educational concepts. On the one hand, reference is made to the fact that children have rights and they, as other citizens of a democratic state, are to be able to voice their opinion (which is to be taken into consideration) on issues affecting them. Here, children are viewed as principally competent, who are not *becoming* human beings to be taken seriously, but rather already *are* human beings. On the other hand, reference is made to the necessity of a modern democracy to be able to rely on people who have learned at an early age to deal with freedom, to make own decisions, to take on the responsibility for their own lives (to take their own lives in their own hands), to act 'responsibly' and to abide to the rules of equal and respectful social interaction. In the sense of these reasonings, participation is understood as a form of technology, which is to do justice to the rights, interests and abilities of children as well as the exigencies of a democratic society.

This sounds good and measured against an education understood in this sense there really is much to do in the existing educational institutions. However a problem is also based in this. If participation is understood as means or technology the questions arises, who utilizes these means or this technology and in what context is it used. Children may wish for more respect for their person and views and more influence on their surrounding and life, but generally they will not understand this and argue for it in the way mentioned above. They will imagine more freedom as liberation, more influence as an increase in power or a step to more equality, but not as a means for a better life or education.

Understood as technology, participation is 'applied', and this by those who already have power and influence and who desire to achieve goals that are surely well meant in most cases. In existing educational institutions, this leads to a dilemma, that participation becomes a norm 'from above' which is to be followed, or to a gift or even mercy that provokes new dependencies. In order to dissolve this dilemma, participation can be understood and recognized not as technology, but rather as practice of the powerless themselves. For educational institutions, this would mean that they would no longer be seen as mere educational institutions but rather that education itself is seen as a self-elected part of life. In schools, as we know them today, this is unimaginable, unless they stop being schools.

If participation is seen as part of the educational process, it takes place in a certain institutional context, which plays a decisive role in the meaning it has for every individual. As 'granted' participation, it contributes – no matter which intentions are behind it – to the integration of the participant in the existing framework and to bind him or her to it. If – as generally is the case in educational institutions – it is a hierarchical context, the participation can extend the scope of activity and possibly even balance power relations, but a complete balance of power is not reached immediately. In order to achieve this, the institution itself would have to be in the hands of those who should participate in it. Understood in the usual way, this would not be participation anymore.

In an institution, which makes participation a rule, all people who belong to it are asked 'to behave as participants, to present and shape themselves as participants and also to consider and approach others as such' (Masschelein & Quaghebeur, 2005: 56). This expectation is not an obligation or even a constraint – as this would undermine the principle of participation itself – but rather wins authority precisely by calling on the free will of the subject and promises the subject an increase in freedom and co- if not self-determination. 'This means that, in its claim to realize freedom, this interpellation requires of the subject that she submits herself to certain norms, that she adopts certain truths for her own identity, that she follows guidelines inscribed in the discourses and techniques of participation' (ibid.). In other words, participation does not simply open the possibility for the subject to reach a 'natural', non-estranged, free and self-determined identity but can serve to prescribe a certain 'participative' identity in which participation becomes a moral obligation. To evade it seems all the more abject, as participation apparently 'happens' by free will. However, when participation is made a moral norm, the question arises: what happens with those who – in the existing context and offered form – do *not* wish to participate? There can be many good reasons for this, for instance, not wanting to be absorbed for goals which are not seen as desired or one's own, or simply wanting to use one's time and energy in another way.

This difficulty is not limited to educational institutions and educational processes; it can also be seen in any imaginable social area and field of action insofar as they are marked by social and generational inequality and power imbalances. In order to find answers, in our view, a differentiated concept of political participation is needed, which is not limited to certain institutions and which does justice to the special social situation and position of children in each respective society and local context.

Children's political participation

If we use the term *political participation,* we do not understand it solely in the frame of institutionalized political processes but see it inherent in people's everyday life. This understanding is especially important in the case of children who do still not have franchise. Children cannot take on political responsibility in political parties, national or municipal institutions. Focussing on children, it is of particular importance to investigate their chances to genuinely influence political decisions, and the way they make use of these limited opportunities.

Research commonly focuses on children's interaction with their closer social environment, for instance, the municipal public space and educational facilities. The main question is how they can participate in and influence the result of decision-making processes on topics affecting them in these social contexts. In this field, different, mostly pedagogic, concepts have been developed which aim at expanding children's potential for participation. Almost all of these concepts have been devised and are being implemented by adults. We now want to turn to ways to interpret different understandings of children's political participation emphasizing the particular relevance of different social and cultural contexts.

It is now widely considered a particular achievement of the CRC to have included the right to contribute to political decision-making processes among the newly granted participatory rights. However, the question arises of whether the specific ways in which these rights are framed are capable of doing justice to the actual instances of children's political agency in different social and cultural contexts. Certainly, Article 12 of the CRC generally formulates the children's right to be heard on *all* questions concerning them, but when assessing its implementation into practice there are no convincing indications that this right is understood as one to extensive political participation (see Hinton, 2008: 287; Wyness et al., 2004). Its dominant interpretation seems closely related to the specifically Western conception that children first must be prepared and introduced to political life and are only to be granted access to power and the political sphere on 'adult-bestowed terms' (John, 1995: 106; see also John, 2003). Correspondingly, the specific participatory models and projects developed for children with reference to the CRC mostly differ from adults' political activities, are (or are meant to be) realized separately from the latter and do not take real effect on the wider polity.

This 'child-specific' comprehension of political participation as 'apprenticeship' (Wyness et al., 2004: 84) obstructs the view on children's political self-image and agency, that is enacted among a society or a social group of 'adults' and which is often initiated by children themselves. For instance, when children take part in political resistance and protest movements, it is conceived not as a form of political participation, but above all, and sometimes even solely, as an undesirable development or as a threat to the children.

> Most NGOs and scholars issue unqualified condemnations of children's participation in political movements. Their critiques are based – explicitly or implicitly – on an assumption that children can only be victims, never victimizers; only acted upon, never actors. (Peterson & Read, 2002: 226)

One study that takes this critique into consideration is Anne-Marie Smith's (2007) research on children's involvement in the protests by the Loxicha, an indigenous community in the Mexican State of Oaxaca.[7] The author primarily looks at ways in which children's agency is perceived and depicted in the media and is subjugated to a discourse that distorts both the children's self-image and their agency's content. She notices that the media do, in fact, report on the demonstrations and even raise awareness of police brutality, but that they remain silent on children's involvement.

> This is not in any way to suggest that the children ought to be harassed by police, but rather to highlight their invisibility in this political struggle. Their participation is thus not only subsumed in the adults' activities, but fails to fit into an acceptable form of 'children's participation'. (Smith, 2007: 37)

Although politics and resistance are essential elements of their childhood, the children's presence is, at best, depicted as a lamentable fact. In contrast, Smith emphasizes:

> The combined elements of resilience, agency, happiness, freedom and flexibility which characterize the children's lives present a challenge to prevailing notions of childhood, a challenge that requires close attention if we are truly to take children and what they do seriously. (Ibid.)

It appears as if children's political participation officially only gets approved of and acknowledged when it takes place in contexts such as they usually are predefined by NGOs or governments. Beyond such delimited forms, the activities of children are not noticed in the participation debate.

> The children of Loxicha are not part of a children's group set up to empower them or to promote their participation, they do not attend strategy meetings, do not have 'agendas', do not plan protest actions, have not been given titles or roles by the adults around them (e.g., 'group leader' or 'young MP'), and they have not been politicized in a specified or agency-led format. They have grown up within a politically charged environment, where protests, marches, sit-ins, press photo calls, and hunger strikes are all part of their childhoods. (Ibid.: 50)

The variously shaped lives of children and the political dimension of their agency therefore can only be understood if they are studied with an open concept of childhood that takes its starting point in local realities. The normative notions of childhood that are usually contained in aid activities and media coverage conflict with such an appraisal and make it impossible to link the child rights discourse with children's lives.

That they work and contribute to the family income, are responsible for feeding and looking after younger siblings or go on political marches is not at any point identified by the Loxicha children as exceptional elements of their lives. Nor do they define such roles as a movement between the established worlds of childhood and adulthood. This may be simply because children do not question the ins and outs of their childhood to the extent that adults do. Another explanation is that these are only 'exceptional' activities if they are viewed from a normative and fixed standpoint. Therein also lies a crucial issue at the core of the debates: it is adults who lead discussions about 'who' children are, 'what' childhood is and 'how' children should participate in society.

> The Loxicha children do not fit a neat research category such as 'street child' or 'working child'. They move between worlds – they are indigenous children from a rural home who now move in an urban environment, they are displaced as the result of a situation of political violence, they are involved in a day-to-day struggle for the recognition of the rights of their community, they go to school, they feed and care for younger siblings, and they sometimes work. They do not fit into most local NGOs' criteria for inclusion in their programs. While some adults may argue that the Loxicha children's participation in marches and sit-ins does not constitute 'political activism', the fact that these activities are difficult to categorize does not mean they do not 'count'. (Ibid.: 52)

For Anne-Marie Smith, the reason why the ways in which the Loxicha children take part in their community's political struggle are belittled is that they do not fit neatly into the professional criteria of 'nice' participation, especially those on which NGOs mostly base their work. As conclusion, Anne-Marie Smith points out:

> The lives of the Loxicha children in Oaxaca clearly present a 'type' of children's participation not envisaged by the CRC and its ideals. An acknowledgment of the roles children can play in political activity has not been forthcoming in the advocacy for children's rights, in particular within debates around their participation rights. Their voices are being listened to and their views incorporated into many areas of decision-making, facts that would have been inconceivable at the beginning of the twentieth century. It is perhaps time, however, for notions of children's participation to move beyond the present vision which, while having opened hitherto unexplored territory for many young people, remains nonetheless carefully contained by clear (and adult-imposed) conceptual and linguistic parameters. (Ibid.: 52)

This is similarly valid for children's 'nonconformist' or 'deviant' behaviour. The British sociologist Brian Milne (2007) has raised attention to the fact that, especially in the case of children, the distinction between *'good citizens'* and *'bad citizens'* is readily made. Children reliably complying with their duty to attend school, and to standards of conduct and performance applying to children are classified as *'good citizens'*, whereas those skipping lessons, 'smearing' walls with graffiti, 'hanging around' on the streets or 'fooling around' are considered to be *'bad citizens'*. On the matter of political participation, Milne considers it essential to regard children's activities as expressions of political opinion, even if they are possibly 'against the rules', and to assess their legitimacy in relation to the influence children have in society. Not reducing the possible political meaning and legitimacy of children's participation to the words they voice, but also including their actions, would have to be a part of that.

Conclusion

The question is whether the economic and – to a lesser extent – political responsibilities that children assume in many majority world societies and communities can be conciliated with the very specific understanding of participation contained in the CRC. We agree with Gerison Lansdown's (2010: 11–13) request for more clarity on the meaning of participation in the context of children's rights, but in view of how the CRC has become the crucial conceptual framework to think about children and the variety of childhoods worldwide, we would warn against an uncritical endorsement of the constrained notion of participation as established in its Article 12 (right to be heard in decision-making) as it poses the risk of muting the many instances of children's participation that take place in the economic and the political. As we have tried to demonstrate in this chapter by means of cultural comparison, the fact that it is considered adequate to speak of economic and political participation in relation to adults only, while that of children is predominantly understood in terms of the much more limited activities enumerated in the CRC, must itself be understood as a reflection of a specific generational order that positions children as economic and political dependents and subalterns.

Following from this, being careful to retain a perspective on children's participation that is sensitive to the different dimensions in which children possibly take part in their respective social contexts is not only a question of 'intercultural sensitivity', but more importantly essential for conceiving of possible avenues to the social changes necessary for at least reducing the social marginalization that children experience worldwide. Despite the many valid critiques raised against oversimplifying expectations put on the idea and practice of participation in relation to social transformation (see e.g. Cleaver, 1999; 2004; Kothari, 2001; Mohan & Stokke, 2000), it is not by coincidence that the term retains an important place in current debates on, among others, development, democratic justice and active citizenship. In this line, one of the major theoretical conceptions recently contributed to the philosophical debate on social justice (Fraser, 2000; 2003; 2009) has as its core the notion 'parity of participation', according to which social 'justice requires social arrangements that permit all (adult)[8] members of society to interact with one another as peers' (Fraser, 2003: 36). Importantly for our discussion, in Nancy Fraser's account of social justice, participation is pluri-dimensional: obstacles to participatory parity can be situated in relation to culture, the economy and the political (Fraser, 2000: 116). Only by addressing all dimensions and their complex interactions can one adequately devise strategies about the best way to redress injustice (ibid.: 119).

With this in mind, the debate on what constitutes children's participation and its relation to children's rights should not be considered as having found a definite conclusion with the specific notion of children's participation enshrined in the CRC. We do not at all suggest abandoning the approaches focused on codified participatory rights, i.e. programmes and projects aimed at strengthening the voice of children within their immediate and wider social contexts. But first, these approaches should be implemented with at least an openness to the fact that children's participation can encompass wider meanings and practices than the minority world idea of children suggests, and secondly, codified children's rights in general should self-reflectively be evaluated and possibly modified in relation to the place that 'non-verbal' forms of children's participation have within a project interested in improving the lives and social positions of children. As we have already discussed in preceding chapters, children and youth involved in the rights project, both in the majority and the minority worlds, for a number of reasons propose part of an answer concerning the latter interrogation: they demand a better acknowledgement of their economic participation in the form of a right to work (see Chapter 9).

Notes

1. Theis (2007) and West (2007) describe such instrumentalist instances of participation projects exercised with children, for instance, in Vietnam and China.
2. We are aware that we refer only to a small segment of social philosophical thinking.
3. Our understanding of political participation is not restricted to the formally regulated (for instance, voting rights) exerting of influence on the polity but includes regulated and informal influencing of decisions in all spheres of life, for instance, in associations, in the family or at the workplace. By 'economic participation', we mean the exercise of activities that contribute to the material provisioning and reproduction of a society or community and its members.
4. One example is the election of an 11-year-old boy as mayor (*jilaquata*) of a village with 5,000 inhabitants in the Bolivian Andes. For one year, he became the highest authority of the small polity, and his advice was widely respected, including in relation to personal matters. Answering to the question of whether adults also went to him in cases of personal conflict (for instance marital conflicts), he answered: 'Yes, then they are looking for me. "Solve it", they say to me, "I want to get divorced". But I admonish them not to quarrel. "If you come to blows one more time", I and my mother told them, "then there is really no solution left". And then I advise them to take care of their children, to see to it that they go to school, so that one day they can be teachers or something like that. What I like most in the end, is that persons follow the advice. "We are willing to agree" they then say. Then we solve the problems and they thank us and go home.' (Quoted from the review *Protagonistas*, ed. by Defence for Children International, Bolivia, No. 9, 1999) Similar occurrences are also reported from other rural communities in Bolivia and Peru.
5. For instance, see the differentiation of social 'levels' and correspondingly different extents of economic participation and voice of children in Girling's (1960) description of the Acholi of Northern Uganda.
6. We are aware that there are different variations of CRP. On CRP devised from the NGO *Save the Children* and problems of its implementation in Asian regions, see Theis, 2007.
7. A similar study on a protest movement of another indigenous community in Mexico has been carried out by Yolanda Corona and Carlos Pérez (2000). The American psychologist Robert Coles (1986) was one of the first researchers to argue for the recognition of children's engagement in, and understanding of, political processes. The fact that children do not have a right to vote, he argued, does not mean that they are secluded from, or not interested in, political life.
8. Reproducing the exclusion of children from full social membership that is characteristic for dominant cultural representations of children, Nancy Fraser (2003: 36, 45) bars non-adults from her conception of social justice. As this happens without

any explication, we can only guess as to whether Fraser assumes that the binary social division into adult or child cannot harbour injustices, deems such injustice either legitimate or irrelevant or has other reasons for the differential treatment of adults and non-adults. But what becomes evident in Fraser's theory is an at least awkward variation on the claim to a universalist reach (ibid.: 45) as well as a rather inconsequential postulate that her conception of social justice presupposes the 'the equal moral worth of human beings' (ibid.: 77).

11
Children's Citizenship – Observed and Experienced
Manfred Liebel

> Adults miss the point. When is a child considered skilful enough to contribute and participate actively? If you do not give them the opportunity to participate, they will not acquire the skills. Give us the chance early and see how we fly.
>
> > (Khairul Azri, 17, Malaysian delegate to the UN 'Special Session on Children' in 2002; UNICEF, 2002: 1)

> Citizens before the revolution were apathetic and careless. We didn't care about what is happening because we felt the country was not ours. But now the revolution has succeeded, everyone feels this country is theirs and that's why we will try to rebuild it and make it a better place.
>
> > (Jihad, 14, Cairo, Egypt, April 2011; http://www.bbc.co.uk/ news/education-13312429; date accessed 10 May 2011).

In today's political discourse on the role of children in society, it would be a breach of etiquette not to emphasize children's citizenship. Most of the time, the discussants limit themselves to insist on children being citizens, without specifying or supporting their assertion. Where children's citizenship is further described, it is usually defined as a 'status in the making' which children can acquire in a step-by-step process. The acquisition of citizenship is depicted as a learning process through which the children must go by themselves or be guided by an educator. In this context, children are invited to fight for their interests by participating in activities and programmes organized for them. To engage in such a programme is seen as a practical test to prove that children are on the verge of turning into citizens or just became citizens.

This understanding of citizenship, and the practices it entails, rarely coincide with children's expectations and life experience. Most notably, this concept does not appeal to socially disadvantaged children with limited access to social and cultural capital. These children perceive of this kind of participation as meaningless exercises with little or no relevance for their lives. They do not see how these participation exercises would have an impact on their situation and hence perceive it as pointless. As a result, any kind of citizenship which is conceived and offered in this way will remain a 'privilege' of privileged children. It further intensifies the exclusion of those already marginalized. What is more, it adds to the prejudice that children from 'lower social strata' have little to no 'interest in politics' and are unable to comply with the requirements of 'democratic', 'active' and 'independent' citizenship.

In our contribution, we will advocate for a definition and conception of citizenship which takes into account the situation that children are living in and their experience of life. We will argue that such a concept would be more attractive to children as the existing citizenship practices. We will discuss different proposals of citizenship developed over the past years, such as *citizenship-as-practice*, *citizenship from below* and d*ifference-centred citizenship*. Finally, we will try to show that, not least in relation to children, any meaningful concept of citizenship which renders concrete results must take into account power structures in society and must answer the question of how it can contribute to more social equality and social justice.

Citizenship-as-practice

The British social scientists Robert Lawy and Gert Biesta (2006), having in mind children and young people, developed a concept of citizenship they call *citizenship-as-practice*. The researchers contrast their concept to one they call *citizenship-as-achievement*, and which they view as predominant in the discourse on child policies (at least in Great Britain) (see Such & Walker, 2005). This second concept defines citizenship as a status acquired only after passing through a process of development and education. It is linked to a set of expectations of how a person develops into a citizen. Children are perceived as future citizens or citizens-in-the-making rather than fully fledged citizens. According to Lawy and Biesta, the most important weakness of this concept is that it does not coincide with young people's understanding of citizenship. The two researchers sketch their concept as follows (Lawy & Biesta, 2006: 43):

> Citizenship-as-practice does not presume that young people move through a pre-specified trajectory *into* their citizenship statuses or that the role of the education system is to find appropriate strategies and approaches that prepare young people for their transitions into 'good' and contributing citizens. Indeed it makes no distinction between what might otherwise be regarded as a status differential between citizens and *not-yet-citizens*. It is inclusive rather than exclusive because it assumes that *everyone* in society including young people are citizens who simply move *through* citizenship-as-practice, 'from the cradle to the grave'.

Lawy and Bista's concept does not aim at giving young people the same social responsibility as adults. Instead, they demand recognition of young people as an integral part of society and admission that their lives are integrated into its socio-political, economic and cultural order. Their life experiences, the authors claim, not only qualifies children to take part in society, it also supplies a great variety of opportunities to social participation today. It follows that citizenship cannot simply be learned in schools or other institutions. Instead, citizenship manifests itself through day-to-day practice. The idea of citizenship-as-practice respects young people's claims and interests as social actors within a set of formal relationships. It does not force upon them a particular interpretation of citizenship. It starts from the interpretation that young people have of themselves, the world they are living in and how they choose to act in it.

> Young people do not qualify as citizens through some magical mechanism or 'rite of passage' nor by engaging in a particular mantra or by reproducing a set of practices. Their citizenry is not a status or possession, nor is it the outcome of a developmental and/or educational trajectory that can be socially engineered. It is a practice, embedded within the day-to-day reality of (young) people's lives, interwoven and transformed over time in all the distinctive and different dimensions of their live. (Ibid.: 47)

According to Lawy and Biesta, both citizenship concepts – citizenship-as-achievement and citizenship-as-practice – differ in how they understand the relationship between citizenship and learning. Instead of defining citizenship as the result of a learning process, they argue that the dynamics of acquiring citizenship are intimately related to young people's every day living experience. This is why citizenship learning cannot be seen as a one-dimensional process. It is grounded in the complex and multi-facetted experiences that young people make each day. In order to understand fully what it means to be a citizen in a democratic society, Lawy and Biesta demand to recognize 'that citizenship is an *inclusive* and *relational* concept which is necessarily located in a distinctive socio-economic, political and cultural milieu' (ibid.: 46).

Lawy and Biesta's concept has the advantage that it takes children and young people seriously in their role as acting and reflecting subjects and that it understands citizenship as a part of their everyday lives. However, the reference to 'young people' and the understanding of praxis remain defuse and abstract. The specific nature of this practice *as citizenship* remains unclear. In addition, the concept does not specify how *children's* actions are influenced by existing socio-economic, political and legal practices and how their action could, in return, impact upon them. For instance, it would be obvious to establish a link between the specific situation of children and their difficulties to make themselves heard in society. Especially in the case of children, it would be appropriate to consider a form of citizenship 'which looks at relations within civil society and how children are positioned, then new relations are revealed and new questions of power, requiring justification, emerge' (Roche, 1999: 476). In our conceptual proposal of citizenship from below, we address these issues of power and rights.

Citizenship from below

Even before we knew the work of Lawy and Biesta, we developed a partially similar concept of children's citizenship, which we called 'citizenship from below' (Liebel, 2007c; 2008). Just like Lawy and Biesta's, this concept does not link citizenship to normative prerequisites but rather defines it as part of everyday life. However, our concept takes into account the structures and power relations which impact upon this life. Citizenship is different for those who possess social privileges and power as opposed to those who are socially underprivileged and excluded from power. Citizenship from below may start from a situation in which (young) people are powerless and even without rights. It is a form of everyday action that may appeal to rights but also can take place totally independently of these, for instance, in protest movements with deliberate infringements of rules, whose actors do not wait for their rights to be granted to them.

Citizenship from below means that children knowing that they are deprived of their rights (or that their rights are not being respected or implemented) act as if they were already fully fledged citizens. As a rule, by such action, children incur the accusation of being 'bad citizens' (Milne, 2007; Smith et al., 2005: 437), and it is therefore important to take note of the manner in which this citizenship is performed and to recognize the way 'in which children do resist and challenge adult practices, though not necessarily in obvious or constructive ways' (Roche, 1999: 478). Faced with a world of adults in which children are hardly ever heard, and their political rights are largely refused, they do not have many opportunities to take part in recognized political action. 'Children have to start from where they are socially positioned. This means that they have to make their own space in spaces not of their making' (ibid.: 479).

One constant topic in literature on children's rights is the fact that children and young people have a profound feeling of impotence and exclusion (see Lansdown, 2002; Hill et al., 2004; Wyness et al., 2004). And the question arises, what this means for the view of children as subjects or actors which is a central element of the childhood studies today. Are children degraded to the status of objects by exclusion, marginalization and the withholding of political rights, or is the feeling of impotence and exclusion precisely an indication of the fact that children regard themselves as subjects, which prevents them from resigning themselves to being reduced to the status of objects? In other words, can one imagine that children could effectively influence political life, or at least attempt to do so, despite their feeling of impotence and inadequate political rights?

We see the key to the answer to this question in the fact that children are becoming aware of, or being involved in many ways in, social and economic life today. This participation frequently takes on forms which, as shown above, bring disadvantages rather than advantages for the children, and as a rule does not meet with appropriate recognition. But it can form a basis for children to be assured of their importance to society and to claim a role that is not merely recognized but is also influential in society.

In all societies – whether in the minority or the majority world – 'children are social participants – participating in homeworking, child labour, political protest, caring, keeping the family "on the road", etc.' (Roche, 1999: 484). This participation takes very diverse forms; ranging from participation in the 'functional' sense of acting out different predefined roles or the social integration into the existing society and its improved functioning[1] to the 'transformational' sense of the critical exertion of influence aiming at an improvement of living conditions and social recognition. For this kind of citizenship, the local (municipal) environment and the nation state are just as relevant as a global perspective which takes into account the evolving process of globalization and the increasing global interdependence.

In this sense, Citizenship from below is not an individual matter, subject to the whim of individual children. It only has a chance of being realized where an awareness of common interests comes about among the acting children. This is not possible for all children in the same way or to the same extent, for common interests are not only a question of a common age group (for instance, a three-year-old and a 13-year-old may not have much in common, but they certainly share the desire for distinction). Great differences might also separate a child living in poverty form one who does not lack any material goods. As with adults, with children a fusion of interests must first take place, in which similar experiences are put together in a push for common action.

Children's social movements in countries of the majority world (see Liebel, 2004: 19–37; Liebel, 2007a) are instructive examples of how such a union of interest might occur and what can result from it. These movements are organized by children who, at first sight, start from the worst conditions for claiming attention self-confidently. In their lives, they face multiple challenges: as children, they are not being taken seriously; as children living in poverty, they have comparatively few educational opportunities, are frequently discriminated against socially and have few opportunities to making positive experiences which would increase their self-esteem. Children from ethnic minorities, in addition, face racist prejudice and exclusion. Girls are often prevented from taking part in social activities outside the house which involve young people of their same age group.

In the children's movements of the majority world, what is doubtless the main motor of common action is the shared experience of fulfilling vital tasks in everyday life despite widespread disadvantage and discrimination. The necessity to do something in order to survive leads many children to take part in the spontaneous formation of groups whose self-help is frequently denigrated and criminalized as an early or concealed form of delinquency. While these spontaneous groups often see themselves in the paradoxical situation of offending laws in order to realize their rights, in the more organized forms of children's movements a marked sense of justice arises. Children act intrepidly, expressly demanding the realization of rights and, in some cases, even formulating such themselves (see Chapter 8).

This is remarkable inasmuch as thinking in terms of codified 'rights' is alien to children in everyday life. In general, they have a sceptical attitude towards everything to do with the law and laws, or show little interest in them. The sphere of laws is a domain of adults. Children can (up to now) neither pass laws nor be involved in jurisdiction. As a rule, laws are accompanied by unpleasant experiences for children, by primarily restricting their freedom of action, either by certain actions being prohibited for them as 'minors' or by laws, when they involve advantages, only applying to adults (from a particular age). For instance, African children are confronted by laws dating from the colonial era which forbid them to engage in 'hawking' or 'loitering' in the street in order to sell things or beg (see Coly & Terenzio, 2007). At present, Children who work in the street in Latin America are experiencing how laws and conventions which are supposed to be for their protection lead to harassment by the police or 'social cleansing' operations.[2] Such laws place children, particularly those who live in poverty and try to assist their families, in a state of 'illegality' that means still greater problems for them than that of merely having 'no rights' (see Liebel, 2004).

If, nevertheless, they appeal to their rights and insist on rights, this is no doubt to do with the fact that with their movements they have fought for and acquired social domains of their own, in which they can experience mutual respect and the application of their own rules. The rights that they formulate are, it is true, influenced by the discourse on children's rights that, since the passing of the CRC, has been welcomed by the children too, but these rights are primarily founded on their own experience, and are immediately related to the reality of their lives. They are not formulae of compromise or general principles that leave broad, almost unlimited scope for interpretation, but concrete programmes of action in experienced or conceivable situations in life.

Difference-centred citizenship

In the case of citizenship the question of how to account for differences between adults and children has to be answered. These differences are not simply determined biologically. To a large extend they are 'socially constructed' and, therefore, historically and culturally variable. While in some cultures children take on social responsibilities from an early age, in other cultures, namely modern western cultures, they are viewed as fragile beings in need of care and protection. This is why in western countries children are commonly believed to be citizens according to formal law at best, but that, in reality, they cannot be seen as 'equal' citizens. Special 'child-size' concepts of 'partial' or 'semi-citizenship' might be developed. These grant children specific rights and obligations which lag behind adult's rights and responsibilities or are seen as preparation towards a future citizenship and, hence, represent some kind of learning process (see Jans, 2004; Wyness et al., 2004; for a critical appraisal see Liebel, 2008).

So-called *differentiated* or *relational* concepts take a different approach to citizenship which has been developed mainly by feminist authors. According to these concepts 'children should be regarded as equal citizens with the right to belong as "differently equal" members of society' (Lister, 2006: 25; on the relationship to feminist discourse see Lister, 2003). Children do not have to be understood and treated like adults, rather they can find recognition on the basis of 'social difference'.

From this a concept of citizenship can emerge that does not only focus on the dependence of children on adults, but also brings out the mutual interdependence of children and adults (as a rule concealed) in the sense of 'giving and taking' (Alderson, 2008a: 62). Or, in the words of Tom Cockburn (1998: 109–10):

> Children are clearly dependent upon others [...]. However, all members of society are dependent upon children for their society's continuation and future existence. [...] A starting point for any reformulation of citizenship must begin with a re-evaluation of citizenship not as property centred but rather based on solidaristic, non-contractual interdependence.

This also applies to quite young children who, although they are more dependent on adults than older children, can be also important to the adults. Parents can learn from them how to treat their 'following' children (for instance younger siblings), or educators in public institutions can be relieved of the daily burden by children participating actively. Furthermore, as Priscilla Alderson (2008b: 117) points out, the taking over of tasks and self-responsibility of children from an early age, can contribute to making the services 'more cost-effective', meaning it can have immediate economic impact:

> [A] review of children's under-recognized citizenship and economic contributions to their families and communities suggests that concepts of "delivering" health care and education services misunderstand the

crucial contributions that children can make within more cost-effective public services.

The Canadian social scientist Mehmoona Moosa-Mitha (2005) elaborated a differentiated approach to citizenship with a view to children. She contrasts it with individualistic concepts in the tradition of liberalism, in which citizenship is understood as the individual possession of formal (legal) rights and privileges. These concepts define children as 'not-yet-citizens' because they orient their concept of autonomy and equality solely to the (presumed) competences of adults.

The difference-centred concept, on the other hand, acts on the assumption that it is possible to conceptualize children's citizenship without measuring it against a predefined, adult-centred standard. It does not define citizenship through normative categories, which are usually thought of as inherent to citizenship – for instance marriageability, aptitude for military service, participation in the labour market – and it rejects the normative demeanour of the liberal citizenship model with its understanding of citizens as 'right-bearer' and 'virtuous' in the sense of fulfilling civil obligations. This model stands for a fluent and pluralistic understanding of citizenship in which citizens can take on the position of a variety of subjects, in which, for instance, class membership, gender and race can combine to overcome experiences of oppression in solidarity.

The difference-centred concept of citizenship seizes the experience of belonging and participation and takes both seriously without measuring them against the model of a universal individual having a defined set of rights. Accordingly, citizenship means the 'acceptance' of the different characteristics of different groups of citizens, with their individual historical circumstances, vulnerabilities and interests. Additionally, citizenship means 'membership' through the recognition of the individual desire to be a fully fledged member of society without the imposition of normative criteria for citizenship. The basis of this difference-centred approach is a vision of social change which includes the individual grasp of the necessity of self-empowerment, as well as the changing power structures in any one society. Open and hidden forms of resistance are understood as participation.

The self(-concept) of citizens is redefined in two ways. On the one hand, a citizen is characterized as an independent person capable of acting (agency); on the other, the citizen is seen in his or her relationship to 'others', a relationship which is understood as being the root of life-sense. Action is defined as a dialectical relationship between the individual life-sense and common activities. This self should not be confused with the 'responsible' self of neoliberal concepts. Self in difference-theory is 'a responsive being showing its ability to act in interaction with the reality it experiences. It is not a responsible being that moves along predefined lines of normative expectations of civic duties' (Moosa-Mitha, 2005: 375).

With regard to children and their rights, Moosa-Mitha distinguishes among three theoretical approaches which she contrasts with a difference-centred approach of child rights and citizenship. All approaches revolve around the contradictory rapport of equality and difference. The approach of the *child liberationalists*, which was very popular in the US during the 1970s (Farson, 1974; Holt, 1974), underlines the equality of children and adults and concludes that children should have the same rights as adults. The approach of the *child protectionists* (Goldstein et al., 1973a; 1973b) emphasizes the difference between children and adults in the sense of children 'not-yet-being-adults'. The third approach, called *liberal paternalistic* by Moosa-Mitha (Freeman, 1983; 1992; 1997), tries to strike a balance between the former two approaches. It does see a difference between children and adults, but it does not define this difference using fixed categories. Difference is sketched out for each and every individual case, the more so in the case of older children (see Chapter 4).

The contradictory relationship of equality and difference causes a whole bundle of other contradictions, such as the parental right to autonomous decisions and the child right to equality or between the protection of children and the children's right to participation. The difference-centred approach claims to avert these dichotomies by accepting childhood as an important phase in life without referring to adulthood as a norm or standard. Instead of degrading children to 'not-yet-adults', it understands the differences to adulthood, be they real or constructed, as being equally valid phases.

Children's freedom rights are understood not in terms of individual autonomy but in their interactive relatedness to other human beings of any age. Likewise, the ability to act and participate is not linked to a level of competence, since 'competence' is a constantly changing category and because it reflects adult ideas of what children do (not) know or need. Children are special not because of a lack or insufficiency of competences but 'because they do not have the authority or the authorial presence, where their views or presence is taken seriously in society' (Hughes, 1988: 72). Participation in this approach does not carry the normative meaning of entailing obligations and responsibilities as would be expected of an adult. It uses a broader concept of participation which comprises all action initiated and supported by children.

> Thus children may not be responsible for the way the world is, and they may not have the psychological wherewithal to make 'rational choices', but they certainly respond, mitigate, resist, have views about and interact with the social conditions in which they find themselves. Even infants, for example, have a presence and express their agency in a multitude of ways by making their needs, desires, likes and dislikes as well as their joy expressed through acts of crying, laughing and other verbal and non-verbal means of communication. (Moosa-Mitha, 2005: 380–1)

Moreover, children's participation rights are understood in the broader terms of the multiple interdependent relationships that children have in society. Moosa-Mitha gives more importance to interdependent relationships than to autonomy insofar as the former taken to mean being independent of relationships to adults or even having overcome such relationships. What counts is that children have 'presence' in their relationships, for instance, that they are neither subdued nor marginalized. Following Judith Hughes (1988), Moosa-Mitha (2005: 281) defines presence as

> [...] the degree to which the voice, contribution and agency of the child is acknowledged in their many relationships. Presence, more than autonomy, acknowledges the self as relational and dialogical, thereby suggesting that it is not enough to have a voice; it is equally important to also be heard in order for one to have a presence in society. Not to recognize the presence of a citizen, be it a child or a black man, is itself a form of oppression.

It is due to the normative and adult-oriented assumptions about participation and citizenship that factual participation and action of children are still largely overlooked in society. Child rights to protection, as they are most commonly accepted today, ignore the presence of children in their multiple relationships and localize children in the participation/protection dichotomy in such a way as to make protection equal to non-participation. This results in a situation where children are denied their right to protection exactly when they most need it (see Stasilius, 2002). According to Moosa-Mitha (2005: 382),

> Children's rights of participation must address and empower children's agency in resisting the oppression that they may be facing in ways that have their basis in an acknowledgement of children's right to participate on this resistance and not by overlooking it through a construction of children as victims.

While participation is indispensable for children's freedom rights, the concept of belonging is central to their equality rights. Equality is more than the possession of formal rights. After critical scrutiny, it is localized in the lived experiences of exclusion and marginalization to which people are subjected if they are different and do not belong to a certain group. To overcome this situation, one should not recur to normative assumptions about participation and the preconditions and characteristics necessary for it. Children's 'presence' and their will and ability to act should be recognized and strengthened. The outlines of the child's right to equality become clearer if it is understood as the right to be accepted into society as 'differently equal' members. This understanding must go beyond the dichotomy private/public which, more often than not, leads to the marginalization and neglect of children's interests and needs arguing they are of 'private' nature.

In case of the concept of difference-centred citizenship, the question arises of whether social inequality within the same generation of children and existing social structures and through which social inequality and different power relations are reproduced, receive sufficient attention. Likewise, it must be investigated whether the concept of autonomy which the difference-centred approach rejects really is incompatible with the recognition of interdependencies.

Conclusion: latent and manifest citizenship

The different concepts of citizenship presented in this chapter strive to enable children to participate fully in all social matters and according to their own free will. Children's citizenship, as introduced here, is not limited to 'child-specific' issues, it encloses all aspects of society. It is not attached to certain – adult set – preconditions. On the contrary, it parts from the assumption that the difference between children and adults is not an obstacle to children's equal participation. This differences result principally from unequal power relations giving children's citizenship unique and specific imprint. It is not understood as a *status* granted to children or bestowed upon them but rather as a *factum* resulting from *children's daily life experience* which challenges *adults' advantages in power relations*. Children's citizenship – be it as *citizenship-as-practice*, *citizenship from below* or *difference-centred citizenship* – represents a demand to change: social recognition as well as freedom and equality in relation to those who, until now, dispose of the decision monopoly in social and political matters.

All concepts focus on the relationship that children have with adults, or rather the difference between children and adults. Neither concept inquires into the different circumstances under which children live, nor how children's interest in participation might be explained. It remains open how the concept of citizenship can be put into practice; in other words, how the *latent* citizenship present in children's everyday activities can be transformed into a *manifest* citizenship, granting children direct influence on decision-making. We shall pursue this question at this point.

Differences in children's life situation are important insofar as they impact their opportunities to improve their standing in society – in the words of Judith Hughes (1988) – to have 'presence'. The child rights codified in the CRC, for instance, apply to all children in equal measure. But they can be interpreted differently. Likewise, children's ability to claim those rights depends on the situation they live in. A concept of citizenship centred on children's living experience and everyday practice must pay special attention to social disadvantages and violations of rights. It cannot limit itself to evoking the advantages of citizenship, but it must show which impact its implementation has for the group of children to whom it is addressed It also must find and exemplify ways to enable socially disadvantaged children and children whose rights are most notably violated to increase their presence and standing in society.

This might mean that the predominant criteria for competence must be assessed critically insofar as they result in a devaluation of the agency of the children with limited cultural capital, and in attesting deficiencies and the status of victims (unable to act) to these children. It might also mean that children's practices which are discriminated against, or even criminalized under dominant legal practice, must be re-evaluated in view of their life situation. This might result in the legitimization of these practices. It also could challenge a currently legitimate socio-political system which systematically produces social discrimination and in which children from particular groups of society (for instance, migrants or ethnic minorities) or children living contrary to established norms (for instance, children in street situations or working children) are discriminated against systematically and prevented from claiming their human rights. In other words: this citizenship concept must define its position claiming more social equality and justice.

Children's interest in citizenship could result from a feeling of dissatisfaction and unjust treatment in connection with the expectation that one's own actions can contribute to changing one's situation. The concepts of citizenship which have been presented are characterized by the fact that they not only grant children symbolic participation but also promise real influence on social issues. They are therefore likely to be interesting for children who are dissatisfied with their situation. In order to be attractive to children, this auspicious citizenship must be linked back to children's real-life situation and to their living experience. To embrace the idea of citizenship, children must gain the impression that citizenship brings them social recognition and furthers their social standing. This can only be done if the position of disadvantaged children is advocated, opening up social spaces in which they can recognize and articulate their common interests.

Such a concept of *appropriation* of citizenship could be linked to the fact that children, especially those in disadvantaged life situations, take up a variety of tasks in their environment. They do productive household work, they do breadwinning job or they volunteer in their neighbourhoods. But because the value of these activities is not acknowledged socially, the extent to which they gain life experience, their self-assertion and resistance are not recognized – even often by the children themselves. A concept of citizenship which is in touch with reality could draw upon the experience of 'being needed' and the contribution these children make to their social environment, thus making it easier for the children to recognize their own 'value'. In order for such everyday behaviour of children to be interpreted in this way, a concept of citizenship would need a stringent socio-psychological theory and adequate categories.[3]

The question of how the conceptualized citizenship can be put into practice, respectively, how latent citizenship can be transformed into manifest citizenship, is directly linked to the question of autonomy. The interdependent relationship between adults and children, which is of special importance to the difference-centred approach, is important for understanding the importance that children have for adults. But it entails the risk of overlooking that, at least in today's societies, we find an unequal relationship in which children are more dependent on adults than vice versa.[4] This is why the claim to autonomy is especially important if the thought of difference on the basis of equality is to be taken seriously. Particularly, for socially disadvantaged and marginalized children who are being denied spaces of autonomous action, citizenship can only become practice if they have the opportunity to articulate and assert their own individual and collective interests in society – especially if these interests are contrary to the views of the dominant adults. A frame for this sort of articulation can be set by pedagogical projects aiming at the empowerment of children and the advancement of their self-confidence, as well as by social movements which have been organized and are run by the children themselves (often with help from adults showing solidarity).

Notes

1. In development politics, functional participation is seen as a prerequisite to the efficiency and effectiveness of projects.
2. As has happened in Bolivia, Paraguay, Peru, Ecuador, Colombia and other countries in Latin America, with reference to the ILO Convention No. 182 on the 'worst forms of child labour', occasionally in connection with laws or regulations against begging.
3. The concepts discussed here only come close to this goal but do not achieve it. A socially critical and inter-culturally reflected concept of resilience (see Boyden & Mann, 2005; Ungar, 2005) might be helpful.
4. Katherine Hunt Federle (1994: 356) makes the educated guess 'that feminist concerns about the importance of connection and social relationships actually mask the power (perhaps the only power) that women have'.

Part IV

New Frameworks for Children's Rights from Below

12
The Role of Children in Shaping New Contexts of Children's Rights

Manfred Liebel

I am Prema from Uppunda Panchayat. When we went to do the survey, the teacher who had taught me said: 'Now you have become very sharp'. Then I said, 'When I used to come to the school, you had told me that I was good enough only to break fish necks. I am the same girl'.

(Our Survey Story, by Bhima Sangha and
Makkala Panchayat, India, 2001)

We understand 'children's rights from below' in a double sense: on the one hand, we emphasize that children in the societies known to us – for whatever reasons – are a subordinated and powerless social 'group' who are reliant on rights which they can use to overcome generational and other social inequalities. On the other hand, we emphasize, in view of children as individuals, that they, like adults, have specific capacities that change constantly during a lifetime and enable them to exercise their rights. These capacities can be different from those that adults have, but they cannot be understood as biological fact or expression of physical development per se but are, as cognitive, moral and social capacities, also products of specific living and generational relations. In all their possible differences, they are neither inferior nor 'worth' less than the capacities ascribed to adults. Their lesser 'weight' as typically seen characteristic of children is, itself, an expression of the social power relations, which are to be faced by the acknowledgement and 'equality' of children as subjects. Children's rights can help to bring about this change.

In this chapter, we attempt to reveal that this is not only a child-friendly idea but that in different parts of the world, processes are taking place that point in this direction. While having mentioned, in Chapters 8 and 9, concrete examples how children actively participate in the construction of their rights, we attempt to depict here ways and circumstances under which the agency of children can be manifested cross-culturally by the claim of their rights.

We will discuss three approaches for thought and action which have developed over the past decades and are mutually interrelated: a) children as protagonists for social transformations, b) children as actors in new economies of solidarity, and c) children as researchers on their own behalf. In order to clarify that these new approaches for thought and action are not made of 'thin air', we will first depict some globalization processes which demonstrate the emergence of historically new childhood patterns.

New childhoods?

There are children everywhere around the globe. If one looks beyond the European or North American borders, one will realize very quickly that the circumstances in which they live and grow up are as different as can be imagined. The same holds true for existing imaginations, how a successful childhood should be or how children themselves see their life and try to form it.

The still-dominant conception of childhood, which emerged in Western Europe, represents the power claims and privileges of the bourgeois class and, within this, predominantly the masculine part. It is not universally valid even though it often serves to measure the way of children's lives in other – mainly the southern – parts of the world and to impute deficits to them (see Balagopalan, 2002). This concerns mainly the aspect of whether children are mainly involved in preparing themselves for 'life's seriousness' in pedagogical institutions specifically constructed for them, or whether they take on responsible roles in their communities and societies from a very early age. This touches the question of the relations between generations as well as the relations between work and education, present and future.

Most recently, with the rapid progression of the globalization process and the widespread dissemination of electronic media, children living in different parts of the world are no longer isolated from each other but are confronted with measures, expectations, dangers and prophecies from other world regions and must face them (see Katz, 2004; Bühler-Niederberger, 2008; Wells, 2009).

Today, young people around the globe more or less insist on living a life of individual responsibility, in which their desires and peculiarities are respected. Many of them no longer follow given traditions unquestioningly but rather develop their own ideas and practices in which they are at times in 'the driver's seat'. Such processes of 'autonomization' start at an age which is generally depicted as childhood and which is according to dominant Western concept marked by dependence and the need for protection. In addition, a number of children around the globe no longer see themselves as dependents of adults but rather as persons in their 'own right', whose dignity is to be respected and who have 'something to say'. Of course, the ways in which children from different regions of the world 'pipe up', bring about their own cultures and social movements and meddle with the world of adults vary drastically and require us to rethink the familiar perceptions and thought patterns. This holds true for the term 'childhood' as well as for the ways in which children can be understood as 'subjects', 'actors' or 'agents'.

In social studies of childhood of the past two decades, children have often been seen as 'outsiders', and with a critical view on societal relations and relations between generations, a stronger consideration of their interests and needs and their participation is necessary. Simultaneously, there are diagnoses, which state a 'comeback of children into society', that however often see a higher risk for the children in this that must be confronted with educational and social policies, or rather with measures of child protection.

Some academics understand the children's status of outsiders as a manifold structural disadvantage, including the lack of a chance to say anything. In this sense, the German sociologist Franz-Xaver Kaufmann (1980: 767) remarked as early as the beginning of the 1980s, 'Children [...] are structurally excluded from all areas of modern life, save those institutions which are specifically created for them.' Others similarly point to the exclusion from the dominant 'adult society' set out in the bourgeois childhood conception and the appointment of a special status which is marked by dependence and lack of power for influence. One indicator of the exclusion of children is that children are seen and treated merely as developing creatures, who will reach recognition only when they are adults or 'are not even the main actors in the spaces created for them' (Zinnecker, 2001: 10). According to this view, there are denied economic and political participation rights and, in particular, respective possibilities for action.

Others, however, understand the children's status of outsiders as denial of protection, which children require due to their age-specific physical and psychological needs. In this sense, the society is understood/seen as 'child-unfriendly'. Or, more specifically, the social disadvantages and discrimination with which groups of children are increasingly confronted due to their social origin or immigrant status is pointed to , as well as them being hindered, in certain circumstances, from claiming social welfare services or participating in the educational system. Today 'child poverty' and 'street children' are seen as significant for this kind of outsider status.

Obviously, both views are based in differing normative ideas about childhood and children's appropriate and strived-for role in society. Both views reflect social changes that emerge from new structures of societal production and development, including changes in generational relations.

It belongs to the peculiarities of the discourses on childhood that the children's status as outsiders is seen especially where children come back to society and take on tasks or exercise social functions reserved for adults, at least according to the 'modern' western understanding. In this context, it is argued, for instance, that children who are involved in economic activities as working children are per se overwhelmed and hindered from learning, or that children who desire to participate in the political process of decision-making are made to believe they are not (yet) competent enough to do so. When, by contrast, the British sociologist Nick Lee (2001) refers to 'children out of place',[1] he means that children understand and live their lives more and more not only as *becomings* but (also) as *beings*. He sees in both the majority and minority world's societies tendencies of childhood research transcending the familiar opposition of becoming and being and creating a new mode of childhood(s) united both aspects. As these tendencies transcend in contradicting ways, he speaks of the ambiguity of childhood(s) today.

'Children out of place' – as we and Nick Lee understand – are neither 'outsiders' nor 'fringe groups' nor 'minorities', which would simply differ from dominant concepts of childhood. Rather, they embody a growing tendency of change within that concept of 'childhood' that has not yet been appropriately 'discovered' and 'understood'. For instance, one could ask what exactly this new type of 'childhood out of place' implies for the children characterized in this way. Does it affect their lives? In other words, does that term express discrimination or disadvantage? Or may it lead to new spheres of activity that previously have been restricted to adults? Perhaps such questions cannot be answered clearly with a simple 'yes' or 'no' but need to be examined with the help of sophisticated categories of analysis and a distinct set of evaluations.

We are convinced that the long-standing western concept of childhood as a time of development and shelter from the harsh aspects of life, which kept children out of adults' lives and in dependent relationships, has perished. Nowadays, children again participate directly and abundantly – although, compared to earlier evolutions of society, differently – in social life and, through their 'independent' behaviour, they reveal that the old patterns of 'childhood' have become invalid for good.[2] If those processes are interpreted by the public and, partly, by the social sciences as being highly inadequate and unreasonable, it becomes apparent that this perspective still represents a limited eurocentric point of view.

This view becomes especially evident if we not only focus on the welfare societies or post-industrial societies of the minority world but also turn to the societies of the majority world and take into account the implications of the processes of globalization. One distinctive feature of globalization is the growing insecurity and uncertainty which affects an increasing number of people worldwide. With regard to children, Nick Lee (2001) points out that the mechanism which removed children from direct contact with society in order to 'preserve' them for the future was not some sort of social force but the 'developmental state' that originated from Europe. It is well known that children have been assigned to distinct (educational) constraints (especially the family and school) and that their contact with social life had been mediated through, and ensured by, adults. This social localization never applied to all children, but in the 'age of uncertainty' (Lee, 2001) the number of children who detach themselves from that classification is evidently increasing. At the same time, the national 'authorities' are losing their authority to 'educate' subsequent generations for the future by assigning them to a subordinate position through the execution of traditional patterns.

By citing the example of 'street children', Lee illustrates the problem that is characteristic of this 'age of uncertainty':

> Such children have failed to become 'becomings', but [...] that does not mean they are understood as 'beings'. Rather, to the extent that states aspire to being developmental states, such children cannot be recognized as beings. Since these children do not easily fit into either the category 'being' or 'becoming', they are a source of confusion for any who think in terms of those categories. Their ambiguity is profoundly disturbing to adult authority and, in many cases, such children pay a high price for authorities' confusion. Neither 'becomings' nor individual 'beings', these children [...] are frequently understood as troublesome or malevolent packs or gangs to be managed or even eliminated collectively. (Ibid.: 58; emphasis by the author)

Lee predominantly detects the phenomenon of 'street children' in the majority world. He sees it as a result of a global development policy that imposed the western concept of childhood on southern nations without providing the proper financial resources that are needed to install the familiar and institutional frameworks necessary for the successful implementation of the concept. Thus, 'a tension was set up between desired standards and lived realities. The result was that many southern children could not fit neatly into the "becoming" category that had come to seem their common place' (ibid.: 60). For Lee, the 'street children' do not represent a singular phenomenon; their existence, rather, must be understood as the tip of the iceberg beneath which is lurking a new type of 'ambiguous' childhood that no longer conforms with the prescribed categories of order that underlie government policy.

In the treatment of working children, one can see how powerless and, sometimes, aggressive state- and quasi-state policies react on this new mode of childhood(s) (for which it is also responsible). The fact that children's work is seen as a sort of sacrilege to the promises of the western childhood paradigm which – under the ideologically-laden label 'child labour' – is banned by most governments with a prohibition of these essential and economically beneficial activities. In this context, children are – at best – seen as victims, without acknowledging (or accepting) that through this policy – and contrary to full-bodied promises – children's marginality is pushed to its extreme.

According to Deborah Levison (2000: 127), it is the common adult-centred and the adult-dominant view on children that led to a distorted perception and underestimation of the diversity and significance of children's economic activities.

> Children's lack of power has led economists to overlook the importance of their paid and unpaid work and thus to support policies which not only undermine children's well-being within their work contexts but also threaten their ability to be contributing and appreciated members of families, communities, and societies.

Corroborating this, other research findings reported by McKechnie and Hobbs (1999) on the UK and other minority world countries suggest that, instead of reflecting an empirical fact, the absoluteness of assumptions on the 'disappearance' of children's employment from the minority world rather must be considered the result of dominant representations of childhood making children's paid economic activities invisible. Further evidencing how dominant accounts on children mute those elements of lived childhoods incompatible with social representations of childhood, Virginia Morrow (2008: 112) empirically shows, in relation to children's responsibilities in the domestic sphere, how widespread assumptions about children's dependency 'have arguably precluded acknowledgment of the extent to which children have responsibilities in their everyday lives, in the here and now'.[3]

Zelizer (2002: 376) points out that 'the looming image of child labour as a corrupting force has [...] inhibited careful examination of children's economic activity'. In a vein similar to Levison, she interprets it as the manifestations of an adult perspective.

> When we start to examine social life with regards to aspects that are far more important from children's point of view, we can discover a wide range of economic activities that are very differentiated in the children's context and their social relationships. (Ibid.: 379)

In Zelizer's view, it is important to see the 'unequal exercises of power' within the extensive relationships between children and the 'adult-dominated spheres of production, consumption and distribution'. At the same time, one should recognize that 'despite adult efforts to contain them [the children], they also establish segregated, partly autonomous spheres of production, consumption and distribution on their own' (ibid.) and 'work out their own moral views and strategies' (ibid.: 382). By the same token, she suggests that 'multiple other forms of peer production remain invisible', while they are 'catalogued as child play' (ibid.: 383). Thus, she concludes: 'Like that of their elders, children's production takes place within negotiated sets of social relations, and varies significantly as a function of those social relations' content and meaning' (ibid.: 384).

In an earlier edition of her book *Pricing the Priceless Child*, Zelizer (1985/1994) had examined how the appraisal of children and childhood by adults in the United States had changed since the nineteenth century. Now, in a chapter called 'The Priceless Child Revisited', she points out the necessity to focus on the children's experiences and their perspective:

> When we do so, we discover that the creation of an ostensibly useless child never segregated children from economic life in general. Under changed symbolic and practical conditions, the priceless child remained a consumer, producer and distributor. What's more, [...] children engaged actively in bargaining, contesting and transforming their own relations with the economy. (Zelizer, 2002: 391)

With regard to the United States – and especially to the ever-growing inequality of income, the rise of child poverty, and the ongoing hidden child labour of immigrants – Zelizer even asks whether 'the era of the priceless child ended' (ibid.; see also Zelizer, 2005; 2011). So far, this question cannot be answered. But even if adults evaluate children as being 'priceless' and 'economically useless', 'they cannot deny children's substantial economic activity. Thus, a new agenda for research on children's economic experiences emerges from the old' (Zelizer, 2002: 392).

To counteract the ideological instrumentalization of the children's urge for an independent and influential social role, it would be important to analyse the actual economic and social relevance of their activities without neglecting the children's own perspective. Then it might become apparent that the vital necessity of work not only can be measured in terms of exploitation or plight but also that it can exist under dignified conditions and be absolutely voluntarily. To reach that point, we certainly need more than an 'unbiased' evaluation of 'economic roles' of children nowadays. Stronger collective efforts for a society which is no longer based on exploitation and instrumentalization are under way.

The newly perceived 'childhoods' often emerge from distress, especially in societies of the majority world. They are characterized by the fact that children must take responsibility for themselves, and often for their families, at a very early age. This can be associated with extraordinary burdens and sometimes excessive strain. But it is also possible that children acquire unconventional abilities which are of at least the same importance as those abilities and experiences which are conveyed to them by schools and other educational institutions. That way, many children gain independence and an active role in society that they do not intend to relinquish afterwards. These concepts can be understood as forms of participation that exceed our usual connotations of that term (see Chapter 10). They challenge us to reassess our understanding and the practice of 'help', 'shelter' and 'advocacy' and to search for new approaches that do justice to these 'childhoods'. In the following, we will discuss three of these approaches.

Discourses and realities of children's protagonism

The debate on the role of children as protagonists ('children's protagonism') emerged in the late 1970s in Latin America (see Cussiánovich, 2001) and is widespread today in other parts of the majority world (see, e.g., Reddy & Ratna, 2002; Coly & Terenzio, 2007). The debate expresses the fact that children can no longer be understood as mere creatures in need of help and shelter, but that they play an important role in their respective communities and societies, or at least that they *could* play such a role. Connected to this are ideas of participation and citizenship that do not assign the children to special spheres, in which they could manage their affairs on their own authority, but in which they are granted the right and the ability to interfere with the social and the political sphere in general. Thus, children not only raise their voice in anticipation of being 'heard' and 'respected' but also demand the possibilities of self-determination and equality within the social and political sphere. To highlight this aspect, these claims are occasionally called 'protagonist participation' or 'protagonist citizenship' (Cussiánovich & Márquez, 2002; Liebel, 2007a; Cussiánovich, 2009; 2010a).

Historically, the term 'children's protagonism' draws from the 'popular movement' that actively fought for liberation and better life conditions for excluded and exploited population groups (for instance, people without land, inhabitants of poor urban neighbourhoods, minorities and black and indigenous populations). The concept of protagonism is considered a criticism and alternative to the concepts of 'paternalists' and 'developmentalists' (based on the so-called 'modernization theory') that see the poor and ethnic minorities as underdeveloped people who are uncivilized and culturally backward. As with popular protagonism, which underlines the sovereignty and creativity of these classes and people, children's protagonism increases awareness of young people's capabilities and demands their independent and influential role in society. Since the 1980s, the discourse on children's protagonism has been particularly linked to the rise of the social movements of working children and adolescents.

In this context, two types of children's protagonism are usually differentiated: *spontaneous* and *organized*. Spontaneous protagonism manifests itself daily, individually and collectively. It is expressed, above all, in the survival strategies of children in life-or-death situations. The most common examples are children who live on the street and support themselves on their own. However, spontaneous protagonism is also expressed when children rebel against unfair treatment in their homes; when they demand to be taken seriously and be respected; when they must take care of the household and their younger siblings because their mother must work outside the home or because their parents have died ('child-headed households') (see Tolfree, 2004; Couzens & Zaal, 2009; van Breda, 2010; Germann, 2011); when against their will they must work and help support the family economically or must guarantee their survival by themselves. Daily life is full of such examples of children's protagonism.

The organized form of protagonism is observed when children establish a relationship of solidarity in order to advance their interests and rights. Children's social movements represent an ideal form of this kind of protagonism. They are directed by children themselves, and the structures and norms are constructed in the same manner, allowing children's participation and even questioning prejudices and discriminations by sex, age or skin colour. The group often becomes a reality through mutual respect and solidarity measures. The highest level of organized protagonism is achieved when children's movements have gained qualitative and quantitative weight in society, and young people can influence the social and political decisions that affect them (see Chapter 9).[4]

In educational discourses, there is an ongoing discussion about the ways in which spontaneous forms relate to organized forms of protagonism. Those who consider spontaneous protagonism to be an immature form of organized protagonism are criticized because this measure of protagonism is based on adults' criteria rather than children's. This view reflects an implicit belief in an age hierarchy that limits children's opportunities to be appreciated as protagonists if they have not reached the age and experience level that would allow them to be formally organized. This is a common problem in educational projects that regard organized protagonism as the ultimate goal of, or even the opposite of, 'spontaneous' practical forms. In these cases, educators often demand the power to stipulate what is good or bad, desired or rejected. Children's daily experience and acquired capabilities are inevitably undervalued as they are considered irrelevant or counterproductive to the 'real' children's protagonism. This happens, for example, when adult educators attempt to formalize children's groups that sprang forth spontaneously on the street. Here, the adults focus on changing the elements of the group that they consider problematic (for instance, violence or sexism) and ignore those that are uniquely powerful (for instance, mutual help). The adult goal of this educational experience is to give children a new identity that departs from their 'previous life'.

To counteract this, it is necessary to calibrate adults' and children's views of the advancement criteria of children's protagonism through dialogue in which children have the same power of definition as adults, and in which children's protagonism is encouraged (Cussiánovich, 1997). This means that these criteria cannot be regarded as absolute values but must be linked to the context in which they develop. Any attempt to measure the advancement of protagonism must take this into consideration and account for children's possibilities in various contexts – including their age, sex and life conditions – and what they themselves consider desirable and appropriate. There are two possible responses to the question of what conditions lead to the rise and easiest development of children's protagonism.

One position understands children's protagonism to be the result of educational intervention. This view contends that while children have specific characteristics that make protagonism easier or harder, such as their age or life conditions, it is only through educational intervention with educators in power that children's protagonism is expressed and reaches its highest level. Children are seen as human beings who do not yet have the necessary, fundamental capabilities to confront their reality in a direct and adequate way and thus cannot solve their problems without adult help. For example, while it may be recognized that working children are capable of assuming responsibility for their family's well-being, they are not believed to be capable of developing awareness of the value of their work and the eventual risks to be exploited. Rather, the necessary elements of their formation and self-awareness can only be transmitted, according to this position, by capable and experienced adults who coordinate a methodical and directed educational process. A technical variation of this position views children's protagonism as an educational method in itself. Protagonism is thereby reduced to a type of proposal for children to take initiatives and assume responsibilities, step by step, in an educational process intended to achieve a goal pre-established by their educators. In this form, the concept of protagonism has been corrupted into a type of motivation stimulus.

The other view of the necessary conditions for protagonism attributes an important supportive role to education but, above all, assumes that children's protagonism is derived from children themselves. In this paradigm, the roots of children's protagonism are based in their reality and their daily practice, which they interpret in their own way, even when they cannot or would not articulate it in a way understood by adults. Thus, to understand children's protagonism, their anthropological, cultural and social conditions must be taken into consideration. These create and change historic processes and are not the same for all societies or for all children. In a cross-cultural manner, we see four basic conditions that set the stage for children's protagonism.

The first condition is anthropologically based. The child can be seen as a discoverer of the world from the moment of birth. As soon as children are born, they express desires and articulate themselves as human beings with needs. Soon, they begin to face the world and discover it with curiosity and pleasure. Children act as 'researchers' and 'artists' in the truest sense: they research, interpret and give shape to their immediate reality. However, children are soon exposed to a continuous and layered process of denial of their subjectivity, and their creativity begins to die. It is apparently not until the child is finally subordinated to adult power positions and conceptions of the world that he or she is perceived to be a valid human being. In this way, the child's possibilities for developing recognized agency and personal initiative are reduced. However, these qualities do not disappear completely; rather, they are stimulated through social experiences that inspire them to counteract their total subjugation by adults.

At this juncture, the second basic condition of children's protagonism emerges. Children spontaneously respond to their exclusion and the denial of their subjectivity and dignity by uniting with other children. The institutionalization of childhood through the aggregation of children in specialized educational institutions gives children the opportunity to identify with others in their age group, with whom they share experiences and common interests. At the same time, however, a growing number of children live in quarters and family conditions that leave no personal space for them. Moreover, in almost all families and institutions dedicated to children, adults impose their authority in an absolute way, even through force. These material limitations and authoritarian and paternalistic traditions mold the environment, and children look for alternatives outside educational institutions and their families. Thus, it is on city streets that children form spontaneous groups to establish friendships and alliances, to be protected in case of danger or to obtain daily subsistence. They try to build within the group a fair order and an environment that allows them to develop their subjectivity and have an honourable and safe life. Children do not always achieve what they are looking for, but it is this quest that drives them towards protagonism.

The third basic condition of children's protagonism results from the erosion of adult functions and authority in traditional institutions dedicated to the education and social control of children, particularly the family and the school. These institutions gradually lose influence in relation to other socialization agents, mainly the mass media and other technologies in the environment. In contemporary societies, there is decreasing validity in the ideology that children's world is isolated from the adult world. Children find themselves in the wider world at an early age and must face practically similar problems and risks as adults. Yet, despite all this, as well as all the attempts to manipulate and subordinate children under commercial interests, children now have greater opportunities to access the information and knowledge that previously was solely the privilege of adults. Further, children can adapt to technological and social changes with more flexibility, and they can innovatively adopt the necessary knowledge to orient themselves and stand up in a changing world. Through these processes, the traditional hierarchy between elders and minors is inverted, and children begin to question their subordination (see Buckingham, 2003; De Block & Buckingham, 2007).

Lastly, the fourth basic condition of children's protagonism is specifically pertinent to children who have emerged to take on responsibility for their lives or even the lives of adult relatives. For instance, working children, including those who are involved in care work in their own family, know that they carry a heavy weight of responsibility because they must contribute to their family's survival or because they must support themselves through their work. Children who work always develop a certain seriousness – no matter how expressive or passionate they are – and they give the impression of being 'older' than children who have not had to assume such responsibilities. Work experience gives children an earlier independence, not only in the sense that they have money to spend, but also because they become sharp and capable of survival and have the opportunity to feel capable and productive. In this way, they help to dissolve paternalistic subordination based exclusively on their age. Children who work are not freer than the children who do not work, but they experience an internal demand for respect, have a more influential role in society and achieve more equal terms in their relationships with adults and other traditional authorities (see Liebel, 2004).

While the basic conditions of children's protagonism discussed above are necessary, they are not enough to produce it. Other elements are needed for children's protagonism to be expressed, particularly social spaces where children can communicate and express themselves freely. Adults can contribute towards the expression and development of children's protagonism by creating children's spaces and facilitating better conditions for communication and self-expression among children.

Further, there are certain aspects of children's protagonism that have been little addressed before now, such as whether the youngest ones are capable of exercising it. Discussions almost always refer to adolescents, but we also should ask in what sense and in what ways smaller children can act as protagonists, as well as the ways they can further their articulation and organization processes. The French sociologist Jean-Claude Chamboredon (1975: 4–5) was one of the first who noticed that the child can no longer be regarded as 'pre-cultural being' but must be seen from birth onward as a 'cultural subject' or 'artistic being' who learns through spontaneous play and can 'become itself'. It is acknowledged that, from an early age, the child has a creative 'interpretative competence' which could also be exemplary for adults. In a similar way, the French psychotherapist Caroline Eliascheff (1993: 186), who studied the social behaviour of 'autistic' babies and small children, stresses that one must regard 'each child as an independent being, having autonomous wishes long before really being able to be autonomous, and one must not equate the lack of experience and the inability to speak with nothingness'.[5]

Another little-discussed aspect is girls' protagonism. In-depth studies are needed to understand the ways in which protagonism can be developed and promoted among girls. Girls are to be found as leaders in the working children's and other children's movements; there are efforts of girls to guarantee equal rights and opportunities among boys and girls, and several movements even practice a 50:50 quota. However, in general girls are still less active than boys. It is likely that, due to their life conditions, socialization and educational worlds, as a rule girls seem to be less prepared and encouraged to play public roles. Other aspects of children's protagonism that deserve more attention are the differences between urban and rural children, and the specific influences of different cultures such as indigenous cultures and cultures of colour. How are children socialized in these cultures? In what ways are boys and girls involved in the responsibilities of their families? How are children valued? These are a few of the questions that must be examined if children's movements are to be more represented and more influential as a social force.

Children's protagonism, as conceived in this chapter, can be understood as an answer to paternalism in all its manifestations (see Liebel, 2007a). It requires that society amplify children's possibilities to participate not only in 'children's matters' but in all issues of society; in other words, it requires that society recognize children as citizens (see Chapter 11). What we understand here as children's protagonism does not exclude the protagonism of other subjects, and it is not directed against adults in general. To the contrary, it calls for solidarity and collaboration with adults as well as children's own protagonism. This presentation of the appropriate conditions and criteria for children's protagonism does not establish norms to say that children's protagonism can rise in one place but not in others. Children's protagonism can always exist, albeit in different forms and levels. It can be discovered if one listens to and observes the daily lives and practices of boys and girls. This explanation of the conditions, initiators and criteria for children's protagonism may serve as a basis for considering the particular experiences of children in each social and cultural context and help determine adequate interventions.

Children as actors within new modes of economy

The children's' protagonism manifests itself in the fact that children play an active role in the development of new economic modes, which are based on relationships of solidarity. So far, little attention has been given to children as part of social movements and networks. Their actions are not limited to political demands; rather, they try to reorganize their living conditions by creating an economic foundation. These serve primarily as self-help in situations of adversity and are intended to ensure survival. However, they also refer to a different, better way to live, work and manage which may function as a practical and forward-looking alternative to established social circumstances.

Such alternative approaches to work and economic activity are well known under different terms such as 'social economy', 'solidarity economy', 'alternative economy' and 'local economy'. These concepts manifest themselves in different types of organization, for example, as cooperatives, local exchange trading systems, soup kitchens, local workshops or self-governing companies. From time to time, these organizations are satisfied with bridging emergencies, and they dissolve when the distress is resolved. Some organizations take their niche within the ruling capitalist economy as an informal or parallel economy, without calling for further changes in society; others explicitly refuse economic exploitation and social exclusion and see themselves as an alternative to those concepts.

The idea of a social economy based on principles of solidarity accompanied the idea of capitalism from the very beginning (see Black, 1984). It has been early expressed through the demands and initiatives of the so-called utopian socialists, later on through the different models of cooperative movements, the ideas of anarcho-syndicalism and finally through various 'alternative movements'. Since then, a variety of suggestions, initiatives and projects have developed that are rooted in urgent emergencies or in the discontent about labour and living conditions (see Razeto, 1997; Miller, 2005; Neamtan 2005; Santos, 2006; Amin, 2009; Curl, 2009).

It is less known that even children act this way. With their participation and partly as a result of their own initiative, since 1990 many small companies have been founded in countries of the majority world, which are organized cooperatively and based on principles of solidarity. (On the following, see also Liebel, 2006: 227–53; Schibotto, 2009.) In most cases, these companies are organized as cooperatives (though usually not legally registered), where consumer goods for the neighbourhood (such as furniture, soap, bread and other foods) or for tourists (such as jewellery and candles) – sometimes even for export (such as greeting cards and hand-crafted products) – are produced. Sometimes the children work together with family members or other adults from their neighbourhood (for instance, transport service from marketplaces to households and public houses) or they pursue a type of tourism by showing visitors and tourists hidden locations of their region and by allowing them to participate in their everyday life (for instance, by providing alternative hostels administered by children and young people). Occasionally, banks and microcredit-funds have been founded, which are managed by or with the assistance of children. Most small-scale enterprises of that kind emerge from associations of working children or on the initiative and with the support of child help foundations (NGOs) or neighbourhood associations.

The children's initiatives for a social economy can vary. Since they are designed to alleviate the children's working and living conditions, they differ depending on the circumstances under which the respective children must live. These initiatives mostly aim at overcoming individual or collective emergencies, but they can also aim at reaching a freer and more autonomous life. They usually can be found where children must look after themselves in order to survive and where they use public parks and streets to do so. Substituting non-existent or inaccessible social security instruments or market insurance to secure themselves from individual emergencies, they often found a collective fund that can be used for financial support of other children who have become ill or who were involved in an accident. Sometimes children – with assistance from adults – found a mutual savings bank where they can deposit small amounts of money on a regular basis. That way, especially indigent children get the opportunity to access public schools, medical care or educational programs. Especially amongst children who work on public streets cooperative organizations of work exist (for instance, by shoeshine boys), which help to secure or even expand their freedom of action. For instance, they make special temporal and spatial agreements about their work, or they syndicate in order to fend off adult or non-adult competitors.

If further associations of working children can be implemented, more decisive and more complex attempts to create modes of work that enable more individuals to participate in cooperatives at the same time might emerge. In the context of children's movements, those attempts exceed the usual forms of mutual cooperation in everyday life. They are understood as collective attempts to replace types of labour that are based on exploitation by other concepts of work that ensure the ethical maxims of solidarity, respect and dignity. That way, elements of economic practice emerge, which allow children to work under largely self-determined circumstances to make a living. They manage their working conditions and time in a way that allows them to visit schools, to relax or to participate in the activities of child help organizations. Some companies founded by children or adolescents are purposefully associated with educational facilities and training programs where learning and working are reciprocally connected (see Chapter 9).

Almost every time, the foundation of a company that is based on the economic principles of solidarity is preceded by processes in which children become increasingly interested in forms of cooperative economy and in which they become prepared to take corresponding initiatives. This interest stems from the fact that an increasing number of children must fulfil vital tasks without experiencing appropriate appreciation by society. In the course of globalization, the number of children who are directly or indirectly connected to economic processes as producers is increasing (see Levison, 2000; Zelizer, 2002; 2011). This development partly progresses as children more often must contribute to family maintenance or when they recognize their work as an opportunity to become more autonomous and to gain access to social participation. Both aspects may be connected, particularly when the children can only work in marginalized sectors under especially precarious conditions or when they cease to be 'working children' and become 'unemployed youth', respectively.

When children of the majority world talk about their work, they mostly emphasize that it is not the work itself but the working conditions that pose a problem. They thus explicitly differentiate between *necessity* and *constraint*. Constraint means that they are forced to distinct activities by adults, to whom they are in a relationship of dependence. Necessity means, though, that their work fulfils a vital function – mostly in the family context. If children must work due to necessity – for instance, because their families are poor – they might suffer from limited options, but they have the opportunity to decide for themselves, at least partly, how and how long they must participate in work-life. Furthermore, the fact that their contribution is necessary gives them a feeling of being needed. For that reason, many working children regard their work as meaningful and positive (see examples in Liebel, 2004; Hungerland et al., 2007; Bourdillon et al., 2010).

Thus, for most of the working children of the majority world, there is no question of *whether* they should work, but *how* they do so. That raises the question of how these working conditions under which they must work can be influenced, or, to be more precise: must these conditions be improved, or must they find alternative forms of work? In many cases, the possibilities to improve working conditions are extremely limited or are dismissed by the children as inappropriate or unsatisfactory. If children see the possibility to reach for alternatives to their present labour, they usually strive for a kind of work which allows them to act in a more self-determined way. This desire is often accompanied by the expectation that the new activity is not only less tough and exhausting and better paid, but that it is also more interesting, more diversified and more communicative, while it might open up educational opportunities for them. Though these expectations are usually quite modest, they can increase to the same degree as the opportunity for better alternatives becomes apparent.

At this point, cooperative economic activities become interesting for children, and it is certainly no accident that corresponding initiatives mostly emerge from groups or associations of working children. Here, they have more opportunities to think about alternatives to their present occupations and to take initiative along with other children – often with the support of adults showing solidarity. Therefore, the formation of companies that are based on principles of solidarity always depends on specific preconditions. It must be preceded by specific experiences and learning processes (subjective aspect), and a promoting environment (objective-structural aspect) is needed.

Children who are organized in cooperative economic structures have usually experienced unsatisfactory working conditions before, and they have realized that alternatives exist. To this end, it might play a role that they have learned to have own rights and accepted them as being helpful. They developed a consciousness for the relevance of injustice and exploitation and came to believe that they may earn money through more beneficial activities. In this way, the desire for different social relationships (mutual respect, self-determined life, participation and mutual support) has developed. A shared experience of participation in a child help organization that strengthens confidence in abilities and personal rights can encourage the foundation of a cooperative company.

To create a company based on the principles of solidarity, children need the acceptance and the support of adults (parents, neighbours, NGOs and other economic networks). Their development benefits from the public's appreciation and its acceptance of children's rights. It is also promoting when children are explicitly allowed to work under non-exploitative conditions. To accomplish the foundation of an enterprise, educational and financial programs – that are first and foremost dedicated to children – are of prime importance. Likewise, international support and assistance may be helpful, for instance, by selling export goods to wealthy countries.

With children in mind, the whole debate on cooperative economic activities only makes sense if one is convinced that children's work is a significant – be it inevitable, be it desired – experience and means much more than a mere pastime or a source of pocket money. Two reasons account for that: On the one hand, on a worldwide scale, an increasing number of children work out of necessity. On the other hand, more and more children have the desire to work – for different reasons that f from the will to support their parents to the expectation of playing a more influential and more respected role within society.

With their initiatives for self-determined forms of work oriented to solidarity, the movements of working children embody experiences and mediate messages that are important for other children, too. They unveil the fact that work does not inevitably derogate or restrain children but that it might even open up new perspectives. It can enable children to free themselves from marginalized social positions and to get on a par with adults, which might lead to the historically unique situation that children can play a decisive role in society without having to refrain from their 'childhood'. Children, who voluntarily produce vital goods within a cooperative framework and who work for their families and/or their respective communities might still be outnumbered, but they could be the precursors of a childhood that is no longer 'out of place'.

Children as researchers on their own behalf

In order to imagine children as researchers, it is advisable to free ourselves from the usual academic research models – to which the strict separation of scientific and artistic ascertainment of the world belongs – and to clarify our understanding of research. We hold research as a fundamentally important means to systematically observe and map elements of reality and thereby to enhance the knowledge on, and understanding of, life to make it more explainable to ourselves and to others (Alderson, 2000; 2001). Research is based on curiosity and can be understood as a sort of systematic curiosity (Liebel, 2009).[6]

In this spirit, even very young children start acting as researchers when they insist on continuously asking about the 'whys' of their observances and experiences and formulate their own philosophical explanations for the world. Research by children encompasses a broad spectrum that can range from early discoveries in their relationship with the mother and other relatives to investigations on personal freedom of children, to child-friendliness of a neighbourhood, to complex, methodically sophisticated investigations about the basis of human life and what or who endangers it. This can be done in theoretical or philosophical, as well as empirical, investigations.[7]

Of course, it is a question of definition which 'discovering' activities of children can be viewed as research. At least the question of which ways of research are possible must be posed and what specific competences children have or can acquire in this respect. With this in mind, a suggestion would be to think about the relation of cognitive and methodical competences on one hand and creative and mimetic competences (that can be pleasure-oriented) on the other. This happens, if at all, in the surroundings of philosophy, for instance, when the American philosopher and pedagogue Gareth Matthews (1994: 17) remarked that it 'should be obvious to anyone who listens to the philosophical comments and questions of young children that these comments and questions have a freshness and inventiveness that is hard for even the most imaginative adult to match.' In the field of empirical research, there is a lot of backlog on the subject.

One key question for child-centred empirical research is to determine the meaning of giving children 'a voice'. Sirkka Komulainen (2007: 23) points out that the 'voice' of children is, without exception, perceived only selectively by adult researchers and is made into an 'object' [...] 'that can be possessed, retrieved and verbalized'. The children's utterances are subordinated to a cognitive interpretation scheme that not only ignores the social conditionality and ambiguity of the communication between children and adults but also only 'listens to' the children's voices when they are verbalized. 'More listening may not inevitably mean more hearing' (ibid.: 25; see also Roberts 2000; Clark, Kjørholt & Moss, 2010; Clark, 2010). An answer to the question of how the 'voices' of children can be adequately appreciated in all their complexity and diversity could be found in children researching their own reality (in which adults by all means can play a supportive role). Identifying an additional difficulty in relation to 'giving a voice' to children, Alison McLeod (2008: 21) points out that adults and children often have a different understanding of listening by making reference to one of her own studies: while listening from an adult's point of view means that they pay attention to children's statements, have an open attitude and respect their feelings, children expect that actions follow the listening.

According to Feinstein and O'Kane (2008: 37), child-friendly presentations of information and materials for research activities could be increased, particularly those that support participation by younger children, children with disabilities and other marginalized groups. Mann and Tolfree (2003: 7) reviewed the experience of involving children in data analysis and research; their analysis raised ethical issues concerning these children's age, gender, experience, education and adult assistance. Their key message is that

> [...] securing the participation of children in research can be empowering and validating for children (and adults) as well as enriching for the research process and its findings. It was found that children's views and experiences are often significantly different from those of adults, even when the latter believe that they are reflecting children's viewpoints.

Research by children can take place in different contexts. It can be developed in the context of pedagogical activities in child day care centres or schools, for instance, when philosophising with children, or when small investigative projects are included in the lessons and classes. They can be embedded in a play-like manner in children's everyday lives and contribute to making it more interesting and to getting to know the environment better. Or they can be implemented by children who (want to) organize themselves, in order to investigate their own situations and those of other children, to get to know the existing problems better and to find approaches to solving problems. It is usually a kind of research that is oriented towards the ideas of action research, as it aims not only at knowing the reality but also at identifying possible solutions to one's own and others' problems and carrying them out.

In some cases, the initiative to engage in research is raised by children; in other cases, adults give the incentive. Often the reason is a pressing necessity or the children's desire to learn more about other children and their living situations. According to Priscilla Alderson (2000: 254), it is not a coincidence that most research by children is done in countries of the majority world.

> Child researchers tend to be more adventurously involved in poor and war-torn countries, in adult work as well as research. [...] The limitations in Europe and North America for research by children seem to lie less therefore in children's (in)competencies, than in adults' limiting attitudes, in constraints, and concern for protection over participation rights.

The geographical gap is possibly also related to the fact that in recent decades, participatory research approaches have found wide application in many majority world countries (see, for example, Chambers, 1994). We will provide some examples to then address some questions that often arise in the cooperation with researching children.

In a rather informative handbook published by Save the Children Sweden that aims to facilitate the participation of children in research on violence against children, various examples demonstrate contexts and ways in which children can act as co-researchers with adults as well as researchers on their own behalf.

Most often, boys and girls participate as respondents in adult-designed studies. It is becoming increasingly common, however, for children to work with older youth or with adults to design research questions, to decide who will be the most appropriate respondents, to conduct interviews and use other data collection methods, and to analyse the results of their investigations. (Save the Children, 2004a: 15)

When I (see Liebel, 1996) was working as a street worker and project consultant in Nicaragua in the early 1990s, a group of children who were working on the streets wanted to animate other children to join their group. To that end, they wanted to know, in which – partly hidden – places other possibly interested children could be found, under which conditions they lived and worked and what they thought of their work. Together with other street workers, I helped the children organize meetings, in which they were able to talk to the approached children and where they could plan future joint activities. Taking as point of departure the leading questions: 'How do we survive? How do we want to live?', structured group discussions were held, the results were fixed in wall papers, wall paintings and drawings, cooperatively elaborated upon and partly published in a newspaper which was designed by all the children involved.

The meetings called 'testimony workshops' (*talleres testimoniales*) were emulated in other places and eventually led to the establishment of a self-determined organization of some thousand working children in the country. Further activities of the now-organized children followed, in which they acted as researchers. For instance, children, with the support of adults, organized data collection in various city districts to get information on the number of children and their state of health, and started a vaccination campaign on the basis of this information, together with neighbourhood associations. Or they encouraged other children to tell about and document important current and past experiences from the streets, work or school, and published them together with comments and advice in the newspaper of the children's organization and eventually even in a book. A further research activity of the children was the documentation of living situations that were seen as typical. With cameras that had been provided to them by street workers, the children made photos which they publicly presented in an exhibition, again complemented by their own comments and explanations.

Another example stems from educative practice in a slum in the Colombian city of Neiva. A municipal elementary school had been established in order to give the children the opportunity to understand their world via their 'own scientific insight'. The teachers described their method as follows:

> The child is involved in a cognitive process that is not – as in the traditional scheme – rooted in the reception of information, but that lets the child become a discoverer of reality in which she lives. Instead of practising the dead letters of schoolbooks, they learn to learn. Instead of giving them fish in a charitable way, this method teaches them to fish themselves (which can obviously never be neutral). (Colectivo de la Escuela Popular Claretiana, 1987: 97)

One important element of schooling, therefore, was 'research excursions' (*salidas de investigación*), in which the children investigated why the river of their neighbourhood was contaminated, what the toxins involved were and how they affected the lives of the inhabitants. Or they investigated the characteristics of mosquitoes, why there were so many of them in the neighbourhood and how they transmit malaria and other illnesses. Or they conducted studies on the effects of the sun in nature. Or they investigated the living and nutrition behaviours of the inhabitants of their neighbourhood and unearthed long-forgotten traditions of a 'healthy nutrition', such as the usage of the *chicha*, a traditional beverage based on maze.

There are similar research reports from India. The first example which pertains to a slum in the capital city of India, New Delhi, and is taken from a report by Sudeshna Chatterjee (2007). According to the report, in October 2002, with the assistance of the NGO *Ankur*, a group of 28 children and young people aged 12–18 engaged in investigations on the origin of the contamination of the river Yamuna flowing through their neighbourhood. The motivation for this research was the fact that the local authorities had accused the people living in the neighbourhood of poisoning the river in order to justify the displacement of the community and the dismantling of the neighbourhood. Collaborators from a research institute showed the children how they could identify and measure the toxins. Afterwards, the children and their adult companions travelled 350 kilometres up the river, where they discovered that the river had been re-channelled to serve various hydroelectric centres and the watering of large plantations – and that this was the origin of the contamination of the river. The children and young people elaborated a report with their field notes, photos and other illustrations and published it with the title *You, Me and Yamuna*. Their report triggered great resonance in the public opinion.

Similar investigative activities are described in a brochure of the Indian child rights organization *The Concerned for Working Children* that is closely connected with the children's trade union Bhima Sangha (Lolichen, 2002; see also Lolichen, 2009 and CWC, 2005). From September 1998 to

May 1999, members of Bhima Sangha conducted a house-to-house-survey in their villages together with other children, in the course of which they reached more than 7,500 households. About 270 children aged 8–18 were actively involved. For the children, the investigation had practical implications. They wanted exact and reliable information on what problems the children in the villages had and what could be done to solve them. The children dedicated themselves to the investigative work with a high degree of commitment although they had to fit in the interviews alongside their work, school and domestic chores. This was not always easy, but by reorganizing their everyday lives, by helping each other and by convincing their employers and/or parents of the importance of the investigation, they succeeded in finding enough time.

The survey was originally initiated by the adult child rights organization that also developed the first draft of the questionnaire. However, the children suggested various modifications. They were responsible for the data collection and decided themselves how to analyse the data. As a result, the children developed a strong feeling of having the process in their own hands. They clearly expressed that this was *their* survey, and they had a very clear idea of what they could do with the results. In the course of the investigation, they discovered a large number of specific problems that affected them as children, as well as relevant to other members of the village communities. They did not stop after having identified the problems but confronted the responsible persons with their findings, with some of the problems eventually being solved. For instance, children of one village targeted the problem that the children from a particular household could not attend school. They negotiated with the school's director and facilitated the immediate school enrolment of the children. Another example was related to the different conditions under which the children worked. On the basis of the survey results, the children elaborated an illustrated brochure, in which suitable and unsuitable work was depicted in a manner adequate for children of different ages (*Work we can and cannot do*). Furthermore, the children used the results of their investigation to demand a prohibition of liquor stores and the prevention of forced child marriages.

In a *Survey Story* written by the children themselves, they elaborated on their experiences and the lessons learned and explained why they also found it important to document the process of the investigation:

> We document because we do not want to keep on repeating mistakes when we do surveys. [...] Others will know that this survey has been done by working children themselves. [...] In the future if children wish to carry out a survey, they need not receive the necessary information from adults, they can get it from us. We have to document all the information because it will help children learn. (Bhima Sangha & Makkala Panchayat, 2001: 22)[8]

Generally, children depend on the advice of adults when they do research. In order to conduct own empirical studies, they usually need access to knowledge on data-collection and -evaluation methods. As most adult researchers would testify to, knowing research tools is useful, for instance, on how an interview outline is designed, how they should behave in the interview situation, how a group discussion is to be moderated and recorded, how recorded conversations are transcribed or data are coded, sometimes including the use of statistic and computer-based evaluation procedures. These skills can be obtained in workshops or tentatively in pilot studies that are led or accompanied by experienced adults.

Children who want to engage in their own research generally require financial resources and logistical support to move around in the research area and to gain access to the places and persons they are interested in. Because children, in contrast to most adult researchers, are not employed and do not have an income as researchers, they require support to access research funds in order to have access to the necessary tools (for instance, recorders for interviews, or a computer for data analysis). The same applies to the dissemination and implementation of their research results. Also they may need adults' support in order to obtain permission from their parents to engage in research and to be legally insured (see Jones, 2004).

Until now, there are only relatively few experiences on how child researchers can cooperate with adults on the same level without pressure and with mutual benefit.[9] Adults who want to give advice to children in their research are confronted, for instance, with the following questions: How much autonomy and responsibility can be expected of the children involved? When should adults intervene to impart the necessary methodical know-how to the children or to cope with difficult situations? Are children to be paid for their research activity? If so, how much? Should children be accompanied when visiting households, in order to protect them from potential abuse? If children are too impressed by authorities whom they have interviewed, should adults encourage them to be more critical? Who should take on the final responsibility for the data and any research reports – the children or the adults, or both together? These are just a few of many potential questions and complications that can occur in the practice of research.[10]

Some questions show that in cooperating with researching children, problems of power, paternalism, exploitation or coercion can arise, that cannot always easily be avoided or solved. These problems are especially likely to appear if children's own research is embedded in institutions where adult pre-eminence is unquestioned. It also cannot simply be assumed that adult consultants intend to act in the children's interest, and even when they do, that they have the awareness and capabilities to act accordingly. Especially in commercial research, children can be given relatively great research independence specifically for getting more insights in the lives and preferences of their peers that eventually can be used for commercial interests.

For instance, children are given disposable cameras in order to take pictures of their friends and family to gain insight into their lifestyles. In a task posed by the sports apparel company Nike, children were sent to their favourite places in order to come back with documentary material about their preferred activities. It is to be assumed that the company used the results for its marketing (see Liebel, 2004: 199–201). The examples point to the fact that research done at the initiative of children, and with relative independence of researching children, cannot necessarily be equated with the guarantee that the research results will not be misused.

Especially because of children researchers' regular dependence on adults and the potential great use of their research for the adult world, ethical maxims are highly important (see Alderson & Morrow, 2004; Alderson, 2004; Hill, 2005; Greig et al., 2007: 168–181; Beazley et al., 2011). Virginia Morrow and Martin Richards (1996: 98) note that 'ultimately, the biggest ethical challenge for researchers working with children is the disparities in power and status between adults and children'. Ethical maxims do not guarantee that children are prevented from abuse and harm; they can, however, contribute to raising the awareness for the conflicts of interest and risks connected to research, including the awareness of the children themselves. One essential expectation in relation to adult co-researchers or consultants is that children are respected as persons with their own rights and competences. Especially in cases of conflict, they should be empowered cautiously, and their self-confidence should be strengthened. The methodical knowledge provided to children must be oriented towards the research interests articulated by the children themselves, and the children must be able to decide on *what* they want to know, *how* they want to acquire the knowledge and what should happen with the research results.

Research by children, as described here, means a challenge to conventional models of research. In contrast to research that turns 'others' into research objects, this approach turns the tables and says, 'We, the children can do it ourselves.' Children who are researching in this sense are not limited to participating in research as 'outsiders' but can determine and handle research questions and results themselves. They conduct research not for 'alien' purposes but to enhance their knowledge of their own realities and to fight for better conditions.

This approach to research is not at all new. In view of investigations of living situations and ways of living of socially disadvantaged and marginalized people, the question of whether the researching 'subjects' can at all 'represent' their researched 'objects' in an appropriate way and by their own interests is posed rather frequently. For instance, such research approaches were developed in which the 'affected speak' for themselves and interpret their own reality (see Haug, 2000), in which researchers and researched find themselves in similar living situations and have similar life stories (see Jones et al., 2002) or in which research is an integral part of the joint actions directed to change (see Rahman, 1993).

In this chapter, we have tried to demonstrate that these research approaches can also be relevant for children and that they open new possibilities for children to find solutions for their problems. They have the advantage that researchers and their addressees are closer together and can develop a relationship of confidence much more easily. Therefore, 'children succeed in getting responses from within their peer group in ways that would not be possible for adult researchers because of power and generational issues' (Kellett, 2005b: 10). The researchers can understand their 'opposite' better or can discover the hidden aspects of social reality better. In contrast to the usual academic, commercial or contracted research, the collected data and findings have a concrete meaning and a practical value for the researchers themselves; they reflect their own reality and can sometimes be implemented right away.

The greatest possible benefit for children who conduct their own research is possibly that they themselves can dispose of the results. Moreover, the gained knowledge of their reality can enable children – especially those who belong to marginalized groups and communities – to have more control over their lives. They not only 'feel' and experience the problems that are part of their reality, but they can possibly now also enhance their knowledge about, and understanding of, these problems. This can help children to try to practically address the problems and possibly to solve them. When they have a clearer understanding of the problems in their lives and their environment, they acquire more self-confidence in their competencies for action and possibility for influencing, and they are more aware of the fact that their social participation can be extended and that their social position can be strengthened. This experience also shows children that the information and findings gained in their own research can be effective means in negotiations and actions.

Conclusion

In this chapter, we intended to demonstrate that children can pro-actively influence the conditions under which their own rights gain practical relevance for them. However, these actions do not come about without preconditions. They are promoted by worldwide social processes that 'lead children back into society' and confront them with new challenges and tasks. These processes question the dominance of the separating, western patterns of childhood, without elevating the generational conditions on a new 'equal' basis. Childhood as a specific stage of life, differing from the arena of adulthood, does not disappear but takes on new forms and brings about new opportunities for children.

Within the framework of children's protagonism, it has been demonstrated how children (may) take advantage of new options for action in order to consolidate their position in society and to exercise their rights in order to increase their influence in society. The participation of children in the reconfiguration of economic and working settings is evidence that the 'return' of children into society need not lead to new forms of subjection and exploitation but can instead allow for new perspectives of participation which are no longer limited to societal fringes or to merely symbolic forms. As producers and researchers in their own right, children can influence their reality and its interpretation and thus acquire the necessary knowledge by themselves in order to fortify their claim for societal participation. In doing so, children contribute in providing the 'material' fundament for their own rights and taking these into their own hands.

Notes

1. He refers to a phrasing that stems from Mark Conolly and Judith Ennew (1996: 133): 'To be a child outside adult supervision, visible on city centre streets, is to be out of place.'
2. Alan Prout (2005) notes that the dichotomy between agency and structure, nature and culture, being and becoming adopted from 'modernist sociology' for the study of childhood is no longer adequate to comprehend the characteristics of childhood today.
3. Both McKechnie & Hobbs (1999) and Morrow (2008) identify how the heterogeneity of lived childhood is shaped by the intersections with other social categories like class or gender, and with geographical locality. This suggests that if the dominant 'Western' representation of childhood ever has fully corresponded to any empirically-lived childhoods, these most probably are lives of white, male, urban children from higher social strata in the minority world.
4. Here we describe a possible, yet not necessary, development which can be observed in the social movements of children. As children are also influenced by their social surrounding and the existing social relations and habits, these can be reproduced also in their groupings. For instance, it is not easy for children in interacting with each other and the surrounding society to avoid violence and discrimination if society is marked by exactly these phenomena.
5. See also the studies of Alderson, Hawthorne & Killen (2005a; 2005b) on 'premature babies'. In one of their studies, regarding children's rights and citizenship, they came to the following conclusion (Alderson et al., 2005b: 80): 'The UNCRC, by not stating any ages, challenges age-stage theories and assumptions that children acquire rights at certain ages. Instead of trivializing children's rights, concepts of babies as agents and aware meaning makers, and concepts of rights along a continuum of human life from cradle to grave, can help to increase respect and care for every person, including those who may be at the edges of citizenship.'
6. In a publication about children as researchers, Mary Kellett (2005b: 8) calls ' "finding out" by collecting data' the essence of research but also emphasizes that it must be 'ethical, sceptical and systematic'. An exact definition is always exclusive and, especially in the case of children's research activities, it is even more problematic, above all if the definition is made by adults.

7. In a way that seems problematic to us, Sandy Fraser (2004: 18) constructs a hierarchy from *philosophical* or *speculative* to *empirical* research. 'Empirical research can be distinguished from speculative or philosophical research because it accepts our experience of the world as a valid way of deriving new knowledge.'

8. There was another project in India, where working children researched traffic and transport problems during their daily work. In this context, an exchange of experiences with child researchers from Ghana and South Africa was realized (Lolichen et al., 2007).

9. Mary Kellett (2005a) was the first to initiate a research project about the relations between child researchers and their adult companions, and about the repercussions affecting children with their own research experiences. Based on her research, she developed a step-by-step guide for teaching children the know-how of social research (Kellett, 2005b).

10. On further questions that must be considered, and some answers for them, see the excellent set of manuals edited by Knowing Children, 2009.

13
The Role of Adults in Supporting Children's Rights from Below

Manfred Liebel

> Time has wrapped itself around the adults – with its haste, its dread, its ambition, its bitterness and its long-term goals. They no longer see us properly and what they do see they have forgotten five minutes later.
>
> While we, we have no skin. And we remember them always.
>
> From the novel *Borderliners*, by Peter Høeg: 144

We began this book describing the important role that outstanding individuals, social institutions and organizations, or the states themselves have played in the promotion and defence of children's rights during the twentieth century. In every chapter, and supported in examples from social research and social theory, we have tried to demonstrate the aptitude that the children must 'discover', 'recreate' and defend their rights for themselves. Further we have demonstrated the scarce recognition that the adult society shows towards such capacities and the ever clearer need for a 'transfer of power' from adults towards children, with a view to allowing the children to be stronger and more in charge, for themselves, for those who form their more immediate relations circle and for society itself.

We have not tried to transmit the idea that adults must feign ignorance of the well-being and the safety of children. On the contrary, children need adults to begin unfolding in the world, but the question of how to deal with it remains, if in the way in which adults (or every adult) interpret the 'best interests' of the child, or in the way in which the girls and boys themselves express and demand them. With the risk of defying the status quo of the conventional thought about the role of children in society, we have chosen to raise a set of topics in a way that might seem slightly orthodox, all of them referring to the status of children in contemporary societies (with special emphasis on children's citizenship and participation). The purpose has been that of questioning, or even disregarding, a large number of beliefs that are usually assumed about childhood and about being a boy or a girl, in order to depict alternative explanations of both, which would entail a modification of the shared visions of childhood as well as of the attitudes towards children.

In this concluding chapter, we will rest again on the experience to show performances of children in different parts of the world, with the intention of trying to understand, and make understood, the meaning and importance that self-organization of children has for putting their human rights into practice and the way in which the adults who accompany them can offer them the best support, since the children need them. The adults, in this case, would be the persons who accompany children's organizations as advisers or collaborators, but also the commissioners or defenders of the rights of the child that, with the ratification of the Convention on the Rights of the Child (CRC), have become institutionalized in almost the whole world.

The children's movements provide to us truly notable examples of the capacity of self-organization of the children. In them, analysing their declarations, their projects and their activities, we have seen how the children not only refer to their rights as children but also point to particular hostile characteristics of the societies they live in and indicate alternatives. Foremost, they consider it to be a thorn in their side that children are systematically excluded from participating and taking on responsibilities in society, and that this is legitimized by their supposedly age-related 'immaturity' and 'imperfection'. They challenge what we see as a fundamental way, namely, the paternalistic model of existing societies, by not only complaining that they are the subordinates (objects) of adults, but also insisting on roles being newly distributed between age groups. It seems that children do not want to understand why 'children's imagination' should be limited to children, and 'responsibility' to adults. With this, they claim for themselves a new position in society, without having to stop being 'children'. And they make it quite clear that a new understanding, we could also say: a new culture of childhood calls for a new culture of adulthood, that means a culture where adults do not feel superior and more competent than children any longer and do recognize children as decision-makers in all affairs affecting them. Only in this way can it be reasoned that adults as well as children can become social subjects and remain social subjects throughout their whole lives.

In Latin America, this understanding of generational order, and the children's personal support for it, became known in the 1970s as *protagonismo infantil,* which only translates badly into English but is easily understood in this context (see Chapter 12). According to it, children do not necessarily just think about themselves and, where they organize in social movements, are concerned not only about individual interests but develop and get involved in ideas about a fairer society. Such a society can no longer fence children off and place them on the 'island of childhood' but rather must offer them opportunities as early as possible to play a serious role (that is, to be taken seriously) in society and accordingly in their surroundings. The understanding of participation expressed under this vision is still far from what children are granted usually as 'participation'.

In some countries, given the image that children's movements have, it has become common to speak in favour of the participation or even the protagonist's role of children. However, there is not always much behind this, and the use of this vocabulary often only leads to veiling the continuation of a practice of little participation. Notably, there is often talk of, for example, engaging children in the process of their own change, which means nothing other than letting children search for the solutions to their problems themselves. Or the participation of children is understood simply as a method to keep children busy or to encourage them to take on activities whose aims and course of action have long been defined by adults. Or participation, under the condition that the child must be 'sufficiently sensible', is perverted into a catch phrase (see Chapter 10).

In the minority world, when children's participation is discussed, one usually thinks of projects or initiatives that adults created for children. In contrast, children's own initiatives that arise out of their everyday life are not generally perceived and recognized as participation. They are, however, often taken up by organizations or institutions that lay in the hands of adults, to 'support' them, make them 'more effective' or otherwise 'accompany' them. The motives and aims of these organizations and institutions can be very varied. They can, for example, aim, in instrumental ways, at using the initiatives of the children for their own image and to justify the existence of their own organization or profession. However, they can also be taken on with the only aim of standing by the side of children and bestowing their initiatives with more stability and efficacy. Ultimately, the children are dependent on accompaniment and support and happily take up corresponding offers. The issue to be looked at here is in what ways the intervention of adults, regardless of their intentions, can affect active children. For this purpose, we will refer to a study from the South Asian country Bangladesh and then will take another look at my own experience in the 1990s in Latin America, which I will try to interpret anew from today's perspective. Finally, we shall delineate some conclusions aspiring to the advocacy of adults, which might also be relevant in a minority world context.

The risks of advocacy: an example from Bangladesh

In a study of a group of children called *Amra* working on the streets in Bangladesh, Sarah White and Shyamol Choudhury (2010; see also White, 2007) explore how the aims and working methods of the group had changed under the influence of an NGO. The group that originated in the 1990s on the children's own initiative was at the beginning of the investigation made up of a core of eight to ten boys who, in turn, worked together with around

70 children in various locations. About 30 adolescents, some of whom had earlier belonged to the children's group, supported them. In the slum where they lived, the boys tried to teach other children to read and write and stood up for better health care in their neighbourhood. The group organized festivities with the children in the surrounding area and planned a contact point and complaints office for children whose rights were violated.

In their activities, the group constantly faced problems and hindrances, which mainly resulted from the ubiquitous violence of the area and the complex informal and formal political structures that were usually also touched by violence. In Bangladesh, the slums are usually 'ruled' by so-called *Mastaans*, whose power is based on a mixture of offers of protection and the spreading of fear, and who control access to all-important resources. In order to achieve something in the neighbourhood, the children's groups consistently had to carry out a balancing act of coming to arrangements with individual *Mastaans* without being identified with one or another, and having to protect themselves from becoming tools of the local politicians for their purposes. The children constantly had to interrupt and postpone their activities, to survive the conflicts among the various power groups of the neighbourhood. Considerable energy was also put into tackling the problems of the individual members and the protection of their group identity as the main basis of their solidarity, and in doing so, securing their independence.

Some difficulties also arose in the attempts to establish relationships with the young persons in the direct surroundings. After having at first actively supported the group, some ultimately tried to use it as a drug trafficking spot and as a basis for illegal businesses. The earlier members of the group got caught up in the attempt to become a kind of Proto-*Mastaans* themselves. Moreover, because of evictions in the neighbourhood, most of the members of the group had to make use of the meeting room as a place to sleep. Some of the young people of the neighbourhood saw an opportunity in this to establish a kind of club where they could drink, smoke, consume drugs and watch videos. The younger members of the group were afraid to defend themselves, and the older neighbours put enormous pressure on the 'club' to close. This crisis could only be overcome by lengthy talks and negotiations with all sides, where an adult, who had been accompanying the group in a solidarity-orientated way, played a key role. The group's standing and influence is seen in the fact that, despite all hindrances, the group finally managed to succeed, with the agreement of the local authorities and informal power groups, to gain the support of some NGOs for their fight for better living conditions in their neighbourhood. What is particularly impressive about this is the ability of the children to organize neighbourhood meetings and to activate many people from the neighbourhood. The initial reluctance to be mobilized by children, quickly faded to give way to amazement and recognition for the great aptitude of the group in setting up a well co-ordinated and active network. Ironically, it was neither resistance towards the participation of children nor hostility of the residents of the neighbourhood that ultimately undermined the network but rather the manner in which the NGOs intervened.

The NGOs saw a good opportunity to reach other children in the neighbourhood through the children's group *Amra*, and they invited the group to take part in vaccination campaigns, research programmes and consultations of children. The backdrop for these kinds of activities, which took off around the year 2000, was the increased pressure on local NGOs to bring their work on children's rights into line, in particular to boost the participation of children and thereby demonstrate their legitimacy inwardly and outwardly. The interventions of NGOs had conflicting consequences for the children. On the one hand, they gave the children's groups the opportunity to convey their views and concerns to a broader public. On the other hand, the media attention attained by NGOs, the visible prominence, experiencing personal recognition, the availability of better food, and the investment of sums of money for the children that until then had been simply unimaginable, were big temptations for the children. The outcome was that participation in the activities of the NGOs gradually replaced the hard, uncomfortable grassroots work on the streets, which brought little recognition. Over time, the orientation of the children changed: from direct action to advocacy, from groups to individuals, from the slum to the NGOs.

The daily experience of poverty, the organizational experience with the group, and the constantly active relationship with other children in the neighbourhood allowed the members of the children's group to emerge as highly efficient advocates and were, in the eyes of the NGOs, an important complement to the program's activities. However, the danger that accompanied this model of child participation, was that the activists of the children's group distanced themselves more and more from the other children in the neighbourhood. The more opportunities they had in 'participation' and 'advocacy', the greater the distance to the other children. The clearest example was offering *Amra* members the opportunity to travel to international meetings abroad. Wherever they showed up, they were celebrated as the 'true' representatives of the poor children of their country and praised. Although, as delegated persons, they initially upheld their principles and, for example, insisted on always being re-elected 'by the base', after returning from the events they were seen in another way by the other children and unintentionally estranged themselves from them.

The new type of activities was reflected by changes in the group culture. In the interviews that they did with the children and adolescents four years later, Choudhury and White observed a stronger interest in more comfort and consumption. The children hardly spoke of their activities in the neighbourhood anymore but rather emphasized their desire for grants, good food, travel and monetary allowances and, above all, their connection to 'important' people who later may be able to get them better jobs. For a select few, the recognition as 'child-activists' had a stimulating effect, which was accompanied by increased self-confidence, but for most it resulted only in vague expectations of an easier life and an actual new dependence. The most marked effect was seen in a growing difference in power relations among the children. The core group hardly had any connections to the other children anymore. The younger and worse-off children of the neighbourhood hardly had the heart to go to the meeting place anymore, and if they did go, they only seldom spoke up at meetings. By trying they risked scornfulness. *Amra* – so they say – had become a *borolok*, that is to say, a rich organization. White and Choudhury conclude that the dynamics of this model of participation are as concentric as they are exclusive: the few celebrated persons distanced themselves through this kind of participation bit by bit from those whose speaker they had become.

In practice, the self-directed actions of the children's group were replaced by the input and initiatives of the NGO-workers. This does not mean that the children simply became passive objects. During the process, they enjoyed taking part in the new 'participatory' projects, doing street theatre and making videos, calendars or statements for the media to produce. Two or three of them could even fulfil a widespread childhood dream to find work 'in film'. Indeed, the notion that the children are 'autonomous' vanished into thin air. Ultimately, it depended on the available opportunities and forms of support.

White and Choudhury see here a new form of 'office-centred' models of participation, which they categorize as part of the 'theatre for development'. It was made-up of an efficient use of time and minimum discomfort. The numerous meetings satisfied the bureaucratic need for activities that can be represented, and the creation of media products demonstrated tangible and quantifiable results. However, all of these demonstrative participatory practices could also bring some individual benefits for the children but inured first to the benefit of the representatives and employees of the NGOs. They gained in repute and in this way procured new opportunities to attain lucrative jobs or to place friends as advisors.

> The attraction of such approaches over the hard, low-capitalised, relatively invisible and highly uncertain work at street level, are very clear. [...] Despite the rhetoric of bottom-up development and the importance of local responsiveness, in the world of development the major financial and esteem rewards, both corporate and individual, derive not from the local but from the global 'community'. (White & Chouhury, 2010: 47)

The analysis of White and Choudhury draws attention to the fact that it is not enough to ask *whether* children participate but *in what*, under *what framework*, for *which aim* and in *whose interest* they do this. This leads to the question of what the implicit rules are that determine what counts as participation. In the case discussed above, a participation regime was established, which was far away from the daily reality of the children and followed 'superimposed' rules that did not reflect this reality. This type of participation can lead to personal benefits for individual children, but it is not adapted to lead to changes in living conditions.

To make the latter possible, it is necessary first to give careful consideration to the complex, conflicting and difficult life context of the children, and in particular their life experiences must be respected. This includes the fact that, on a local level, there are big differences in power and often violent conflicts – also among the children and adolescents themselves – and that the children move in a field in which they cannot act as they wish, and absolutely not according to pre-set recipes. They have – like adults – the potential to come to grips with their daily problems and to organize themselves for this purpose and to overcome these problems. But for this, they need their 'own space' and in the long run, not to be surrounded by (adult) persons who seek to understand, support, defend and, at any rate, encourage them. This calls for not a desire to 'teach them participation' but rather to recognize that they already practise this in their daily lives, usually of a kind and in a way not foreseen by 'participation models'. 'If we are serious about learning from child participation we need to "follow their feet" when marginalized children leave their air-conditioned office and design programmes that address the world they go and live within' (ibid.: 49).

From advocacy to self-organization?
An example from Nicaragua

We will take this opportunity, having discussed the study by White and Choudhury, to once more reflect on my own experiences made in the 1990s in my work with children in Latin America, initially in particular in Nicaragua.

When I started working as a street worker in the early 1990s, working with children who mainly earned their living on the streets or at markets, a government that aligned its policies with neoliberal dictum had just taken power. Within a few weeks, many children turned up on the streets looking for any opportunities to make money or to obtain food. Some of these children begged, others robbed, others collected half-rotten fruit and vegetables at the markets or ravaged the waste bins for cans, bottles, scrap metal and similar things, whilst others made an effort to get odd jobs or thought up some services in order to earn some money in a 'dignified' way, and many children also did many of these things simultaneously. Some of the street workers quickly concluded that their street education work was too narrowly considered. For every child for whom they cared in a project, within a short time came five, 10 or 20 further children they should have included in their work. Their conclusion was that they should no longer advise the children that they can rely on the help of the street workers, but rather that they should group together to tackle their problems jointly and improve their awkward predicament. We, the street workers, would support them in this.

We based our thoughts on our observation that many children had already organized in small groups in order to better face their situation. However, they often found themselves in competition or in conflict with one another. Many other children had or saw no other way than to get by on their own account. Our attempt to bring together the children, with whom we had dealt in various projects or whom we knew from the streets, was met with a positive response surprisingly quickly and unanimously. We invited children to workshops, which they could largely mould themselves. From these workshops sprung the initiative for a first larger meeting, in which around 100 boys and girls from numerous towns would take part. At the meeting, which lasted two and a half days and was also largely organized by the children themselves, the decision was reached to form the 'Movement of Working Children and Adolescents of Nicaragua' (later called NATRAS) and to allure other children into participating. (On the formation of the movement, see Liebel, 1994: 91–118.)

At the meeting, it was demonstrated that the children were very efficient in producing their own ideas on how to organize themselves and what they wanted to achieve with their organization. As they, for example, voted an executive committee, they came to an agreement on the criterion that the members of the committee should fulfil. Amongst others, they had to be active, be able to speak, take initiatives, be honourable, be responsible, be serious, be respectful and not be a braggart; they should not be fearful and should not have any 'hair on their tongues'; that is to say, they had to trust themselves to speak up even in unwanted situations; they should respect all children and defend their interests; they should fulfil the task at hand and be able to direct and instruct the children; and ultimately they should also see eye to eye with the adult co-workers of the movement (who, at the time, were still called 'educators'). In a heated debate, the attending girls managed to ensure that they were represented in equal numbers in the executive committee and that the younger children were also taken into consideration. (The attending children were between the ages of 10 and 16.) In light of the everyday experiences of the children, which were wrought with degradation, discrimination and violence, we were initially astonished at the self-confidence with which they took things into their own hands, and at the thoughtful way in which they interacted with each other. We put this down to the fact, that at the meetings (like earlier at the workshops), they had experiences which for them were probably very surprising, that (most) of the attending adults trusted them, treating them respectfully, and that they really could act in self-determined ways.

Of course, it was not all sunshine and roses. There were arguments and heartaches. Some at first tried to dominate others. Girls had to defend themselves against boys' 'macho' attitudes, and some boys beat each other up for futile reasons and much more. But the first really serious problems did not come about among the children, but rather between them and some adults. The reason therefore lay in the fact that some of these adults, who were mainly acting as educators for projects of NGOs or church communities, despite best intentions, could not get used to the independence of the children and their way of managing the meetings, and therefore tried time and again to have unsolicited influence over the children. The adults had already been made to understand this at previous meetings, at which a part of them held the view that in the case of the formation of the children's movement, the adults should be integrated as quasi 'equal' members. Others held the view that the children's movement should be an 'autonomous' endeavour of the children and that the adults should, in coordination with the children, find their role as 'outsiders' who support or advise the children.

Once the children had begun to publicly draw attention to their situation and to make accusations about the violation of their rights, they reaped some friendly commentaries, but it must also be noted that they were not taken very seriously. Only once they started to pester journalists and politicians (for example, by paying unannounced 'visits' to their offices) were they granted serious attention. Some media, for example, soon no longer spoke of 'street children', 'bummers' and 'no-good-ers' but rather of 'working children' whose parents stood by their side, or it was increasingly requested that the children be heard, and their rights respected. But the difficulties and attacks quickly accumulated. It was alleged either that the children had been manipulated by adults or they were accused of behaving in an improper manner, showing a lack of respect towards adults. Some even saw 'order' or 'culture' as being under threat and called for a timely 'clamp down' and the restoration of 'authority'.

To our astonishment, the children were in no way intimidated by these attacks. They seemed to know them from their daily lives or saw them as a sign that they were finally being taken seriously. It also became clear, however, that the children felt that they were dependent on allies in the adult world. In particular, they had very high expectations of us adults, who accompanied them as 'educators' and ensured our solidarity. These sometimes went so far that they idealized us as a kind of surrogate father or mother, who would stand by their side unconditionally and whom they could trust almost without limits. The children expected active support also from the NGOs, which had since added children's rights to their banners. One key issue turned out to be how the relationship between the autonomy that accompanied the children's movement, and which was the children claimed, and the actual and perceived independence of the adults showing 'solidarity' and the 'co-operative' NGOs would develop.

With the growth of the children's movement, in which, in the meantime, up to 3,000 children were active, the self-awareness and the collective claim to autonomy of the children grew, but paradoxically the dependency on the adults also increased. The children's movement was increasingly dependent on space and money, to be able to plan and realize their activities. All of this could only be provided by adults, as only they had the necessary contacts and the right to sign the contracts that the financial provider or loaner usually insisted upon. The local UNICEF office, for example, offered financial support out of delight about the engagement of the children for their own rights, but placed the condition that an NGO or contract partner act as an intermediary (which, at the time, the children rejected).[1] However, meanwhile understanding better our role as adult co-workers of the children's movement, we succeeded in convincing some child help organizations or private persons to accept this movement as direct partners even in granting money, but as middlemen we felt the risk to end up in the role of powerful benefactors, on whose benevolence the children depended. Despite the occasional unease, we had long underestimated the imbalance resulting from this and the one-sided labelling.

No less serious, it turned out that some local NGOs and some of their appointed educators saw the children's movement as unfair competition, be it because they worried that the finances that they desperately needed for their own work would be snatched away from them or because they did not want their monopoly over 'pedagogy' or the 'fight for children's rights' to be taken out of their hands. If already a children's movement, then it should subsist under their banner and the control of the NGO and 'their' educators and make public appearances. Behind this hides both various institutional and personal interests and differing views on what is to be understood as children's rights and, in particular, the right to participation. We would like to use an example to clarify the challenges and expectations of the claim for autonomy of the children's movement and the way it was implemented.

With the increasing quantity of activities, the children faced the dilemma of no longer having enough time for all organizational affairs, all the more so as their time was highly demanded by their work, school and sometimes family. To confront this dilemma, two 'experienced' and trustworthy adults were to be appointed for the centre of the children's movement[2] to continuously look after the 'bureaucratic things'. The applicants – mostly educators and social workers looking for jobs – found themselves in the unusual situation of appearing before a selection committee that was mainly made up of children, to demonstrate their suitability and to stand up to interrogation. This took some overcoming for most, but as they waited over an hour for the decision of the committee, which meant subjecting themselves to the judgement of the children, almost all of them left in panic. This demonstrates how deeply-rooted, even amongst adults who were allocated to the children and who wanted to advocate for their rights, the conviction was that children should not decide over adults, but adults over children, and should have the last word.

This tenor can be reinforced in organizations and institutions where adults are amongst themselves, however convinced they are about the significance of children's rights and the participation of children. In particular, where their work and existence are dedicated to children's rights and form the basis for their economic existence, to assume that they give much consideration to the question of how to stay in power lies at hand. The children's movement learnt this the hard way through countless attempts to secure NGOs' support. The support offered or accorded was either restricted to verbal demonstrations of sympathy or was subject to the condition that the children renounce their decision-making autonomy. The reason that was given for this was almost always that the children did not command the necessary competencies to keep their organization alive and to manage with the corresponding duties. Every now and then, this came to a head with the allegation that the children were too impetuous or 'actionistic' and not sufficiently proficient in the 'strategic' intricacies of the 'political business'. In other words, it was suggested to them that they would do themselves and the 'children's right cause' more harm than good if they did not entrust experienced specialists from the NGO.

This reflects more than just a generational problem. The interests of the NGOs in legitimating their own 'professional' actions also had a class-specific component. When it came to, for example, negotiations with the health ministry and police head office, in which the children called for more consideration for their particular situation as working children and for better protection, some agents of the NGOs accused them of using 'vulgar speech' and lack of courtesy. Instead of respecting the forms of communication of the children and the strengths these have, they tried to impose on them 'cultured' behaviour that matched their own social world better than that of the children. In doing so, they contributed – possibly unintentionally – to devaluing the life experiences of the children and eroding their gradually increasing self-confidence, which was an essential base for the autonomy of action of their organization.

Their claim to autonomous action, which the children consistently voiced, was based on the experience of finding themselves in a situation of subordination from which they were seeking to free themselves. The subordination consisted, for one, in that as children, they were refused recognition as equal partners, and also in that they were disesteemed and discriminated against time and again as *working children* or *children living on the streets*. Their own organization allowed them to abstract themselves from this double subordination, at least for a time, and to experience mutual respect and mutual recognition. These experiences that were novel for the children were constantly making their self-confidence take wing, gave them back their sense of dignity and allowed them to see their everyday life and work with new eyes. To the extent that they saw, for example, their way of working or living no longer as a defect in their childhood but rather as being valuable and a source of pride, their desire for respect and recognition of what they were, and how they saw themselves, grew. The refusal of the children to let themselves be put off by promises about a later phase in life or a better future took on the form of a phrase they often used: 'We are the present'.

One problem that was difficult to solve presented itself in the attempt to conciliate the autonomy demanded and practically achieved by the children's movement with the everyday local reality. As a social place, in a way the children's movement presented a kind of counter-reality to the daily indignity experienced. At their meetings, the children were amongst themselves and could feel free there most of the time. However, this new awareness of life could also lead to the children hoping, through the children's movement, to escape their previous lives and to secure certain privileges albeit modest ones. In order not to be removed from reality, they had to constantly ascertain that the reason for the movement lay not in escaping problems but that they should be the basis for an improvement of everyday life.

The question that repeatedly arose was how to guarantee that the children, who as (usually elected) delegates of other children participated in meetings and assemblies of the children's movement, disseminated the conclusions reached communally and the communally developed ideas and demands, and engaged in their local implementation. It was shown that the movement only had value insofar as it could demonstrate their autonomy and ability to act locally as well. On the contrary, it was also shown that the children acting locally were only taken seriously and could only gain influence to the extent to which the children's movement showed general public presence and 'made a name' for itself. For this, stable locally comprehensive structures and forms of actions in turn proved essential.

At the meetings of the children's movement, these problems were contemplated again and again in a self-critical way, and methods of self-correction were sought. Some examples: Delegates who had not fulfilled their duties or who showed signs of arrogance were criticized or even discharged. When children (mostly girls) could not take part in meetings, because their parents feared for their welfare, a delegation would be sent to their home in order to convince the parents (which usually succeeded). As a 12-year-old girl, who belonged to the executive committee of the children's movement, no longer wanted to go to school (she did not feel she was taken seriously there), she was reminded that she was partially responsible for the credibility of the children's movement, which advocated the right to education for all children, and that she must be an example for other children. To reduce the dependence of the children's movement on financial aid, festivities with raffle and merchandising were organized in various city districts to provide the local group with the necessary financial base.

In the search for solutions to problems that arose, the advice and support from adults were also drawn on. Their advice was usually taken up when it did not conflict with the 'frequency' of the children's movement and respected the decision-making autonomy of the children. However, in the case of children's movements, this autonomy always remains vulnerable, as it does not rescind the existing social power imbalances between children and adults and as it always also – as shown above – involves dependencies. Therefore, over time, ideas developed in different children's movements across Latin America on which demands were to be made of 'empathic' adults or organizations: the adults should consider themselves 'co-protagonists', who not only respect the independent existence and form of organization and communication of the children's movement but also act in their own field in the same way as they expect it from children. The co-protagonism of adults is spoken of 'to designate the interdependence that makes us free and autonomous' (Cussiánovich, 2008: 71). In this sense, 'autonomous' networks of 'co-workers' of children's movement, that is, not dependent on NGOs, parties or institutions, have since appeared, which should promote both self-critical thinking and the social and legal recognition of children's movements.

Conclusion with view to the minority world

From a 'northern' perspective, the thoughts set out in this chapter (and other parts of the book) may sound exotic, as for the most part it does not seem to be about putting an 'impetuous' children's movement on track but rather prompting children to actually first create their own initiatives and increase their engagement for their own rights. But such an approach overlooks that the alleged lack of engagement by children is also a consequence of a lack of opportunities and not least a childhood concept that 'infantilizes' children and largely seals them off from the adult world.

A society in which the participation of children becomes a reality would not have much in common with the societies known up until today. Children alone cannot bring about such a fundamental change, however well organized they are. They are dependent on allies. But the children who are organizing themselves contribute to making the adults more aware that a childhood that is not based on exclusion, but rather that shapes society, offers them the chance to be a social subject, too.

That is perhaps a rather naive thought. As we have demonstrated in Chapters 10 and 11, participation is not a clear thing, on which there is agreement, and it does not only touch on the relationship of children and adults. But the quintessential is still topical: if participation is to be attractive for children and something to be taken seriously, it cannot only be conceded by adults. Children must be under the impression, that their actions are not inconsequential but can produce something. This is not only the question of arranged occasions and opportunities for participation, but regards the social position and the everyday lives of children in general. Only where children are allocated vital responsibilities and activities will they see sense in 'bending over backwards' for it. It would then also become apparent that the differences in power and competences between adults and children are not natural and absolute, but rather social products, relative and situational.

The manner in which the advocacy of children and their rights have been discussed until now does not always take this into consideration. It often remains tightly trapped in the idea that children cannot represent their interests and rights by themselves. The practice of a child rights commissioner or a child rights observatory is usually conceptualized so that adults act *instead of* children, or the corresponding facilities are seen as a walk-in centre for children, where they can go with their worries and requests. Here the unequal power dynamic between adults and children is untouched and not questioned, and sometimes even (unintentionally) reinforced.

There is no doubt that representative acting can be useful for children, in particular where they have little self-confidence or are severely limited in their ability to act (for instance, very young or 'disabled' children who nowadays are referred to as children with 'special needs'). The same goes for situations in which children find themselves in a weak position and the decisions of adults are more or less provided (for instance, in custody proceedings in family courts). But here it also holds true that the advocacy of children only makes sense where it is applied to work against the subordination of children and wherever possible, to strengthen the social position of children. In this sense, forms of 'non-paternalistic' advocacy are favoured in international discussions nowadays, which are understood as being advice and encouragement of children and are directly oriented to the extension of their possibilities to be of influence (see, e.g., Oliver & Dalrymple, 2008). Thereby, a difference is made between case-by-case advocacy, on the one hand, and systemic or cause-related advocacy on the other hand, in order to underline the fact that the individual support of children quickly reaches its limits, which in turn can only be overcome through structural changes in the balance of power. Adults, who want to act as advocates for children in this way, will not only insist on their independence (see Lansdown, 2001) but also must also understand themselves – as in the case of the children's movements in Latin America – as 'co-protagonists' of the children.

We hope that this book has contributed to an open-minded and more contextualized understanding of children's rights as human rights, in a theoretical as well as in a practical sense. Surely, if we want 'to promote [...] the sociological analysis of children's rights' (Alanen, 2010: 7), and if we want to do it with serious consideration of children's viewpoints, perspectives and agency, much more empirical research and theoretical reflection is needed. For instance, we need more knowledge about the conditions under which, and in which ways, the participation of children can really contribute to the transformation of the paternalism and adultism in contemporary societies and communities; or under which conditions children's movements have a chance to obtain continuity without losing their autonomy, and what could be their short-term and long-term impact, internally for the socialization and learning process of the children involved as well as for the intended and claimed external impact on the transformation of societies. These and other topics of research are relevant and needed with regard to not only the majority world but also the minority world.

Notes

1. Here it was demonstrated that the right to participation accorded by the CRC, to form an association, is worth little if this association is not legally able to act. However, precisely this is excluded in all countries by legislation.
2. It served not only as an office but also as a kind of self-regulated child and youth centre, where the children met to talk and play, to celebrate festivities, to do tasks for school or to plan activities.

Bibliography

Adams, Paul (1971) *Children's Rights. Towards the Liberation of the Child* (New York: Praeger).

AGJ (ed.) (2010) *First Children and Young People's Report. On UN Reporting on the Implementation of the UN Convention on the Rights of the Child in Germany* (Berlin: Arbeitsgemeinschaft für Kinder- und Jugendhilfe), http://www.national-coalition. de/pdf/Kinder_und_Jugendreport_engl-EV.pdf, date accessed 20 April 2011.

Ahmadu, Fuambay (2000) 'Rites and Wrongs: An Insider/Outsider Reflects on Power and Excision' in B. Shell-Duncan & Y. Hernlund (eds) *Female 'Circumcision' in Africa. Culture, Controversy, and Change* (Boulder: Lynne Rienner), pp. 283–412.

Ainsworth, Martha & Deon Filmer (2006) 'Inequalities in Children's Schooling: AIDS, Orphanhood, Poverty, and Gender', *World Development*, 34(6), 1099–128.

Alaimo, Kathleen (2002) 'Historical Roots of Children's Rights in Europe and the United States' in K. Alaimo & B. Klug (eds) *Children as Equals: Exploring the Rights of the Child* (Lanham, Maryland: University Press of America), pp. 1–23.

Alanen, Leena (1992) *Modern Childhood? Exploring the 'Child Question' in Sociology.* (Jyväskylä: University of Jyväskylä).

Alanen, Leena (1994) 'Zur Theorie der Kindheit. Die Kinderfrage in den Sozialwissenschaften', *Sozialwissenschaftliche Literatur Rundschau*, 17(28), 93–112.

Alanen, Leena (2010) 'Taking Children's Rights Seriously', *Childhood*, 17(1), 5–8.

Alanen, Leena & Berry Mayall (eds) (2001) *Conceptualising Child-Adult Relations* (New York: Routledge).

Alderson, Priscilla (2000) 'Children as Researchers. The Effects of Participation Rights on Research Methodology' in P. Christensen & A. James (eds) *Research with Children* (London & New York: Falmer Press), pp. 241–57.

Alderson, Priscilla (2001) 'Research by Children', *International Journal of Social Research Methodology*, 4(2), 139–53.

Alderson, Priscilla (2004) 'Ethics' in N. Fraser et al. (eds) *Doing Research With Children and Young People* (London: SAGE & Open University), pp. 97–112.

Alderson, Priscilla (2005) 'A New Approach to Studying Childhood' in Helen Penn (ed.) *Understanding Early Childhood* (Maidenhead: Open University Press), pp. 127–40.

Alderson, Priscilla (2008a) *Young Children's Rights. Exploring Beliefs, Principles and Practice*, 2nd edition (London & Philadelphia: Jessica Kingsley).

Alderson, Priscilla (2008b) 'When Does Citizenship Begin? Economics and Early Childhood' in A. Invernizzi & J. Williams (eds) *Children and Citizenship* (London: SAGE), pp. 108–19.

Alderson, Priscilla, Joanna Hawthorne & Margaret Killen (2005a) 'The Participation Rights of Premature Babies', *International Journal of Children's Rights*, 13(1/2), 31–50.

Alderson, Priscilla, Joanna Hawthorne & Margaret Killen (2005b) 'Are Premature Babies Citizens with Rights? The Edges of Citizenship' in A. Invernizzi & B. Milne (eds) *Children's Citizenship: An Emergent Discourse on the Rights of the Child*, Special Edition 9 of the *Journal of Social Sciences* (Delhi: Kamla-Raj), pp. 83–99.

Alderson, Priscilla & Virginia Morrow (2004) *Ethics, Social Research and Consulting with Children and Young People* (Bakingside, Essex: Barnardo's).

Alston, Philip (1994) 'The Best Interest Principle: Towards a Reconciliation of Culture and Human Rights', *International Journal of Law, Policy and the Family*, 8(1), 1–25.

Alston, Philip & John Tobin (2005) *Laying the Foundations for Children's Rights. An Independent Study of some Key Legal and Institutional Aspects of the Impact of the Convention on the Rights of the Child* (Florence: UNICEF Innocenti Research Centre).

Amin, Ash (ed.) (2009) *The Social Economy: International Perspectives on Economic Perspectives* (London: Zed Books).

AMWCY (2009) *Working Children and Youth Face the Challenge N° 9. Annual News Bulletin of the African Movement of Working Children and Youth* (Dakar: ENDA Tiers Monde).

Anderson, Gary L. (1998) 'Toward Authentic Participation: Deconstructing the Discourses of Participatory Reforms in Education', *American Educational Research Journal*, 35(4), 571–603.

Apostel, Leo (1989) 'Children's Rights and Needs or/and Human Rights and Needs. Open Problems and Personal Convictions' in E. Verhellen & F. Spiesschaert (eds) *Ombudswork for Children. A Way of Improving the Position of Children in Society* (Leuven: Acco), pp. 47–85.

Aptekar, Luis (1991) 'Are Colombian Street Children Neglected? The Contributions of Ethnographic and Ethnohistorical Approaches to the Study of Children', *Anthropology and Education Quarterly*, 22, 326–49.

Archard, David & Colin M. Macleod (eds) (2002) *The Moral and Political Status of Children*. (Oxford: Oxford University Press).

Archard, David (2004) *Children: Rights and Childhood*, 2nd edition (London: Routledge).

Ariès, Philippe (1960) *L'enfant et la vie familiale sous l'Ancien Régime*. Paris: Plon (published in English translation as: Ariès, Philippe (1962) *Centuries of Childhood*. London: Cape).

Austria (2004) *Ein kindgerechtes Österreich, Nationaler Aktionsplan zur Umsetzung der Kinderrechte* (Wien: Bundesregierung der Republik Österreich).

Balagopalan, Sarada (2002) 'Constructing Indigenous Childhoods: Colonialism, Vocational Education and the Working Child', *Childhood*, 9(1), 19–34.

Balagopalan, Sarada (2012) 'The Politics of Failure: Street Children and the Circulation of Rights Discourses in Kolkata (Calcutta), India' in K. Hanson & O. Nieuwenhuys (eds) *Living Rights: Theorizing Children's Rights in International Development* (Manuscript submitted for publication).

Baranco Avilés, María del Carmen & Juan José García Ferrer (eds) (2006) *Reconocimiento y protección de los Derechos de los Niños* (Madrid: Instituto Madrileño del Menor y la Familia).

Barranco Avilés, Maria del Carmen (2007) 'Globalización y Derechos de la infancia y la adolescencia' in M. Calvo García & J. Guilló Jiménez (eds) *Globalización y derechos de la infancia y la adolescencia* (Madrid: Save the Children), pp. 11–24.

Bauer, Joanne & Daniel Bell (eds) (1999) *The East Asian Challenge for Human Rights* (Cambridge: Cambridge University Press).

Baxi, Upendra (2006) 'Politics of Reading Human Rights: Inclusion and Exclusion Within the Production of Human rights' in Saladin Meckled-Garcìa &Başak Çalı (eds) *The Legalization of Human Rights: Multidisciplinary Perspectives on Human Rights and Human Rights Law* (London & New York: Routledge), pp. 182–200.

Baxi, Upendra (2007) *Human Rights in a Posthuman World* (New Delhi: Oxford University Press).

Bayart, Jean, Stephen Ellis & Béatrice Hibou (eds) *The Criminalization of the African State* (Oxford: James Currey).

Beazley, Harriot, Sharon Bessell, Judith Ennew & Roxana Waterson (2011) 'How are the Human Rights of Children related to Research Methodology? in A. Invernizzi & J. Williams & (eds) *The Human Rights of Children. From Visions to Implementation* (Farnham, Surrey: Ashgate), pp. 159–78.

Bellamy, Carol & Jean Zermatten (eds) (2007) *Realizing the Rights of the Child*, Swiss Human Rights Book, Vol. 2, (Zurich: Rüffer & Rub).

Benhabib, Seyla (1999 'Nous' et 'les Autres' in Ch. Joppke & S. Lukes (eds) *Multicultural Questions* (Oxford: Oxford University Press), pp. 44–64.

Bentley, Kristina Anne (2005) 'Can There Be Any Universal Children's Rights?', *International Journal of Human Rights*, 9(1), 107–23.

Bhabha, Jacqueline (2007) 'A "Vide Juridique"? – Migrant Children: The Rights and the Wrongs' in C. Bellamy & J. Zermatten (eds) *Realizing the Rights of the Child*, Swiss Human Rights Book, Vol. 2 (Zurich: Rüffer & Rub), pp. 206–19, Notes pp. 279–82.

Bhima Sangha & Makkala Panchayat (2001) *Our Survey Story* (Bangalore: The Concerned for Working Children).

Bilgin, Pinar& Adam David Morton (2002) 'Historicising Representations of "Failed States": Beyond the Cold War Annexation of Social Sciences?', *Third World Quarterly*, 23(1), 55–80.

Black, Anthony (1984) *Guilds and Civil Society in European Thought from the Twelth Century to the Present* (London: Methuen).

Bodenstein, Jobst (2007) *Report on the State of Community-Based Paralegal Advice Offices in South Africa* (on file with author Wouter Vandenhole).

Bourdillon, Michael F.C., Ben White & William E. Myers (2009) 'Re-assessing Minimum-Age Standards for Children's Work', *International Journal of Sociology and Social Policy*, 29(3/4), 106–17.

Bourdillon, Michael, Levison, Deborah, Myers, William & White, Ben (2010) *Rights and Wrongs of Children's Work* (Brunswick, NJ & London: Rutgers University Press).

Boyden, Jo (1997) 'Childhood and the Policy Makers: A Comparative Perspective on the Globalization of Childhood' in A. James & A. Prout (eds) *Constructing and Reconstructing Childhood* (London & Bristol: Falmer Press), pp. 190–229.

Boyden, Jo, Birgitta Ling & William Myers (1998) *What Works for Working Children* (Stockholm: Rädda Barnen/Save the Children).

Boyden, Jo & Gillian Mann (2005) 'Children's Risk, Resilience, and Coping in Extreme Situations' in M. Ungar (ed.) *Handbook for Working With Children and Youth. Pathways to Resilience Across Cultures and Contexts* (Thousand Oaks, London & New Delhi: SAGE), pp. 3–25.

Brems, Eva (1997) 'Enemies or Allies? Feminism and Cultural Relativism As Dissident Voices in Human Rights Discourse', *Human Rights Quarterly*, 19(1), 136–64.

Brems, Eva (2007) 'Children's Rights and Universality' in C. M. Williams (ed.) *Developmental and Autonomy Rights of Children. Empowering Children, Caregivers and Communities* (Antwerp, Oxford & New York: Intersentia), pp. 11–37.

Brighouse, Harry (2002) 'What Rights (if any) do Children Have?'in D. Archard & C. M. Macleod (eds) *The Moral and Political Status of Children* (Oxford: Oxford University Press), pp. 31–52.

Buckingham, David (2003) *After the Death of Childhood. Growing up in the Age of Electronic Media* (Cambridge: Polity).

Bühler-Niederberger, Doris (2008) 'Persisting Inequalities: Childhood between Global Influences and Local Traditions', *Childhood*, 15(2), 147–55.

Burr, Rachel (2006) *Vietnam's Children in a Changing World* (New Brunswick, NJ & London: Rutgers University Press).

Butler, Jennifer (2000) 'The Christian Right coalition and the UN Special Session on Children: Prospects and Strategies', *The International Journal of Children's Rights*, 8(4), 351–71.

Butterwegge, Christoph & Michael Klundt (eds) (2003) *Kinderarmut und Generationengerechtigkeit. Familien- und Sozialpolitik im demografischen Wandel* (Opladen: Leske + Budrich).

Butterwegge, Christoph (2007) 'Ursachen von und Maßnahmen gegen Kinderarmut' in Deutsches Kinderhilfswerk e.V. (ed.) *Kinderreport Deutschland 2007. Daten, Fakten, Hintergründe* (Freiburg: Deutsches Kinderhilfswerk), pp. 177–84.

Calvo García, Manuel & Juan Guilló Jiménez (eds) (2007) *Globalización y derechos de la infancia y la adolescencia* (Madrid: Save the Children).

Camilleri, Joseph A. & Jim Falk (1992) *The End of Sovereignty? The Politics of a Shrinking and Fragmenting World* (Aldershot: Edward Elgar).

Campbell, Tom D. (1992) 'The Rights of the Minor: as Person, as Child, as Juvenile, as Future Adult', *International Journal of Law and the Family*, 6, 1–23.

Cantwell, Nigel (2007) 'Words that Speak Volumes. A Short History of the Drafting of the CRC' in J. Connors, J. Zermatten & A. Panayotidis (eds) *18 Candles. The Convention on the Rights of the Child Reaches Majority* (Sion: Institut international des droits de l'enfant), pp. 21–9.

Cantwell, Nigel (2011) 'Are Children's Rights still Human?' in A. Invernizzi & J. Williams & (eds) *The Human Rights of Children. From Visions to Implementation* (Farnham, Surrey: Ashgate), pp. 37–59.

Chambers, Robert (1994) 'The Origins and Practice of Participatory Rural Appraisal', *World Development*, 22(7), 953–69.

Chamboderon, Jean-Claude (1975) *Le métier d'enfant : vers une sociologie du spontané* (Paris: Centre pour la recherche et l'innovation dans l'enseignement).

Chatterjee, Sudeshna (2007) 'Children's Role in Humanizing Forced Evictions and Resettlements in Delhi', *Children, Youth and Environments*, 17(1), 198–221.

Cheney, Kristen E. (2012) 'Malik and His Three Mothers: AIDS Orphans' Survival Strategies and How Children's Rights Hinder Them' in K. Hanson & O. Nieuwenhuys (eds) *Living Rights: Theorizing Children's Rights in International Development* (Manuscript submitted for publication).

Cheru, Fantu (1997) 'The Silent Revolution and the Weapons of the Weak: Transformation and Innovation from Below' in S. Gill & J. Mittelman (eds) *Innovation and Transformation in International Studies* (New York: Cambridge University Press), pp. 153–69.

Chinkin, Christine (1998) 'Torture of the Girl-Child' in G. van Bueren (ed.) *Childhood Abused. Protecting Children against Torture, Cruel, Inhuman and Degrading Treatment and Punishment* (Aldershot: Ashgate), pp. 81–106.

Christensen, Pia & Allison James (eds) (2000) *Research with Children* (London & New York: Falmer Press).

Clark, Alison (2010) 'Young Children as Protagonists and the Role of Participatory, Visual Methods in Engaging Multiple Perspectives', *American Journal of Community Psychology*, 46(1–2), 115–23.

Clark, Alison; Anne Trine Kjørholt & Peter Moss (eds) (2010) *Beyond Listening. Children's perspectives on early childhood service*, 3rd edition (Bristol: The Policy Press).

Cleaver, Frances (1999) 'Paradoxes of Participation: Questioning Participatory Approaches to Development', *Journal of International Development*, 11(4), 597–612.

Cleaver, Frances (2004) 'The Social Embeddedness of Agency and Decision-Making' in S. Hickey & G. Mohan (eds) *Participation: From Tyranny to Transformation* (London & New York: Zed Books), pp. 271–77.

Cockburn, Tom (1998) 'Children and Citizenship in Britain: A Case for a socially interdependent model of citizenship', *Childhood*, 5(1), 99–117.

Cohen, Howard (1980) *Equal Rights for Children* (Totowa, NJ: Rowman and Littlefield).

Cohen-Kohler, Jillian Clare; Lisa Forman & Nathaniel Lipkus (2008) 'Addressing Legal and Political Barriers to Global Pharmaceutical Access: Options for Remedying the Impact of the Agreement on Trade-Related Aspects of Intellectual Property Rights (TRIPS) and the Imposition of TRIPS-Plus Standards, *Health Economics, Policy and Law*, 3, 229–56.

Colectivo de la Escuela Popular Claretiana (1987) *Filodehambre. Una experiencia popular de innovación educativa* (Bogotá: Dimensión Educativa).

Coles, Robert (1986) *The Political Life of Children* (Boston: Atlantic Monthly Press).

Coly, Hamidou & Fabrizio Terenzio (2007) 'The Stakes of Children's Participation in Africa: The African Movement of Working Children and Youth' in B. Hungerland et al. (eds) *Working To Be Someone. Child Focused Research and Practice With Working Children* (London & Philadelphia: Jessica Kingsley), pp. 179–85.

Concerned Women for America (1997) *U.N. Convention on the Rights of the Child. A Treaty to Undermine the Family*, http://www.cwfa.org, date accessed 23 July 2001.

Conolly, Mark & Judith Ennew (1996) 'Introduction: Children out of place', *Childhood*, 3(2), 131–47.

Cornwall, Andrea (2008). 'Unpacking "Participation": Models, Meanings and Practices', *Community Development Journal*, 43(3), 269–83.

Cornwall, Andrea & Celestine Nyamu-Musembi (2004) 'Putting the "Rights-Based Approach" to Development into Perspective', *Third World Quarterly*, 25(8), 1415–37.

Corona Caraveo, Yolanda & Carlos Pérez Zavala (2000) 'Infancia y resistencia culturales. La participación de los niños en los movimientos de resistencia comunitarios' in N. del Río (ed.) *La Infancia Vulnerable de México en un Mundo Globalizado* (Mexico: UAM-UNICEF), pp. 127–45.

Correa, Carlos M. (2002) 'Public Health and Intellectual Property Rights', *Global Social Policy*, 2(3), 261–78.

Couzens, Meda & F. Noel Zaal (2009) 'Legal Recognition for Child-Headed Households: An Evaluation of the Emerging South African Framework', *International Journal of Children's Rights*, 17, 299–320.

Cox, Robert W. (1999) 'Civil Society at the Turn of the Millennium: Prospects for an Alternative World Order', *Review of International Studies*, 25(1), 3–28

CRIN (2009a) *Measuring Maturity: Understanding Children's 'Evolving Capacities'* (London: Child Rights Information Network), http://www.crin.org/docs/CRIN_review_23_final.pdf, date accessed 15 October 2009.

CRIN (2009b) *Non-discrimination toolkit*, http://www.crin.org/discrimination/, date accessed 25 October 2009.

CRIN (2009c) *Global Report on Status Offences* (London: Child Rights Information Network), http://www.crin.org/docs/Status_Offenses_doc_2_final.pdf, date accessed 25 October 2009.

CRIN (2009d) *Guide to Non-Discrimination and the CRC* (London: Child Rights Information Network), http://www.crin.org/Discrimination/CRC/index.asp, date accessed 8 February 2011.

Curl, John (2009) *For All the People: Uncovering the Hidden History of Cooperation, Cooperative Movements, and Communalism in America* (Oakland, CA: PM Press).

Cussiánovich, Alejandro (1997) *Some Premises for Reflection and Social Practices with Working Children and Adolescents* (Lima: Rädda Barnen/Save the Children Sweden).

Cussiánovich, Alejandro (2001) What Does Protagonism Mean?' in M. Liebel et al. (eds) *Working Children's Protagonism: Social Movements and Empowerment in Latin America, Africa and Asia* (Frankfurt & London: IKO), pp. 157–70.

Cussiánovich, Alejandro (2008) *Treintaidos años de vida y acción de los NATs por la dignidad en el Perú* (Lima: Universidad Nacional Federico Villarreal & Ifejant).

Cussiánovich, Alejandro (2009) *Ensayos sobre Infancia. Sujeto de Derechos y Protagonista* (Lima: Ifejant).

Cussiánovich, Alejandro (2010a) *Ensayos sobre Infancia II. Sujeto de Derechos y Protagonista.*(Lima: Ifejant).

Cussiánovich, Alejandro (2010b) 'Evaluación e incidencia de la Convención sobre los Derechos del Niño a veinte años de su aprobación 1989–2009', *NATs – Revista Internacional desde los Niños/as y Adolescentes Trabajadores*, n° 18, 15–25.

Cussiánovich, Alejandro & Ana María Márquez (2002) *Toward a Protagonist Participation of Boys, Girls and Teenagers* (Lima: Save the Children Sweden).

CWC (2005) *Taking a Right Turn: Children Lead the Way in Research* (Bangalore: The Concerned for Working Children).

De Block, Liesbeth & David Buckingham (2007) *Global Children, Global Media. Migration, Media and Childhood* (Basingstoke: Palgrave Macmillan).

De Feyter, Koen (2007) 'Localising Human Rights' in W. Benedek, K. De Feyter & F. Marrella (eds) *Economic Globalisation and Human Rights* (Cambridge: Cambridge University Press), pp. 67–92.

De Feyter, Koen (2011) 'Sites of Rights Resistance' in K. De Feyter, S. Parmentier, C. Timmerman & G. Ulrich (eds) *The Local Relevance of Human Rights* (Cambridge: Cambridge University Press), pp. 11–39.

De Gaay Fortman, Bas (2006) ' "Adventurous" Judgments – A Comparative Exploration into Human Rights As a Moral-Political Force in Judicial Law Development', *Utrecht Law Review*, 2(2), 22–43.

De Gaay Fortman, Bas (2008) 'Beating the State at its Own Game. An Inquiry into the Intricacies of Sovereignty and the Separation of Powers' in I. Boerefijn & J. Goldschmidt (eds) *Changing Perceptions of Sovereignty and Human Rights. Essays in Honour of Cees Flinterman* (Antwerp: Intersentia), pp. 41–55.

De Gaay Fortman, Bas (2011) *A Political Economy of Human Rights: Rights, Realities and Realization* (London: Routledge).

De Langen, Miek (1992) 'The Meaning of Human Rights for Children', in M. Freeman & Ph. Veerman (eds) *The Ideologies of Children's Rights* (The Hague: Martinus Nijhoff), pp. 255–64.

Dean, Caroline (2002) 'Sketches of Childhood: Children in Colonial Andean Art and Society' in T. Hecht (ed.) *Minor Omissions. Children in Latin American History and Society* (Madison: The University of Wisconsin Press), pp. 21–51.

Dekker, Jeroen J.H. (2000) 'The Century of the Child Revisited', *International Journal of Children's Rights*, 8, 133–150.

Detrick, Sharon (ed.) (1992) *The United Nations Convention on the Rights of the Child. A Guide to the 'Travaux Preparatoires'* (Dordrecht: Martinus Nijhoff).

Dillon, Sara (2010) *International Children's Rights* (Durham, NC: Carolina Academic Press).

Dimmock, Sam (2009) *Maximising Children's Engagement in the Reporting Process for the Convention on the Rights of the Child* (Geneva: NGO Group for the Convention on the Rights of the Child).

Dimock, George (1993) 'Children of the Mills: Re-reading Lewis Hine's Child-Labour Photographs', *The Oxford Art Journal*, 16(2), 37–54.

Dohnal, Jerry (1994) 'Structural Adjustment Programs: A Violation of Rights', *Australian Journal of Human Rights*, 57(1), 57–85.

Donelly, Jack (2006) 'The Virtues of Legalization' in S. Meckled-Garcìa & B. Çalı (eds) *The Legalization of Human Rights: Multidisciplinary Perspectives on Human Rights and Human Rights Law* (London & New York: Routledge), pp. 67–80.

Dünnweller, Barbara (2009) '20 Jahre Kinderrechtskonvention: Zeit für ein Individualbeschwerderecht!' in H. Bielefeldt et al. (eds) *Kinder und Jugendliche. Jahrbuch Menschenrechte 2010* (Vienna, Cologne & Weimar : Böhlau), pp. 113–24.

Eliascheff, Caroline (1993) *À corps et à cris. Être psychanalyste avec les tout-petits* (Paris: Odile Jacob).

Elson, Diane (2002) 'Gender Justice, Human Rights, and Neo-Liberal Economic Policies' in M. Molyneux & S. Razavi (eds) *Gender Justice, Development, and Rights* (Oxford: Oxford University Press), pp. 78–114.

Eltshain, Jean Bethke (1996) 'Political Children', *Childhood*, 3(11), 11–28.

Engebrigtsen, Ada (2003) 'The Child's – or the State's – Best Interests? an Examination of the Ways Immigration Officials Work with Unaccompanied Asylum Seeking Minors in Norway', *Child and Family Social Work*, 8, 191–200.

Ennew, Judith (1985) *Juvenile Street Workers in Lima, Peru* (Report for the Overseas Development Administration, London) [mimeo].

Ennew, Judith (2002) 'Outside Childhood. Street Children's Rights' in B. Franklin (ed.) *The New Handbook of Children's Rights* (London & New York: Routledge), pp. 388–403.

Ennew, Judith (2005) 'Prisoners of Childhood: Orphans and Economic Dependency' in J. Qvortrup (ed.) *Studies in Modern Childhood* (Basingstoke: Palgrave MacMillan), pp. 128–46.

Ennew, Judith (2011) 'Has Research Improved the Human Rights of Children? Or Have the Information Needs of the CRC Improved Data about Children?' in A. Invernizzi & J. Williams (eds) *The Human Rights of Children. From Visions to Implementation* (Farnham, Surrey: Ashgate), pp. 133–58.

Evans, Rosalind (2007) 'The Impact of Concepts of Childhood on Children's Participation: Case of the Bhutanese Refugee Camp', *Children, Youth and Environments*, 17(1), 171–97.

Evans, Tony (2007) 'Disciplining Global Society', *Studies in Social Justice*, 1(2), 108–21.

Evans, Tony (2011) *Human Rights in the Global Political Economy: Critical Processes* (Boulder & London: Lynne Rienner).

Farson, Richard (1974) *Birthrights* (New York & London: Macmillan & Collier Macmillan).

Federle, Katherine Hunt (1994) 'Rights Flow Downhill', *International Journal of Children's Rights*, 2(4), 343–68.

Feinstein, Clare & Claire O'Kane (2008) *Cultivating Children's Participation – Abridged Version of Participation is a Virtue That Must Be Cultivated* (Stockholm: Save the Children Sweden), http://shop.rb.se/Section/Section.aspx?SectionId=2017321&MenuId=74347, date accessed 25 May 2010.

Felstiner, William L.F., Richard L. Abel & Austin Sarat (1980/81) 'The Emergence and Transformation of Disputes: Naming, Blaming, Claiming', *Law and Society Review*, 15(3), 631–53.

Fleischhauer, Johanna (2008) *Vom Krieg betroffene Kinder. Eine vernachlässigte Dimension von Friedenskonsolidierung. Eine Untersuchung psychosozialer Intervention für Kinder während und nach bewaffneten Konflikten am Beispiel Eritreas* (Opladen & Farmington Hills: Budrich UniPress).

Foster, Geoff & John Williamson (2000) 'A Review of Current Literature of the Impact of HIV/AIDS on Children in Sub-Saharan Africa', *AIDS*, 14(Suppl. 3), 275–84.

Franklin, Bob (ed.) (1986) *The Rights of Children* (Oxford: Basil Blackwell).

Franklin, Bob (1998) 'Children's political rights' in E. Verhellen (ed.) *Understanding Children's Rights: Collected Papers Presented at the Third International Interdisciplinary Course on Children's Rights* (Ghent: Children's Rights Centre/Ghent University), pp. 157–73.

Franklin, Bob (ed.) (2002) *The New Handbook of Children's Rights* (London & New York: Routledge).

Fraser, Nancy (2000) 'Rethinking Recognition', *New Left Review*, 3, 107–20.

Fraser, Nancy (2003) 'Social Justice in the Age of Identity Politics: Redistribution, Recognition and Participation' in N. Fraser & A. Honneth. *Recognition or Redistribution? A Political-Philosophical Exchange* (London & New York: Verso Books), pp. 7–109.

Fraser, Nancy (2009) *Scales of Justice: Reimagining Political Space in a Globalizing World* (New York & Chichester: Columbia University Press).

Fraser, Sandy (2004) 'Situating Empirical Research' in N. Fraser et al. (eds) *Doing Research with Children and Young People* (London: SAGE & Open University), pp. 15–26.

Fraser, Sandy; Vicky Lewis, Sharon Ding, Mary Kellet & Chris Robinson (eds) (2004) *Doing Research with Children and Young People* (London: SAGE & Open University).

Freeman, Michael (1983) *The Rights and Wrongs of Children* (London: Frances Pinter).

Freeman, Michael (1992) 'The Limits of Children's Rights' in M. Freeman & P. Veerman (eds) *The Ideologies of Children's Rights* (Dordrecht: Martin Nijhoff), pp. 29–46.

Freeman, Michael (1998) 'Human Rights and Real Cultures: Towards a Dialogue on "Asian values"', *Netherlands Quarterly of Human Rights*, 16, 25–39.

Freeman, Michael (2002) *Human Rights. An Interdisciplinary Approach* (London: Wiley).

Freeman, Michael (2007) 'Why It Remains Important to Take Children's Rights Seriously', *International Journal of Children's Rights*, 15, 5–23.

Freeman, Michael (2009) 'Children's Rights as Human Rights. Reading the UNCRC' in J. Qvortrup, W.A. Corsaro & M.S. Honig (eds) *The Palgrave Handbook of Childhood Studies* (Basingstoke: Palgrave Macmillan), pp. 377–93.

Freeman, Michael (2011) 'The Value and Values of Children's Rights' in A. Invernizzi & J. Williams (eds) *The Human Rights of Children: From Visions to Implementation* (Farnham, Surrey: Ashgate), pp. 21–36.

Freeman, Michael & Philip E. Veerman (eds) (1997) *The Moral Status of Children. Essays on the Rights of the Child* (Dordrecht: Martinus Nijhoff).

Funes, Jaume (2007) 'Niños y niñas de hoy, derechos de hoy' in M. Calvo García & J. Guilló Jiménez (eds) *Globalización y derechos de la infancia y la adolescencia* (Madrid: Save the Children), pp. 59–66.

Funky Dragon (2011) 'Our Rights, Our Story: Funky Dragon's Report to the United Nations Committee on the Rights of the Child' in A. Invernizzi & J. Williams (eds) *The Human Rights of Children. From Visions to Implementation* (Farnham, Surrey: Ashgate), pp. 327–48.

Galvis Ortiz, Ligia (2006) *Las niñas, los niños y los adolescentes – titulares activos de derechos* (Bogotá: Aurora).

Galvis Ortiz, Ligia (2007) 'Reflexiones en torno a la titularidad de derechos' in E. Durán & M. C. Torrado (eds) *Derechos de los niños y las niñas. Debates, realidades y perspectivas* (Bogotá: Universidad Nacional de Colombia), pp. 57–64.

Germann, Jelka Mervi (2011) *Social Dynamics Regarding Child-Headed Household in South Africa – A Case Study from the Gauteng and Mpumalanga Provinces.* Master Thesis European Master in Childhood Studies and Children's Rights (EMCR) at the Free University Berlin [mimeo].

Gewirth, Alan (1996) *The Community of Rights* (Chicago: University of Chicago Press).

Ghai, Yash (1999) 'Rights, Social Justice, and Globalization in East Asia' in J. Bauer & D. Bell (eds) *The East Asian Challenge for Human Rights* (Cambridge: Cambridge University Press), pp. 241–63.

Gill, Stephen (2003) 'Social Reproduction of Affluence and Human In/Security' in I. Bakker & S. Gill (eds) *Power, Production and Social Reproduction: Human In/Security in the Global Political Economy* (Basingstoke & New York: Palgrave Macmillan), pp. 190–207.

Girling, Frank K. (1960) *The Acholi of Uganda* (London: Her Majesty's Stationary Office).

Goldstein, Joseph, Anna Freud & Albert J. Solnit (1973a) *Before the Best Interest of the Child.* (New York: The Free Press).

Goldstein, Joseph, Anna Freud & Albert J. Solnit (1973b) *Beyond the Best Interest of the Child* (New York: The Free Press).

González Contró, Mónica (2008) *Derechos Humanos de los Niños: Una Propuesta de Fundamentación* (Mexiko City: Universidad Nacional Autónoma de México, Instituto de Investigaciones Jurídicas).

Goodale, Mark (2006) 'Introduction: Locating Rights, Envisioning Law between the Global and the Local' in M. Goodale & S. Engle Merry (eds) *The Practice of Human Rights: Tracking Law Between the Global and the Local* (Cambridge, Cambridge University Press), pp. 1–38.

Gottlieb, David (1973) *Children's Liberation* (Englewood Cliffs, NJ: Prentice Hall).

Greene, Sheila & Diane Hogan (eds) (2005) *Researching Children's Experience. Approaches and Methods* (London: SAGE).

Greig, Anne, Jane Taylor & Tommy MacKay (2007) *Doing Research with Children*, 2nd edition (Los Angeles: SAGE).

Griffin, James (2002) 'Do Children Have Rights?' in D. Archard & C. M. Macleod (eds) *The Moral and Political Status of Children* (Oxford: Oxford University Press), pp. 19–30.

Gross, Beatrice & Ronald Gross (eds) (1977) *The Children's Rights Movement. Overcoming the Oppression of Young People* (Garden City, NY: Anchor Books).

Grugel, Jean & Nicola Piper (2007) *Critical Perspectives on Global Governance: Rights and Regulation in Governing Regimes* (London: Routledge).

GTZ (2007) *Female Genital Mutilation in Kenya*, http://www.gtz.de/fgm, date accessed 14 December 2010.

Hall, Stuart (1992) 'The West and the Rest: Discourse and Power' in S. Hall & B. Giebens (eds) *Formations of Modernity* (Oxford: Polity, in association with Open University), pp. 276–95.

Hanson, Karl (2006) 'Repenser les droits des enfants travailleurs' in M. Bonnet et al. (eds) *Enfants travailleurs – Repenser l'enfance* (Lausanne: Page deux), pp. 101–28.

Hanson, Karl (2011) 'International Children's Rights and Armed Conflict', *Human Rights & International Legal Discourse*, 5, 40–62.

Hanson, Karl (2012) 'Rethinking Working Children's Rights' in K. Hanson & O. Nieuwenhuys (eds) *Living Rights: Theorizing Children's Rights in International Development* (Manuscript submitted for publication).

Hanson, Karl & Arne Vandaele (2003) 'Working Children and International Labour Law: A Critical Analysis', *International Journal of Children's Rights*, 11(1), 73–146.

Harris-Short, Sonia (2001) 'Listening to "the other"? The Convention on the Rights of the Child', *Melbourne Journal of International Law*, 2(2), 304–51.

Harris-Short, Sonia (2003) 'International Human Rights Law: Imperialist, Inept and Ineffective? Cultural Relativism and the UN Convention on the Rights of the Child', *Human Rights Quarterly*, 35, 130–81.

Hart, H.L.A. (1998) *The Concept of Law*, 2nd edition (Oxford: Clarendon).

Hart, Jason (2008a) *Business as Usual? The Global Political Economy of Childhood Poverty* (Oxford: Young Lives Technical Note 13).

Hart, Jason (2008b) 'Children's Participation and International Development: Attending to the Political', *International Journal of Children's Rights*, 16, 407–18.

Hart, Roger A. (1992) *Children's Participation: From Tokenism to Citizenship* (Florence: UNICEF Innocenti Research Centre).

Hauck, Gerhard (2004) 'Schwache Staaten? Überlegungen zu einer fragwürdigen entwicklungspolitischen Kategorie', *Peripherie*, 24(96), 411–27.

Haug, Frigga (2000) 'Memory Work: the Key to Women's Anxiety' in S. Radstone (ed.) *Memory and Methodology* (Oxford & New York: Berg), pp. 155–78.

Hawes, Joseph (1991) *The Children's Rights Movement. A History of Advocacy and Protection* (Boston, Mass.: Twayne).

Hecht, Tobias (ed.) (2002) *Minor Omissions. Children in Latin American History and Society* (Madison: The University of Wisconsin Press).

Heesterman, Wiebina (2005) 'An Assessment of the Impact of Youth Submissions to the United Nations Committee on the Rights of the Child', *International Journal of Children's Rights*, 13, 351–78.

Heilprin, John (2011) Fraud Plagues Global Health Fund. Associated Press on the Web, 23 January 2011, http://news.yahoo.com/s/ap/20110123/ap_on_re_eu/eu_ aids_fund_corruption, date accessed 10 February 2011.

Hemingway, Joanne (2004) The Age Discrimination Act 2004 (Australia), http:// www.hreoc.gov.au/age/roadmap_ADA.pdf, date accessed 15 October 2009.

Herman, Didi (2001) 'Globalism's "Siren Song": The United Nations and International Law in Christian Right Thought and Prophecy', *The Sociological Review*, 49(1), 56–77.

Hernández-Truyol, Berta Esperanza & Stephen J. Powell (2009) *Just Trade* (New York: New York University Press).

Hill, Malcolm (2005) 'Ethical Considerations in Researching Children's Experiences' in S. Greene & D. Hogan (eds) *Researching Children's Experience. Approaches and Methods* (London: SAGE), pp. 61–86.

Hill, Malcolm, John Davis, Alan Prout & Kay Tisdall (2004) 'Moving the Participation Agenda Forward', *Children & Society*, 18, 77–96.

Hinton, Rachel (1996) *Health in Transition: The Bhutanese Refugees*. Submitted in partial requirements for the degree of Ph.D. (Cambridge: University of Cambridge).

Hinton, Rachel (2000) 'Seen but not Heard: Refugee Children and Models for Intervention' in C. Panter-Brick & M. Smith (eds) *Abandoned Children* (Cambridge: Cambridge University Press), pp. 199–212.

Hinton, Rachel (2008) 'Children's Participation and Good Governance: Limitations of the Theoretical Literature', *International Journal of Children's Rights*, 16, 285–300.

Høeg, Peter (1994) *Borderliners* (London: The Harvill Press).

Holt, John (1974) *Escape from Childhood. The Needs and Rights of Children* (New York: Dutton).

Holzscheiter, Anna (2010) *Children's Rights in International Politics. The Transformative Power of Discourse* (Basingstoke: Palgrave Macmillan).

Hughes, Judith (1988) 'The Philosopher's Child' in M. Griffiths & M. Whitford (eds) *Feminist Perspectives in Philosophy* (Bloomington & Indianapolis: Indiana University Press), pp. 72–89.

Human Rights and Equality Opportunity Commission (2000) *Age Matters: A Report on Age Discrimination*. Sidney, http://www.crin.org/docs/age_report_australia_2000. pdf, date accessed 8 February 2011.

Hungerland, Beatrice (2010) 'Kindheiten im Kulturvergleich' in M. Liebel & R. Lutz (eds) *Sozialarbeit des Südens, Band 3: Kindheiten und Kinderrechte* (Oldenburg: Paulo Freire Verlag), pp. 31–46.

Hungerland, Beatrice; Manfred Liebel; Brian Milne & Anne Wihstutz (eds) (2007) *Working To Be Someone. Child Focused Research and Practice with Working Children* (London & Philadelphia: Jessica Kingsley).

Ibhawoh, Bonny (2001) 'Cultural Relativism and Human Rights : Reconsidering the Africanist Discourse', *Netherlands Quarterly of Human Rights*, 19, 43–62.

Imorou, Abou-Bakari (2009) 'Rapport d'évaluation de l'appui au renforcement des capacités'. Unpublished Report Presented on the Occasion of the 8th Meeting of the African Movement of Working Children and Youth in Cotonou, Benin [mimeo].

Institut für Sozialforschung (1956) *Soziologische Exkurse* (Frankfurt: Europäische Verlagsanstalt).

Invernizzi, Antonella & Brian Milne (2002) 'Are Children Entitled to Contribute to International Policy Making? A Critical View of Children's Participation in the International Campaign for the Elimination of Child Labour', *International Journal of Children´s Rights*, 10(4), 403–31.

Invernizzi, Antonella & Brian Milne (eds) (2005) 'Children's Citizenship: An Emergent Discourse on the Rights of the Child?', *Journal of Social Sciences,* Special Issue N° 9 (Delhi: Kamla – RAJ).

Invernizzi, Antonella & Jane Williams (eds) (2008) *Children and Citizenship* (London: SAGE).

Invernizzi, Antonella & Jane Williams (eds) (2011) *The Human Rights of Children. From Visions to Implementation* (Farnham, Surrey: Ashgate).

Jaffé, Philip D. & Hélène Rey Wicky (1996) 'Competence? Now really!' in E. Verhellen (ed.) *Understanding Children's Rights: Collected Papers presented at the first International Interdisciplinary Course on Children's Rights* (Ghent: Children's Rights Centre/Ghent University), pp. 99–110.

James, Allison (2007) 'Giving Voice to Children's Voices: Practices and Problems, Pitfalls and Potentials', *American Anthropologist*, 109(2), 261–72.

James, Allison (2009) 'Agency' in J. Qvortrup, W.A. Corsaro & M.S. Honig (eds) *The Palgrave Handbook of Childhood Studies* (Basingstoke & New York: Palgrave Macmillan), pp. 34–45..

James, Allison & Adrian L. James (2004) *Constructing Childhood. Theory, Policy and Social Practice* (Basingstoke: Palgrave Macmillan).

James, Allison; Chris Jenks & Alan Prout (1998) *Theorizing Childhood* (Cambridge: Polity).

Jans, Marc (2004) 'Children as Citizens. Towards a Contemporary Notion of Child Participation', *Childhood*, 11(1), 27–44.

Jenkins, Richard (ed.) (1998) *Questions of Competence: Culture, Classification and Intellectual Disability* (Cambridge: Cambridge University Press).

John, Mary (1995) 'Children's Rights in a Free-Market Culture' in S. Stephens (ed.) *Children and the Politics of Culture* (New Jersey: Princeton University Press), pp. 105–37.

John, Mary (2003) *Children's Rights and Power. Charging up for a New Century* (London & New York: Jessica Kingsley).

Johnson, Victoria, Edda Ivan-Smith, Gill Gordon, Pat Pridmore & Patta Scott (eds) (1998) *Stepping Forward. Children and Young People's Participation in the Development Process* (London: Intermediate Technology Publications).

Jones, Adele (2004) 'Involving Children and Young People as Researchers' in S. Fraser et al. (eds) *Doing Research with Children and Young People* (London: SAGE & Open University), 113–30.

Jones, Adele; Dharman Jeyasingham & Sita Rajasooriya (2002) *Invisible Families. The Strength and Needs of Black Families in Which Young People Have Caring Responsibilities* (Bristol: The Policy Press).

Jones, Branwen Gruffydd (2008) 'The Global Political Economy of Social Crisis: Towards a Critique of the "Failed State" Ideology', *Review of International Political Economy*, 15(2), 180–205.

Katz, Cindi (2004) *Growing Up Global: Economic Restructuring and Children's Everyday Lives.* (Minneapolis: University of Minnesota Press).

Kaufmann, Franz-Xaver (1980) 'Kinder als Außenseiter der Gesellschaft', *Merkur*, 34(387), 761–71.

Kellett, Mary (2005a) 'Children as Active Researchers: A New Paradigm for the 21st Century?', *ESRC National Centre for Research Methods, Methods Review Papers NCRM/003*, http://www.ncrm.ac.uk/publications.

Kellett, Mary (2005b) *How to Develop Children as Researchers: A Step By Step Guide to the Research Process* (London: Paul Chapman).

Kerber-Ganse, Waltraut (2009) *Die Menschenrechte des Kindes. Die UN-Kinderrechtskonvention und die Pädagogik von Janusz Korczak* (Opladen: Barbara Budrich).

Key, Ellen (1909) *The Century of the Child* (New York & London: G. P. Putnam's Sons).

Key, Ellen (1911) *Love and Marriage. With a Critical and Biographical Introduction by Havelock Ellis* (New York & London: G. P. Putnam's Sons).

Kirby, Perpetua (2002) 'Involving Young People in Research' in B. Franklin (ed.) *The New Handbook of Children's Rights* (London & New York: Routledge), pp. 268–84.

Knowing Children (2009) *The Right to be Properly Researched. How to Do Rights-Based Scientific Research with Children. A Set of Ten Manuals for Field Researchers* (Bangkok: Knowing Children, Black on White Publications).

Kohli, Ravi K.S. (2006) 'The Sound of Silence: Listening to What Unaccompanied Asylum-seeking Children Say and Do Not Say', *British Journal of Social Work*, 36, 707–21.

Komulainen, Sirkka (2007) 'The Ambiguity of the Child's "Voice" in Social Research', *Childhood*, 14(1), 11–28.

Korczak, Janusz (1928/2009) *The Child's Right to Respect* (Strasbourg: Council of Europe).

Kothari, Uma (2001) 'Power, Knowledge and Social Control in Participatory Development' in B. Cooke & K. Uma (eds) *Participation: The New Tyranny?* (London: Zed Books), pp. 139–52.

Kränzl-Nagl, Renate; Johanna Mierendorff & Thomas Olk (2003) 'Die Kindheitsvergessenheit der Wohlfahrtsstaatsforschung die Wohlfahrtsstaatsvergessenheit der Kindheitsforschung' in R. Kränzl-Nagl, J. Mierendorff & Th. Olk (eds) *Kindheit im Wohlfahrtsstaat. Gesellschaftliche und politische Herausforderungen* (Frankfurt & New York: Campus), pp. 9–55.

Kupffer, Heinrich (1974) *Jugend und Herrschaft. Eine Analyse der pädagogischen Entfremdung* (Heidelberg: Quelle und Meyer).

Lansdown, Gerison (2001) *Independent Institutions Protecting Children's Rights* (Florence: UNICEF Innocenti Research Centre).

Lansdown, Gerison (2002) 'Children's Rights Commissioners for the UK' in B. Franklin (ed.) *The New Handbook of Children's Rights* (London & New York: Routledge), pp. 285–97.

Lansdown, Gerison (2004) 'Participation and Young Children' in *Early Childhood Matters* edited by Bernard van Leer Foundation, The Hague, N° 103, pp. 4–14.

Lansdown, Gerison (2005) *The Evolving Capacities of the Child* (Florence: UNICEF Innocenti Research Centre).

Lansdown, Gerison (2010) 'The Realisation of Children's Participation Rights: Critical Reflections' in B. Percy-Smith & N. Thomas (eds) *A Handbook of Children and Young People's Participation* (London & New York: Routledge), pp. 11–23.

Latouche, Serge (1993) *In the Wake of the Affluent Society: An Exploration of Post-Development* (London: Zed Books).

Lawy, Robert & Gert Biesta (2006) 'Citizenship-as-Practice: The Educational Implications of an Inclusive and Relational Understanding of Citizenship', *British Journal of Educational Studies*, 54(1), 34–50.

Lee, Nick (2001) *Childhood and Society. Growing Up in an Age of Uncertainty* (Buckingham & Philadelphia: Open University Press).

Leonard, Madeleine (2004) 'Children's Views on Children's Right to Work. Reflections from Belfast', *Childhood*, 11, 45–61.

Levison, Deborah (2000) 'Children as Economic Agents', *Feminist Economics*, 6(1), 125–134.

Levison, Deborah (2007) 'A Feminist Economist's Approach to Children's Work' in B. Hungerland et al. (eds) *Working To Be Someone. Child Focused Research and Practice With Working Children* (London & Philadelphia: Jessica Kingsley), pp. 17–22.

Lewis, Ann & Geoff Lindsay (eds) (2000) *Researching Children's Perspectives* (Buckingham: Open University Press).

Lewis, Norman (1998) 'Human Rights, Law and Democracy in an Unfree World' in T. Evans (ed.) *Human Rights Fifty Years On: A Reappraisal* (Manchester, NY: Manchester University Press), pp. 77–104.

Liebel, Manfred (1994) *Protagonismo Infantil. Movimientos de niños trabajadores en América Latina* (Managua: Ed. Nueva Nicaragua).

Liebel, Manfred (1996) *Somos NATRAS. Testimonios de Niños, Niñas y Adolescentes Trabajadores de Nicaragua* (Managua: Ed. Nueva Nicaragua).

Liebel, Manfred (1997) 'Children Want to Work', *NATs – Working Children and Adolescents International Review*, 3(3–4), 79–81.

Liebel, Manfred (2001) '12 Rights, and Making their Own Way. The Working Youth of Africa Organise Themselves' in M. Liebel, B. Overwien & A. Recknagel (eds) *Working Children's Protagonism. Social Movements and Empowerment in Latin America, Africa and India* (Frankfurt M. & London: IKO), pp. 197–217.

Liebel, Manfred (2003) 'Working Children as Social Subjects. The Contribution of Working Children's Organizations to Social Transformations', *Childhood*, 10(3), 265–86.

Liebel, Manfred (2004) *A Will of Their Own. Cross-Cultural Perspectives on Working Children.* (London & New York: Zed Books).

Liebel, Manfred (2006) *Malabaristas del siglo XXI. Los niños y niñas trabajadores frente a la globalización* (Lima: Ifejant), http://www.ifejants.org/new/docs/publicaciones/MALABARISTAS.pdf

Liebel, Manfred (2007a) 'Paternalism, Participation and Children's Protagonism', *Children, Youth and Environments*, 17(2), 56–73.

Liebel, Manfred (2007b) 'Between Prohibition and Praise: Some Hidden Aspects of Children's Work in Affluent Societies' in B. Hungerland et al. (eds) *Working to be Someone.* (London & Philadelphia: Jessica Kingsley), pp. 123–32.

Liebel, Manfred (2007c) 'Bürgerschaft von unten. Kinderrechte und soziale Bewegungen von Kindern', *Diskurs Kindheits- und Jugendforschung*, 2(1), 83–99.

Liebel, Manfred (2008) 'Citizenship from Below: Children's Rights and Social Movements' in A. Invernizzi & J. Williams (eds) *Children and Citizenship* (London: SAGE), pp. 32–43.

Liebel, Manfred (2009) 'Foreword: Systematic Curiosity' in Knowing Children (ed.) *The right to be properly researched* (Bangkok: Knowing Children, Black on White Publications), Manual 1: 13–16.

Liebel, Manfred (2012) 'Do Children Have a Right to Work? Working Children's Movements in the Struggle for Social Justice' in K. Hanson & O. Nieuwenhuys (eds) *Living rights: Theorizing Children's Rights in International Development* (Manuscript submitted for publication).

Liebel, Manfred, Bernd Overwien & Albert Recknagel (eds) (2001) *Working Children's Protagonism. Social Movements and Empowerment in Latin America, Africa and India* (Frankfurt & London: IKO).

Lifton, Betty Jean (1989) *The King of Children. The Life and Death of Janusz Korczak* (London: Pan Books).

Linklater, Andrew (1998) *The Transformation of Political Community* (Cambridge: Polity Press).

Lister, Ruth (2003) *Citizenship. Feminist Perspectives*, 2nd edition (Basingstoke: Palgrave).

Lister, Ruth (2006) 'Children and Citizenship', *Childright – A Journal of Law and Policy Affecting Children and Young People*, N° 223, February: 22–25.

Lolichen, P. J. (2002) *Children and Their Research: A Process Document* (Bangalore: The Concerned for Working Children).

Lolichen, P. J. (2009) 'Rights-Based Participation. Children as Research Protagonists and Partners in Mainstream Governance' in J. Fiedler & Ch. Posch (eds) *Yes, They Can! Children Researching Their Lives* (Baltmannsweiler: Schneider Verlag Hohengehren), pp. 135–43.

Lolichen, P.J., A. Shetty, J. Shenoy and C. Nash (2007) 'Children in the Driver's Seat', *Participatory Learning and Action*, 56(1), 49–55.

Lowy, Catherine (1992) 'Autonomy and the Appropriate Projects of Children: A Comment on Freeman', in Ph. Alston, S. Parker & J. A. Seymour (eds) *Children, Rights, and the Law* (Oxford: Oxford University Press), pp. 72–5.

Mally, Lynn (1990) *Culture of the Future. The Proletkult Movement in Revolutionary Russia* (Berkeley, Los Angeles & Oxford: University of California Press).

Mann, Gillian & David Tolfree (2003) *Children's Participation in Research: Reflections from the Care and Protection of Separated Children in Emergencies Project* (Stockholm: Save the Children Sweden), http://shop.rb.se/Product/Product.aspx?ItemId=2967683&SectionId=2017321&MenuId=74347, date accessed 2 June 2010.

Masaki, Katsuhiko (2004) 'The "Transformative" Unfolding of "Tyrannical" Participation: The *corvée* Tradition and Ongoing Local politics in Western Nepal' in S. Hickey & G. Mohan (eds) *Participation: from Tyranny to Transformation* (London & New York: Zed Books), pp. 125–39.

Masschelein, Jan & Kerlijn Quaghebeur (2005) 'Participation for Better or for Worse?', *Journal of Philosophy of Education*, 39(1), 51–65.

Matthews, Gary B. (1994) *The Philosophy of Childhood* (Cambridge, Mass. & London: Harvard University Press).

Mayall, Berry (2002) *Towards a Sociology for Childhood* (Buckingham: Open University Press).

McAdam-Crisp; Lewis Aptekar & Wanjiku Kironyo (2005) 'The Theory of Resilience and Its Application to Street Children in the Minority and Majority Worlds' in M. Ungar (ed.) *Handbook for Working With Children and Youth. Pathways to Resilience Across Cultures and Contexts* (Thousand Oaks, London & New Delhi: SAGE), pp. 71–88.

McKechnie, Jim & Sandy Hobbs (1999) 'Child Labour: The View from the North', *Childhood*, 6(1), 89–100.

McLeod, Alison (2008) *Listening to Children. A Practitioner's Guide* (London & Philadelphia: Jessica Kingsley).

Merry, Sally Engle (2006a) *Human Rights and Gender Violence. Translating International Law into Local Justice* (Chicago: University of Chicago Press).

Merry, Sally Engle (2006b) *Human Rights, Gender, and New Social Movements: Contemporary Debates in Legal Anthropology*. October 2006.

Meyer, Schalk (2006) *The Access to Justice Cluster – A Manual for Practitioners* (on file with author Wouter Vandenhole).

Miller, Ethan (2005) 'Solidarity Economics. Strategies for Building New Economies. From the Bottom-Up and the Inside-Out', http://www.geonewsletter.org/files/SolidarityEconomicsEthanMiller.pdf, date accessed 15 March 2011.

Miller, Jenifer (2007) *Children as Agents: Guidelines for Participation in Periodic Reporting on the Convention on the Rights of the Child* (World Vision).

Milne, Brian (2007) 'Do the Participation Articles in the Convention on the Rights of the Child Present US with a Recipe for Children's Citizenship?' in B. Hungerland et al. (eds) *Working to Be Someone* (London & Philadelphia: Jessica Kingsley), pp. 205–9.

Minow, Martha (1986) 'Rights for the Next Generation: A Feminist Approach to Children's Rights', *Harvard Women's Law Journal*, 9, 1–24.

Mohamud, Asha; Karin Ringheim; Susan Bloodworth & Kristina Gryboski (2002) 'Girls at Risk: Community Approaches to End Female Genital Mutilation and Treating Women Injured by the Practice' in PATH *Reproductive Health and Rights: Reaching the Hardly Reached* (Washington: PATH), http://www.path.org, date accessed 15 December 2010.

Mohan, Giles & Kristian Stokke (2000) 'Participatory Development and Empowerment: The Dangers of Localism', *Third World Quarterly*, 21(2), 247–68.

Montgomery, Heather (2008) *An Introduction to Childhood: Anthropological Perspectives on Children's Lives* (Oxford: Wiley-Blackwell).

Moosa-Mitha, Mehmoona (2005) 'A Difference-Centred Alternative to Theorization of Children's Citizenship Rights', *Citizenship Studies*, 9(4), 369–88.

Morrow, Virginia (2002) 'Children's Rights to Public Space. Environment and Curfews' in B. Franklin (ed.) *The New Handbook of Children's Rights* (London & New York: Routledge), pp. 168–81.

Morrow, Virginia (2008) 'Responsible Children and Children's Responsibilities? Sibling Caretaking and Babysitting by School-Age Children' in J. Bridgeman, C. Lind & H. Keating (eds) *Responsibility, Law and the Family* (London: Ashgate), pp. 105–24.

Morrow, Virginia & Martin Richards (1996) 'The Ethics of Social Research with Children: An Overview', *Children & Society*, 10, 90–105.

Mortier, Freddy (1996) 'Rationality and Competence to Decide in Children' in E. Verhellen (ed.) *Understanding Children's Rights: Collected Papers Presented at the first International Interdisciplinary Course on Children's Rights* (Ghent: Children's Rights Centre/Ghent University), pp. 83–98.

Muteshi, Jacinta & Justine Sass (2005) *Female Genital Mutilation in Africa: An Analysis of Current Abandonment Approaches* (Nairobi: PATH), http://www.path.org, date accessed 15 December 2010.

Mutua, Makau (2002) *Human Rights: A Political and Cultural Critique* (Philadelphia: University of Pennsylvania Press).

Myers, William E. (2009) 'Organization of Working Children' in H. D. Hindman (ed.) *The World of Child Labor. An Historical and Regional Survey* (Armonk, NY & London: M.E. Sharpe), pp. 153–7.

National Alliance for the Development of Community Advice Offices (NADCAO) (leaflet on file with author Wouter Vandenhole).

Neamtan, Nancy (2002) 'The Social and Solidarity Economy: Towards an "Alternative" Globalisation'. Background Paper for the Symposium *Citizenship and Globalization: Exploring Participation and Democracy in a Global Context*, Langara College, Vancouver, 14–16 June 2002, http://www.unesco.ca/en/commission/resources/documents/social_and_solidarity_economy.pdf, date accessed 15 March 2011.

Neill, Alexander S. (1953) *The Free Child* (London: Herbert Jenkins).

Nieuwenhuys, Olga (2008) 'Editorial: The Ethics of Children's Rights', *Childhood*, 15(1), 4–11.

Nieuwenhuys, Olga (2009) 'From Child Labour to Working Children's Movements' in J. Qvortrup, W.A. Corsaro & M.S. Honig (eds) *The Palgrave Handbook of Childhood Studies* (Basingstoke: Palgrave Macmillan), pp. 289–300.

Nimbona, Godefroid & Kristoffel Lieten (2007) *Child Labour Unions: AEJT Senegal. A Report for IREWOC* (Amsterdam: IREWOC).

O'Kane, Claire and Ravi Karkara (2007) 'Pushing the Boundaries: Critical Perspectives on the Participation of Children in South and Central Asia', *Children, Youth and Environments*, 17(1), 136–47.

Oliver, Christine M. & Jane Dalrymple (eds) (2008) *Developing Advocacy for Children and Young People. Current Issues in Research, Policy and Practice* (London & Philadelphia: Jessica Kingsley).

Olk, Thomas (2009) 'Children, Generational Relations and Intergenerational Justice' in J. Qvortrup, W.A. Corsaro & M.S. Honig (eds) *The Palgrave Handbook of Childhood Studies* (Basingstoke: Palgrave Macmillan), pp. 188–214.

Olk, Thomas & Maksim Hübenthal (2009) 'Child Poverty in the German Social Investment State', *Zeitschrift für Familienforschung*, 21(2), 150–67.

Oloka-Onyango, J. & Deepika Udagama (2000) *The Realization of Economic, Social and Cultural Rights: Globalization and its Impact on the FULL enjoyment of Human Rights.*

Preliminary Report (Geneva: United Nations Sub-Commission on the Promotion and Protection of Human Rights).

OMCT – World Organization against Torture (2006) 'Statement On Universal Children's Day: Stop Violence against Children', 20 November 2006, http://www.crin.org/resources/infodetail.asp?id=11287, date accessed 23 February 2011.

Oré Aguilar, Gaby (2011) 'The Local Relevance of Human Rights: a Methodological Approach' in K. De Feyter, S. Parmentier, C.Timmerman and G. Ulrich (eds) *The Local Relevance of Human Rights* (Cambridge: Cambridge University Press), 109–46.

Orsi, Fabienne; Cristina d'Almeida; Lia Hasenclever; Mamadou Camara; Paulo Tigre & Benjamin Coriat (2007) 'TRIPS Post-2005 and Access to New Antiretroviral Treatments in Southern Countries: Issues and Challenges', *AIDS*, 21(15), 1997–2003.

Orsi, Fabienne & Cristina d'Almeida (2010) 'Soaring Antiretroviral Prices, TRIPS and TRIPS Flexibilities: A Burning Issue for Antiretroviral Treatment Scale-Up in Developing Countries', *Current Opinion in HIV & AIDS*, 5(3), 237–41.

Packer, Corinne (2002) *Using Human Rights to Change Tradition. Traditional Practices Harmful to Women's Reproductive Health in sub-Saharan Africa* (Antwerp: Intersentia).

Panther-Brick, Catherine & Malcolm T. Smith (eds) (2000) *Abandoned Children* (New York: Cambridge University Press).

PATH (2002) *Reproductive Health and Rights: Reaching the Hardly Reached* (Washington: PATH), http://www.path.org, date accessed 15 December 2010.

Penn, Helen (2005) *Unequal Childhoods. Young Children's Lives in Poor Countries* (London: Routledge).

Percy-Smith, Barry & Nigel Thomas (eds) (2009) *A Handbook of Children's Participation: Perspectives from Theory and Practice* (London & New York: Routledge).

Peterson, Anna L. & Kay Almere Read (2002) 'Victims, Heroes, Enemies: Children in Central American Wars' in T. Hecht (ed.) *Minor Omissions. Children in Latin American History and Society* (Madison: The University of Wisconsin Press), pp. 215–31.

Platt, Anthony M. (1969) *The Child Savers. The Invention of Delinquency* (Chicago: The University of Chicago Press).

PRATEC (2005) *Iskay Yachay. Dos Saberes* (Lima: Proyecto Andino de Tecnologías Campesinas).

Pridik, Heinrich (1921) *Das Bildungswesen in Sowjetrussland. Vorträge, Leitsätze und Resolutionen der Ersten Moskauer Allstädtischen Konferenz der kulturell-aufklärenden Organisationen "Mosko-Proletkult" vom 23.-28. Februar 1918* (Annaberg im Erzgebirge: Neupädagogischer Verlag).

ProNATs (2009) *ProNATsNews* N° 1 (Berlin: ProNATs e.V.), http://www.pronats.de/file-admin/pronats/documents/ProNATsNews-Ausgabe1.pdf, date accessed: 20 April 2011.

Protagonistas, edited by Defense for Children International, Bolivia, No. 9, 1999.

Prout, Alan (ed.) (2000) *The Body, Childhood and Society* (Basingstoke: Palgrave Macmillan).

Prout, Alan (2005) *The Future of Childhood* (London & New York: RoutledgeFalmer).

Pupavac, Vanessa (1998) 'The Infantilisation of the South and the UN Convention on the Rights of the Child', *Human Rights Law Review*, 3(2) 1–6.

Pupavac, Vanessa (2001) 'Misanthropy without Borders: The International Children's Rights Regime', *Disasters*, 25(2), 95–112.

Purdy, Laura M. (1992) *In their Best Interest? The Case against Equal Rights for Children* (Ithaca: Cornell University Press).

Qvortrup, Jens (ed.) (2005) *Studies in Modern Childhood. Society, Agency, Culture* (Basingstoke: Palgrave Macmillan).

Qvortrup, Jens (ed.) (2009) *Structural, Historical, and Comparative Perspectives. Sociological Studies of Children and Youth*, Vol. 12 (Bedfordshire: Emerald).

Qvortrup, Jens; William A. Corsaro & Michael-Sebastian Honig (eds.) (2009) *The Palgrave Handbook of Childhood Studies* (Basingstoke: Palgrave Macmillan).

Raes, Koen (1992) *Ongemakkelijk recht. Rechtskritische perspectieven op maatschappij, ethiek en emancipatie* (Antwerpen: Kluwer rechtswetenschappen).

Rahman, Muhammad Anisur (1993) *People's Self-Development. Perspectives on Participatory Action Research. A Journey Through Experience* (London: Zed Books).

Ratna, Kavita (2000) 'Documenting Bhima Sangha's Process. Oxford Notes for "Children in Adversity: Ways to Reinforce the Coping Ability and Resilience of Children in Situations of Hardship"' (Oxford University) [mimeo].

Razeto M., Luís (1997) *Los Caminos de la Economía de Solidaridad* (Buenos Aires: Lumen-Hvmanitas).

Reaves, Malik Stan (1997) *Kenya: Alternative Rite to Female Circumcision Spreading in Kenya*, http://www.allafrica.com, date accessed 14 December 2010.

Reddy, Nandana (2010) 'Children and the New World. Working Children's Response to Globalisation and Privatisation' in M. Liebel & R. Lutz (eds) *Sozialarbeit des Südens, Band 3: Kindheiten und Kinderrechte* (Oldenburg: Paulo Freire Verlag), pp. 331–43.

Reddy, Nandana & Kavita Ratna (2002) 'Protagonism: A Journey in Children's Participation' (Bangalore: The Concerned for Working Children), http://www.workingchild.org/htm/prota9.htm, date accessed 12 April 2011.

Report Belgium (2001) *That's My Opinion... What do you think? First Report by Children and Young People Living in Belgium for the Committee on the Rights of the Child in Geneva* (Brussels: UNICEF Belgium), http://www.crin.org/docs/resources/treaties/crc.30/belgium_child_ngo_report_eng.pdf, date accessed 9 May 2009.

Report Northern Ireland (2002) *Young People's Submission to the United Nations Committee on the Rights of the Child for Consideration during the Committee's Scrutiny of the UK government's Report* (Belfast: Children's Law Centre & Save the Children Northern Ireland), http://www.crin.org/docs/resources/treaties/crc.31/NI_Young_Peoples_Submission.pdf, date accessed 8 May 2009.

Report UK (1999) *It's Not Fair: Young People's Reflections on Children's Rights* (London: The Children's Society), http://www.crin.org/docs/resources/treaties/crc.31/Children%27s_Society.pdf, date accessed 8 May 2009.

Report UK (2002) *Report to the Pre-Sessional Working Group on the Committee of the Rights of the Child, Preparing for Examination of the UK's Second Report under the CRC* (London: Young People's Rights Network), http://www.crin.org/docs/resources/treaties/crc.31/UK_YPRN_report.pdf, date accessed 8 May 2009.

Republic of Bolivia (2009) *Constitution of 2009*.

Reynaert, Didier, Maria Bouverne-de-Bie & Stijn Vandevelde (2009) 'A Review of Children's Rights Literature since the Adoption of the United Nations Convention on the Rights of the Child', *Childhood*, 16(4), 518–34.

Reynolds, Pamela; Olga Nieuwenhuys & Karl Hanson (2006) 'Refractions of Children's Rights in Development Practice', *Childhood*, 13(3), 291–302.

Roberts, Helen (2000) 'Listening to Children: and Hearing Them' in P. Christensen & A. James (eds) (2000) *Research with Children* (London & New York: Falmer Press), 225–40.

Roche, Jeremy (1999) 'Children: Rights, Participation and Citizenship', *Childhood*, 6(4), 475–93.

Rodham, Hillary (1973) 'Children under the Law', *Harvard Educational Review*, 43(4), 487–514.

Rose, Rudi & Maria Bouverne-de Bie (2007) 'Do Children Have Rights or Do Their Rights Have to be Realised? The United Nations Convention on the Right of the Child as a Frame of Reference for Pedagogical Action', *Journal of Philosophy of Education*, 41(3), 431–43.

Rousseau, Jean-Jacques (1762/1979) *Emile, or On Education* (New York: Basic Books).

Rwezaura, Bart (1998) 'The Duty to Hear the Child: A View From Tanzania' in N. Welshman (ed.). *Law, Culture, Tradition and Children's Rights in Eastern and Southern Africa* (Dartmouth: Ashgate), pp. 57–84.

Sainz Prestel, Patricia Isabel (2008) *Changing Their Lives: The Working Children's Movement in Bolivia*. The Hague: Institute of Social Studies, http://oaithesis.eur.nl/ir/ repub/asset/7056/Prestel%20PPSD%202007-08.pdf, date accessed 12 April 2011.

Sall, Ebrima (2002) 'Kindheit in Afrika – Konzepte, Armut und die Entwicklung einer Kinderrechtskultur' in K. Holm & U. Schulz (eds) *Kindheit in Armut weltweit* (Opladen: Leske + Budrich), pp. 81–101.

Santos, Boaventura de Sousa (ed.) (2006) *Another Production is Possible. Beyond the Capitalist Canon* (London: Verso).

Santos, Boaventura de Sousa & César A. Rodríguez-Garavito (2005) 'Law, Politics, and the Subaltern in Counter-Hegemonic Globalization' in B. Santos & C.A. Rodríguez-Garavito (eds) *Law and Globalization from Below. Towards a Cosmopolitan Legality* (Cambridge: Cambridge University Press), pp. 1–26.

Sanz, Andrés (1997) 'From Kundapur to Geneva: The International Coordination of Working Children', *NATs – Working Children and Adolescents International Review*, 3(3–4), 11–23.

Saporiti, Angelo, Ferran Casas, Daniela Grignoli, Antonio Mancini, Fabio Ferrucci, Marina Rago, Carles Alsinet, Cristina Figuer, Mònica González, Mireia Gusó, Carles Rostan & Marta Sadurni (2005) 'Children's View on Children's Rights. A Comparative Study of Spain and Italy', *Sociological Studies of Children and Youth*, 10, 125–152.

Sarfaty, Galit A. (2009) 'Why Culture Matters in International Institutions: the Marginality of Human Rights at the World Bank', *American Journal of International Law*, 103(4), 647–83.

Sassen, Saskia (1996) *Losing Control? Sovereignty in an Age of Globalization* (New York: Columbia University Press).

Save the Children (2002) *Child Rights Programming. How to Apply Rights-Based Approaches in Programming. A Handbook for International Save the Children Alliance Members* (London: ISCA).

Save the Children (2004a) *So You Want to Involve Children in Research? A Toolkit Supporting Children's Meaningful and Ethical Participation in Research Relating to Violence against Children* (Stockholm: Save the Children).

Save the Children (2004b) 'The Separated Children in Europe Programme. Position Paper on: Returns and Separated Children' (London: Save the Children Alliance).

Save the Children Alliance (2009) *Convention on the Rights of the Child – From Moral Imperatives to Legal Obligations. In Search of Effective Remedies for Child Rights Violations*. Conference Report, Geneva, 12–13 November, http://www.crin.org/ resources/infoDetail.asp?ID=21863&flag=report, date accessed 21 March 2010.

Schibotto, Giangi (2009) 'El niño trabajador y la "Economía de Solidaridad": Del umbral de la sobrevivencia al horizonte del projecto', *NATs – Revista Internacional desde los Niños/as y Adolescentes Trabajadores*, 13(17), 109–128, http://www.ifejants. org/new/docs/publicaciones/revistanats17.pdf

Shell-Duncan, Bettina; Walter Obungu Obiero & Leunita Auko Moruli (2000) 'Women without Choices: The Debate over Medicalization of Female Genital

Cutting and Its Impact on a Northern Kenyan Community' in B. Shell-Duncan & Y. Hernlund (eds) *Female 'Circumcision' in Africa. Culture, Controversy, and Change* (Boulder: Lynne Rienner), pp. 109–28.

Simeunovic Frick, Smiljana (2011) *Children's Rights: Experienced and Claimed. Children's Reports to the UN Committee on the Rights of the Child* (Berlin & Münster: LIT) [forthcoming].

Simon, Thomas W. (2000) 'United Nations Convention on Wrongs to the Child', *International Journal of Children's Rights*, 8(1), 1–13.

Smith, Anne-Marie (2007) 'The Children of Loxicha, Mexico: Exploring Ideas of Childhood and the Rules of Participation', *Children, Youth and Environments*, 17(2), 33–55.

Smith, Noel, Ruth Lister, Sue Middleton & Lynne Cox (2005) 'Young People as Real Citizens: Towards an Inclusionary Understanding of Citizenship', *Journal of Youth Studies*, 8(4), 425–43.

Snodgrass Godoy, Angelina (1999) '"Our Right Is the Right to be killed". Making Rights Real on the Streets of Guatemala City', *Childhood*, 6(4), 423–42.

Spence, Tomas (1796) *The Rights of Infants* (London), http://thomas-spence-society. co.uk/4.html, date accessed 5 May 2011.

Stammers, Neil (2009) *Human Rights and Social Movements* (London & New York: Pluto Press).

Stammers, Neil (2012) 'Children's Rights and Social Movements: Reflections from a Cognate Field' in K. Hanson & O. Nieuwenhuys (eds) *Living Rights: Theorizing Children's Rights in International Development* (Manuscript submitted for publication).

Stasilius, Daiva (2002) 'The Active Child Citizen. Lessons from Canadian Policy and Children's Movement', *Citizenship Studies*, 6(4), 507–38.

Stephenson, Svetlana (2001) 'Street Children in Moscow: Using and Creating Social Capital', *The Sociological Review*, 49(4), 530–47.

Stern, Bertrand (ed.) (1995) *Kinderrechte zwischen Resignation und Vision* (Ulm: Klemm und Oelschläger).

Such, Elizabeth & Robert Walker (2005) 'Young Citizens or Policy Objects? Children in the "Rights and Responsibilities" Debate', *Journal for Social Politics*, 34(1), 39–57.

Swift, Anthony (1999) *Working Children Get Organised. An Introduction to Working Children's Organisations* (London: International Save the Children Alliance).

Swift, Anthony (2001) 'India – Tale of Two Working Children's Unions' in M. Liebel, B. Overwien & A. Recknagel (eds) *Working Children's Protagonism. Social movements and empowerment in Latin America, Africa and India* (Frankfurt M. & London: IKO), pp. 181–95.

Tamanaha, Brian Z. (2000) 'A Non-Essentialist Version of Legal Pluralism', *Journal of Law and Society*, 27(2), 296–321.

Terenzio, Fabrizio (2009) 'Le MAEJT en quelques chiffres: Statistiques 2009'. Presentation Held on the Occasion of the 8th Meeting of the African Movement of Working Children and Youth in Cotonou, Benin [mimeo].

Theis, Joachim (2004) *Promoting Rights-Based Approaches. Experiences and Ideas from Asia and the Pacific* (Bangkok: Save the Children Sweden).

Theis, Joachim (2007) 'Performance, Responsibility and Political Decision-Making: Child and Youth Participation in Southeast Asia, East Asia and the Pacific', *Children, Youth and Environments*, 17(1), 1–13.

Thomas, Nigel (2007) 'Towards a Theory of Children's Participation', *International Journal of Children's Rights*, 15, 1–20.

Tisdall, E. Kay M. & John Davis (2004) 'Making a Difference? Bringing Children's and Young People's Views into Policy-Making', *Children & Society*, 18, 131–42.

Tobin, John (2011) 'Understanding a Human Rights Based Approach to Matters Involving Children: Conceptual Foundations and Strategic Considerations' in A. Invernizzi & J. Williams (eds) *The Human Rights of Children. From Visions to Implementation* (Farnham, Surrey: Ashgate), pp. 61–98.

Tolfree, David (2004) *Whose Children? Separated Children's Protection and Participation in Emergencies* (Stockholm: Save the Children Sweden).

Tomasevski, Katarina (2005) 'Not Education for All, Only for Those Who Can Pay: The World Bank's Model for Financing Primary Education', *Law, Social Justice and Global Development Journal*, http://www.go.warwick.ac.uk/elj/lgd/2005_1/tomasevski , date accessed 26 April 2011.

Turner, Susan M. & Gareth B. Matthews (eds) (1998) *The Philosopher's Child. Critical Perspectives in the Western Tradition* (Rochester: University of Rochester Press).

Twining, William (2009) *General Jurisprudence: Understanding Law from a Global Perspective* (Cambridge: Cambridge University Press).

Twum-Danso, Afua (2005) 'The Political Child', in A. McIntyre (ed.) *Invisible stakeholders: Children and War in Africa* (Pretoria: Institute for Security Studies), pp. 7–30.

UN (2006) *Rights of the Child. Report of the Independent Expert for the United Nations Study on Violence against Children* (A/61/150 and Corr.1) (New York: United Nations).

UN Division for the Advancement of Women (2009) 'Report of the Expert Group Meeting – Good Practices in Legislation on "Harmful Practices" against Women', http://www.un.org/womenwatch/daw/egm/vaw_legislation_2009/Report%20EGM%20harmful%20practices.pdf , date accessed 15 December 2010.

UNATSBO (2010) *'Mi Fortaleza es mi Trabajo'. De las Demandas a la Propuesta. Niños, Niñas y Adolescentes Trabajadores y la Regulación del Trabajo Infantil y Adolescente en Bolivia* (Cochabamba: Union de Niños, Niñas y Adolescentes Trabajadores de Bolivia).

UNGA (2006) *Rights of the Child.* UN Doc. A/61/299.

Ungar, Michael (ed.) (2005) *Handbook for Working with Children and Youth. Pathways to Resilience Across Cultures and Contexts* (Thousand Oaks, London & New Delhi: SAGE).

UNICEF (2002) *State of the World's Children 2003* (New York: UNICEF).

UNICEF (2004) *Summary Report of the Study on the Impact of the Implementation of the Convention on the Rights of the Child* (Florence: UNICEF Innocenti Research Centre).

UNICEF (ed.) (2007) *A World Fit for Us. The Children's Statement from the UN Special Session on Children: Five Years on* (New York: UNICEF), http://www.unicef.org/worldfitforchildren/files/A_World_Fit_for_Us.pdf.

UNICEF Kosovo (2010) *Rückführung aus Deutschland und Reintegration aus der Sicht und Erfahrung von Kindern aus den Minderheiten der Roma, Ashkali und Ägypter im Kosovo,* http://www.bundestag.de/bundestag/ausschuesse17/a04/Anhoerungen/Anhoerung02/Stellungnahmen_SV/Stellungnahme_04.pdf, date accessed 22 August 2010.

UN Committee on the Rights of the Child (2003) *General comment No. 4: 'Adolescent Health and Development in the Context of the Convention on the Rights of the Child'*, UN Doc. CRC/GC/2003/4.

UN Committee on the Rights of the Child (2009) *General Comment No. 12: 'The Right of the Child to be Heard'*, UN Doc. CRC/C/GC/12.

US Department of State (2001) *Kenya: Report on Female Genital Mutilation (FGM) or Female Genital Cutting (FGC)*, http://www.state/og/g/wi/rls/rep/crfgm/10103pf.htm, date accessed 14 December 2010.

Valentin, Karen & Lotte Meinert (2009) 'The Adult North and the Young South. Reflections on the Civilizing Mission of Children's Rights', *Anthropology Today*, 25(3), 23–28.

Van Beers, Henk, Vo Phi Chau, Judith Ennew, Pham Quoc Khan, Tran Thap Long, Brian Milne, Trieu Tri Anh Nguyet & Vu Thi Son (2006) *Creating an Enabling Environment. Capacity Building in Children's Participation, Save the Children Sweden, Viet Nam, 2000–2004* (Bangkok: Save the Children Sweden, Regional Office for Southeast Asia and the Pacific).

Van Breda, Adrian D. (2010) 'The Phenomenon and Concerns of Child-Headed Households in Africa' in M. Liebel & R. Lutz (eds) *Sozialarbeit des Südens, Band 3: Kindheiten und Kinderrechte* (Oldenburg: Paulo Freire Verlag), pp. 259–79.

Van Bueren, Geraldine (1995/1998) *The International Law on the Rights of the Child* (Dordrecht: Martinus Nijhoff).

Van den Berge, Marten (2007) *Working Children's Movements in Bolivia*, http://www.childlabour.net/documents/unionsproject/Unions_Bolivia_2007.pdf, date accessed 15 December 2010.

Van Rooyen, Marissa (2009) *Assessment of Degree to which Children's Rights, and in Particular Child-Headed Households and the Human Rights/Children's Rights Implications Are Addressed by Community Based Paralegals in South-Africa* (on file with author Wouter Vandenhole).

Vandenhole, Wouter; Rudi Roose; Didier Reynaert & Maria De Bie (2008) 'Theorizing Participation and Citizenship of Children: Towards an Embedded Approach of Legal Rights of Children?' Working Paper *ESF Exploratory Workshop on Children's Participation in Decision-Making*, Berlin, 16–18 June [mimeo].

Veerman, Philip E. (1992) *The Rights of the Child and the Changing Image of Childhood* (Dordrecht: Martinus Nijhoff).

Veerman, Philip & Hephzibah Levine (2000) 'Implementing Children's Rights on A Local Level: Narrowing the Gap between Geneva and the Grassroots', *International Journal of Children's Rights*, 8, 373–84.

VeneKlasen, Lisa; Valerie Miller; Cindy Clark & Molly Reilly (2005) 'Rights-Based Approaches and Beyond: Challenges of Linking Rights and Participation', IDS working paper 235 (Brighton: Institute of Development Studies), http://www.ids.ac.uk/download.cfm?file=wp235.pdf, date accessed 3 February 2011.

Verhellen, Eugeen (1994/2000) *Convention on the Rights of the Child. Background, Motivation, Strategies, Main Themes* (Leuven & Apeldoorn: Garant).

Voice of African Children (2001) (Dakar: Enda editions, Occasional Papers n° 217).

Vučković Šahović, Nevena (2010) 'The Role of Civil Society in Implementing the General Measures of the Convention on the Rights of the Child', *Innocenti Working Paper* 2010-18 (Florence: UNICEF Innocenti Research Centre).

Waylen, Georgina (2006) 'Constitutional Engineering: What Opportunities for the Enhancement of Gender Rights?', *Third World Quarterly*, 27(7), 1209–21.

Wells, Karen (2009) *Childhood in a Global Perspective* (Cambridge: Polity).

West, Andy (2007) 'Power Relationships and Adult Resistance to Children's Participation', *Children, Youth and Environments*, 17(1), 123–35.

White, Ben (2009) 'Social Science Views on Working in Children' in H. D. Hindman (ed.) *The World of Child Labor. An Historical and Regional Survey* (Armonk, NY & London: M.E. Sharpe), pp. 10–17.

White, Sarah C. (1996) 'Depoliticising Development: The Uses and Abuses of Participation', *Development in Practice*, 6(1), 6–15.

White, Sarah C. (2002) 'Being, Becoming and Relationship: Conceptual Challenges of a Child Rights Approach in Development', *Journal of International Development*, 14(8), 1095–1104.

White, Sarah C. (2007) 'Children's Rights and the Imagination of Community in Bangladesh', *Childhood*, 14(4), 505–20.

White, Sarah C. & Shyamol A. Choudhury (2007) 'The Politics of Child Participation in International Development: The Dilemma of Agency', *The European Journal of Development Research*, 19(4), 529–50.

White, Sarah C. & Shyamol A. Choudhury (2010) 'Children's Participation in Bangladesh: Issues of Agency and Structures of Violence' in B. Percy-Smith & N. Thomas (eds) *A Handbook of Children's and Young People's Participation. Perspectives from Theory and Practice* (London & New York: Routledge), pp. 39–50.

Wiggin, Kate Douglas (1892/1971) *Children's Rights. A Book of Nursery Logic* (Ann Arbor, Mich.: Gryphon Books).

Willemot, Yves (2003) 'What Do You Think? Children's Reporting on Children's Rights' in *Understanding Children's Rights. Collected Papers Presented at the Sixth International Interdisciplinary Course on Children's Rights*, Ghent University, December 2003, edited by Eugeen Verhellen & Arabella Weyts (Children's Rights Centre, Ghent University, Belgium), pp. 271–86.

Wintersberger, Helmut (1994) ‚Sind Kinder eine Minderheitsgruppe? Diskriminierung von Kindern gegenüber Erwachsenen' in M. Rauch-Kallat & J. W. Pichler (eds) *Entwicklungen in den Rechten der Kinder im Hinblick auf das UN-Übereinkommen über die Rechte des Kindes* (Vienna, Cologne & Weimar: Böhlau), pp. 73–104.

Wintersberger, Helmut (2000) 'Kinder als ProduzentInnen und als KonsumentInnen. Zur Wahrnehmung der ökonomischen Bedeutungen von Kinderaktivitäten' in H. Hengst & H. Zeiher (eds) *Die Arbeit der Kinder. Kindheitskonzept und Arbeitsteilung zwischen den Generationen* (Weinheim & Munich: Juventa), pp. 169–88.

Wintersberger, Helmut (2005) 'Work, Welfare and Generational Order: Towards a Political Economy of Childhood' in J. Qvortrup (ed.) *Studies in Modern Childhood* (Basingstoke: Palgrave), pp. 201–20.

Woldeslase, Wunesh; Mulubrha Berhe & Araya Belay (2002) *Pilot Study on Indigenous Knowledge on Child Care in Eritrea* (Asmara).

Woodhead, Martin (2009) 'Child Development and the Development of Childhood' in J. Qvortrup, W.A. Corsaro & M.-S. Honig (eds) *The Palgrave Handbook of Childhood Studies* (Basingstoke: Palgrave Macmillan), pp. 46–61.

Woodiwiss, Anthony (2006) 'The Law Cannot Be Enough: Human rights and the Limits of Legalism' in S. Meckled-Garcìa & B. Çalı (eds) *The Legalization of Human Rights: Multidisciplinary Perspectives on Human Rights and Human Rights Law* (London & New York: Routledge), pp. 32–48.

World Vision Deutschland e.V. (ed.) (2007) *Kinder in Deutschland. 1. World Vision Kinderstudie* (Bonn: Bundeszentrale für politische Bildung).

Worsfold, Victor L. (1974) 'A Philosophical Justification for Children's Rights', *Harvard Educational Review*, 44(1), 142–57.

Wyness, Michael (2005) 'Regulating Participation: The Possibilities and Limits of Children and Young People's Councils' in A. Invernizzi & B. Milne (eds) *Children's Citizenship: An Emergent Discourse on the Rights of the Child? Journal of Social Sciences*, Special Issue N° 9 (Delhi: Kamla – RAJ), pp. 7–18.

Wyness, Michael, Lisa Harrison & Ian Buchanan (2004) 'Childhood, Politics and Ambiguity: Towards an Agenda for Children's Political Inclusion', *Sociology*, 38(1), 81–99.

Young Equals (2009) *Making the Case: Why Children Should Be Protected from Age Discrimination and How It Can Be Done. Proposals for the Equality Bill* (London: Children's Rights Alliance for England).

Zelizer, Viviana A. (1985) *Pricing the Priceless Child. The Changing Social Value of Children* (New York: Basic Books; 2nd edition, Princeton, NJ: Princeton University Press, 1994).

Zelizer, Viviana A. (2002) 'Kids and Commerce', *Childhood*, 9(4), 375–96.

Zelizer, Viviana A. (2005) 'The Priceless Child Revisited' in J. Qvortrup (ed.) *Studies in Modern Childhood* (Basingstoke: Palgrave), pp. 184–200.

Zelizer, Viviana A. (2011) *Economic Lives: How Culture Shapes the Economy* (Princeton, NJ: Princeton University Press).

Zermatten, Jean (2007) 'The Convention on the Rights of the Child from the Perspective of the Child's Best Interest and Children's Views' in C. Bellamy & J. Zermatten (eds) *Realizing the Rights of the Child* (Zurich: rüffer & rub), pp. 36–52.

Zinnecker, Jürgen (2001) *Stadtkids. Kinderleben zwischen Schule und Straße* (Weinheim & Munich: Juventa).

Index